EDITED BY MARY BANHAM
AND BEVIS HILLIER

A TONIC TO THE NATION

THE FESTIVAL OF BRITAIN 1951

with a Prologue by
Roy Strong

THAMES AND HUDSON
LONDON

To the memory of Gerald Barry

ACKNOWLEDGMENTS · The editors wish to thank the writers of this book, many of whom have contributed invaluable background material, and also those who have loaned their collections of Festival material. In particular our thanks go to Mrs Mary Emett, Sir Leslie Joseph, Peter Kneebone, Edward D. Mills, Max Nicholson, Mrs Vera Russell, Sir Gordon Russell, Prof. Peter Shepheard and Sir Huw Wheldon.
In addition, we gratefully acknowledge the assistance of A. J. Allport, the Architectural Press, John Blake, A. Castledine, Hulme Chadwick, Stirling Craig, Andrew Dempsey, the late Bert Eniver, Alec Gibson, Abram Games, Leslie Julius, James Kennedy, Sir Anthony Lewis, Ian Mackenzie-Kerr, E. L. MacFadyen, Ruari McLean, Maxwell G. Moffett, Frank Newby, Ernst Pollak, Cedric Price, David Price, the Public Records Office, Ann-Louise Riley, Bernard Sendall, Peter Sharp, John Shove, Colin Sorensen, the Offices of Sir Basil Spence in London and Sir Basil Spence, Glover & Ferguson of Edinburgh, Douglas Stephen, Colin S. Stewart, Anthony Swift, Anthony Symondson, Robert Wilkin, Prof. Peter Youngman, and the very willing and helpful members of the staff of the Victoria and Albert Museum.

Designed and produced by Thames and Hudson with the co-operation of the Victoria and Albert Museum.

Filmset and printed by
BAS Printers Limited, Wallop, Hampshire

CONTENTS

Prologue ROY STRONG 6

1 Introduction BEVIS HILLIER 10

2 Recollections of the Festival
GERALD BARRY 20

3 Festival Politics ADRIAN FORTY 26

4 Festival Star WILLIAM FEAVER 40

5 The Role of the Design Council Before, During and After the Festival of Britain PAUL REILLY 58

6 Three Years a-Growing IAN COX

7 A NATIONAL ENTERPRISE

Introduction MARY BANHAM 70

South Bank Exhibition 76
HUGH CASSON; MISHA BLACK
ANTONY D. HIPPISLEY COXE
RALPH FREEMAN
R. D. RUSSELL and ROBERT GOODDEN
VICTOR PASMORE; JANE DREW
F. H. K. HENRION; JOHN RATCLIFF
CHARLES HASLER

Pleasure Gardens, Battersea Park 118
JAMES GARDNER; JOHN PIPER
ROWLAND EMETT; BRUCE ANGRAVE
BARBARA JONES

What Architecture, Housing and Planning Can Do For Us: Lansbury
FREDERICK GIBBERD 138

Exhibition of Science, South Kensington
J. BRONOWSKI; BRIAN PEAKE 144

Land Travelling Exhibition
RICHARD LEVIN 148

Festival Ship 'Campania'
JAMES HOLLAND 150

Exhibition of Industrial Power, Glasgow 152

Ulster Farm and Factory Exhibition, Belfast WILLY DE MAJO 155

8 RECOLLECTIONS

Participants 160
JACK GODFREY-GILBERT
GEORGE BACKHOUSE; T. W. HENDRICK
CHARLES PLOUVIEZ; AUDREY RUSSELL
MARGARET SHEPPARD FIDLER
DIANA ARMFIELD; JOHN WRIGHT
DAVID J. WEBB; MARGARET KNOWLES
K. MOLLIE MONCKTON; EILEEN BAILLIE
FRANK TAYLOR; V. L. FORD

Visitors and Abstainers 176
GEORGE MACBETH; BRIAN ALDISS
JOHN MACKAY; ANGUS MCGILL
GEORGE CLARKE; BERESFORD EGAN
GWENDOLINE WILLIS; G. S. WHITTET
W. Y. CARMAN; MARGARET BEAN
FRANK NORMAN; SHELAGH SPARKS
BARBARA DORF; SYLVIA I. JENKINSON
ROY FULLER; ARNOLD WESKER
HARDY AMIES; M. JUNE MAGGS
D. E. WARREN; EDWARD LUCIE-SMITH

9 The Style: 'Flimsy . . . Effeminate'?
REYNER BANHAM 190

Acknowledgments 199

Index 199

Prologue : Utopia Limited

ROY STRONG

I WAS FIFTEEN when the Festival of Britain blazed its sparkling star across the grey heavens of Britain in the aftermath of the Second World War. All of us who grew up then remember it and its concomitant fête, the Coronation, as culminations of a great reawakening of the arts after years of privation, particularly sharp for those whose formative years were the ones of austerity. The first great art exhibition I ever saw was the French tapestries exhibition at the Victoria and Albert Museum in 1947. This was followed by art treasures from Munich and Vienna and the stupendous exhibitions of Dutch and Flemish painting at the Royal Academy. The opera, the ballet, the theatres and the museums all reopened. No one who lived through this period will ever forget it. Twenty-five years after it still seems heroic. And the Festival of Britain of 1951 is the single gigantic event which crystallizes the whole era. Now, looking down the arches of the years, we can also begin to look back with the knowing eye of history. Even better, most of its creators are still with us, able to tell their version of the saga. No one in 1876 tried to do for the Great Exhibition of 1851 what this book set out to achieve for 1951, namely to compile simultaneously an historical memoir allied to a critical reassessment of the arts of an age within living memory. These are the facets which make up the mosaic of this book.

Inevitably one's first question is, why a festival at all? What was it, why did it happen, why did the ideas it represented take on the form of festival? One's reaction is that of an historian. What is a festival? What are its antecedents in Britain and Western Europe? The answer here is easy but, as far as I know, never before mentioned in relation to the Festival of Britain. The 1951 exhibition must be seen as a lineal descendant of the whole art of festival as it stemmed down from the renaissance. The rulers of renaissance and baroque Europe used triumphal entries into cities, tournaments, water spectacles, ballets, firework displays, masques and pageants as vehicles to express, through visual symbol, temporary buildings and allegorical tableaux, the ideas and aspirations of their rule. These festivals of old Europe sang the praises of the prince. Through his virtues and achievements the Golden Age was brought once more to earth and harmony was maintained in the body politic. For this monarchical propaganda its promoters drew upon revamped medieval romance, the imagery of Sacred Empire and of Christian and classical mythology. In the late eighteenth century a change occurred when propaganda for the prince was transmuted into propaganda for the state. The political fêtes of the French Revolution, with their apotheosis of the new ideals of society, of Liberty, Equality and Fraternity, attendants of the goddess Reason, represented something different and are the most direct ancestors of 1951. They were truly secular state festivals in which government set out to present to the masses the ideals and goals of a new society, framed within a view of history recast in the terms of romantic nationalism.

Although much work has been done in the last twenty years on fêtes down to the French revolutionary period, little study has been made of festivals in the last century and a half. The organizers of the 1951 exhibition only refer to the Great Exhibition of 1851 which ostensibly they were commemorating. But in doing this they at least recognize that they are exponents of a long-lived art form. For them, however, the 1851 exhibition is a red herring. This is supported by the fact that the plans of the Festival on the South Bank site were already very far advanced when someone suddenly spotted that 1851 formed no part of it; so with a last-minute flurry a model of the Crystal Palace was erected. This reveals that the idea of a world trade fair on the lines of 1851 was far from their minds. In my view the true perspective into which 1951 should be placed is the previous state festivals of the Edwardian and Georgian periods in England and, of those, one in particular, the British Empire Exhibition at Wembley in 1924, the Festival of Britain's immediate predecessor.

A special souvenir set of stamps was issued for the Festival.

The 1924 exhibition was staged – just like the Festival – six years after a great world war. Although ironically it was to open with Ramsay Macdonald and a Labour Government in office its programme was the direct expression of the Conservative Governments of Bonar Law and Baldwin. Its symbol was not the insular lady Britannia atop a pointer of the compass but the lion, symbolizing the 'might, dignity, power and prestige of the Empire'. The aim of the exhibition was 'to stimulate trade, to strengthen the bonds that bind the Mother Country to her Sister States and Daughters, to bring all into closer contact the one with the other, to enable all who owe allegiance to the British flag to meet on common ground, and to learn to know each other . . . Wembley presents the British Empire at the summit of its achievement.' The golden casket given to King George V (which was available for purchase by the public in model form) displayed 'the World resting on four British lions indicative of the importance of the British Empire in the affairs of the world'. Extraordinary exotic pavilions and palaces arose over some two hundred and sixteen acres. Each was dedicated to a dominion, a protectorate or a colony, to the arts, youth or engineering and there was even – shades of 1951 – an amusement park. The exhibition reached its climax with a great Pageant of Empire in which 12,000 performers filled the newly built Wembley Arena with a series of re-enactments celebrating the history and destiny of the British Empire. We need hardly add that it was that 'Poet of Empire', Rudyard Kipling, who in 1924 named the pavilions and walks (e.g. The Great Circle, Drake's Way). G. K. Chesterton, writing in the *Illustrated London News*, mused on this spectacle of imperial grandeur staged 'as if we claimed to have a sun and a solar system all to our selves'. In the aftermath of the terrible events of the First World War he hoped that Britain would turn to Europe and regard the Empire not as a mirror to look in but as a window from which to look out on to the world around.

Chesterton was right. 1924 was *au fond* a socio-political fête. It presented war-weary Britain with a mirror not a window. The exhibition set before the survivors, and a new generation, the myth of Empire as a way of life and the future. It presented areas where 'there is a white population of two people to the square mile' which needed to be settled; the lure of India, 'the spell that draws Englishmen in the heyday of their youth to work', Canada, New Zealand and Rhodesia

who extended 'the hand of fellowship . . . to welcome every honest newcomer as an asset'. The Empire's hero was the engineer, 'our imperial adventurer'. Only in a temporary exhibition gallery in the Palace of Art did architecture, town planning and working-class housing make their appearance.

A generation later, in the aftermath of the Second World War, the Festival of Britain offered neither a mirror nor a window but rather an enchanted glass in which somehow the organizers, shorn of the magic of Empire, attempted to reconstitute a future based on a new secular mythology. The South Bank Exhibition set out to tell 'one continuous, interwoven story . . . of British contributions to world civilisation in the arts of the people'. It was no longer written in terms of an apotheosis of the crown and its Empire-sustaining heroes, but of a 'people' whose past was 'like pages torn from a buried book' striving towards an insular self-sufficient Utopia. Worse even than 1924 it not only failed to look towards Europe, already well on the way to forming the European Economic Community, it even virtually eliminated the Commonwealth. Fiercely nationalistic, and anti-imperialist, it was, as Adrian Forty writes, a 'celebration of the achievements of the Labour Government'. For those wearied of war and its aftermath, the austerity, the shortages, the rationing, the never-ending queues, it made visible a brave New World. In the words of its forbear, 'Britain can make it.' For that presiding genius of the Festival, Herbert Morrison, it made tangible to the masses the Utopia of the Welfare State, the salvation of society seen in terms of universal material provision, education and nationalization. It was the world of the Education Act, the Town and Country Planning Act, the National Insurance Act, the New Towns and the National Health Service conjured into a momentary millenary vision.

The iconography of 1951 is inward looking. The visitors were made to pursue a pilgrim's way unfolding 'the tale of the continuous impact that this particular land has made on this particular people, and of the achievements that this people has continued to derive from its relationship with this land'. It is poles away from 1924. Its view of history was patriotic, evolutionary and non-expansionist. All references past or present to divisions of rich and poor, of class, of state as against private education, of state as opposed to private medicine were, of course, glossed over as officially it was non-political. British 'supremacy' over the reconstituted Commonwealth of Nations rested no longer on power but on 'common ideas and ideals'. The vision was of harmony, of men and women heroically one, although descended from different stock (no devolution in 1951!), of a land teeming with natural resources to be tapped by valiant workers in field and factory, where traditional skills and crafts were cherished, where industry and commerce were about to boom and bring a hitherto unknown universal prosperity; above all the past, present and future were seen to be moulded by the British, a 'mixed and versatile folk', whose character combined 'on the one hand, realism and strength, on the other fantasy, independence and imagination'.

The South Bank conjured a *ville imaginaire* which purveyed a remarkably consistent stylistic statement, not an original one, as Reyner Banham and William Feaver point out, but derivative. Its roots were in Scandinavia and in Italy, in the work of the Bauhaus and Mies van

der Rohe, the whole presented in a flight of surrealist fantasy as the life style of the new technological age. The deliberate selection and combination of this type of architecture and decoration as the outward expression of the 'idea' of the Welfare State was to have important repercussions. The Festival was a rare instance in modern times of the British Government setting out to promote a style, and its vitality is reflected by any study of the subsequent creativity of the Department of the Environment (then the Ministry of Works) and Her Majesty's Stationery Office. Indeed, in some areas of official government design the Festival fifties still reign supreme. As William Feaver writes, the Festival epitomized for a whole generation what was modern:

> Braced legs, indoor plants, colour-rinse concrete, lily-of-the-valley splays of light bulbs, aluminium lattices, Cotswold-type walling with picture windows, flying staircases, blond wood, the thorn, the spike, the molecule: all became the Festival Style.

Colours were supposed to match the mood of 1951: 'cheerful'. It was the age of a lick of red, white and blue paint over anything to give it a quick face-lift, most of all over anything Victorian. This was *ab initio* conceived as a classless style for the masses – for the council flat, for the terrace and semi-detached house. Even more it was a style of decoration which, by flushing off doors and chipping away Victorian and Edwardian decorative excrescences, could be superimposed on to the interiors of the decayed suburbs of our nineteenth-century cities.

In spite of all this one still continues to regard it with a certain affectionate nostalgia. A 'narcotic' is how Adrian Forty succinctly categorizes it. And it was. Like all the great fêtes in history it solved nothing, but, for a brief fleeting moment, it presented a mirage of hope. Two years later a different enchanted glass was held up by the Conservative Government whose first task had been to sweep away the South Bank vision. Their vehicle was the Coronation of 1953. This time the Festival Style was redeployed for a hierarchy of crowned heads and coroneted aristocracy. The style was turned to the service of a revamped imperial iconography, motifs salvaged from the historic repertory of British imperialism, transmuted into terms of Commonwealth and the image of a Queen of many lands and many peoples far flung across the globe. As a style for the mythology of modern monarchy it was as remarkably ill-suited as it was for the liturgy of the Church of England. The Festival Style belongs firmly and squarely to the world of the New Towns, to the piazzas and pedestrian precincts, the espresso bars and community centres, to the blocks of council flats and rows of little houses and, above all, to the office buildings of the idea it expressed most, that of the post-war Welfare State.

1 Introduction

BEVIS HILLIER

A FAVOURITE QUESTION in English history examination papers is: 'Was Henry VII the last of the medieval monarchs or the first of the modern rulers?' In the same way, one may ask whether the Festival of Britain, 1951, marked the beginning of something or the end of something.

Dr Roy Strong, Director of the Victoria and Albert Museum, who commissioned an exhibition to celebrate the twenty-fifth anniversary of the Festival, has suggested that 'It was the last really great stylistic statement this country made; it's still having repercussions even now. I think probably in remote hotels in Inverness they're still doing things that were started by the Festival of Britain.' Barbara Jones, much involved in Festival design (pp. 129–32), thinks that 'the Festival had a real and lasting effect on private life in Britain. Clothes, streets, houses and thousands of things in daily use have slowly got brighter and lighter ever since, and this change can be traced directly back.' William Feaver observes that 'Festival mannerisms kept reappearing', and rightly sees in Coventry Cathedral the 'apotheosis' of the Festival Style. Jack Godfrey-Gilbert (pp. 160–1), the architect who was deputy to John Ratcliff in the exhibition of architecture, town planning and building research at Poplar, writes: 'The Dome of Discovery and the Skylon epitomized the production of new thinking, new ideas, a new world, higher standards of design in everything. A new architectural language was born.' And Brian Aldiss, who as a science fiction writer must have exacting standards of anticipation, regards the Festival as 'a memorial to the future'.

Cover of New Worlds, *autumn 1951: the main features of the South Bank architecture were thought 'futuristic' enough to form the background to a science-fiction maiden on a surrealist motor-scooter (see pp. 176–8).*

But many people – among them, surprisingly, leading organizers and architects of the Festival – take a quite contrary view. Ralph Tubbs, the architect of the Festival's main and perhaps most revolutionary building, the Dome of Discovery, saw the Festival as the culmination of what the Mars Group had been trying to achieve in the 1930s: the habilitation in Britain of new architectural concepts from the Continent. June Bottomley, who worked on the Festival site at the age of nineteen, writes: 'Although those promoting and working on the Festival were mostly optimistic and responsive to its demands, I do not recall that it made much impact on suburbia or that the nation's mood was particularly festive. . . . I would not say the Festival left a lasting impression except in the display world.' This suggestion is confirmed by the playwright Arnold Wesker who looked in vain for the new Festival materials and design in an East End decorator's shop in 1951. W. Y. Carman (p. 183), a visitor, was disappointed not to find at the Festival the kind of stylistic lead the 1851 exhibition had offered. Charles Plouviez (pp. 165–6), who was in the Festival Office, deplored the chauvinism of the Festival, as against the internationalism of the 1851 exhibition:

It might almost be said to mark the beginning of our 'English disease' – the moment at which we stopped trying to lead the world as an industrial power, and started being the world's entertainers, coaxing tourists to laugh

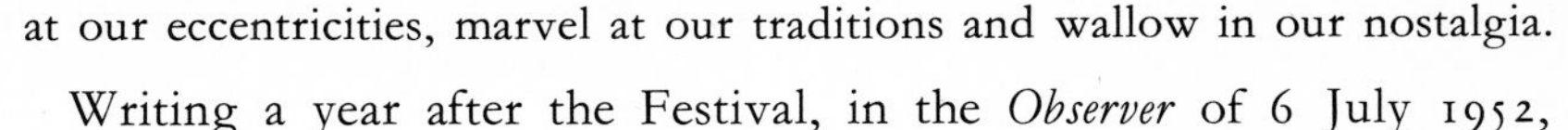
at our eccentricities, marvel at our traditions and wallow in our nostalgia.

Writing a year after the Festival, in the *Observer* of 6 July 1952, Marghanita Laski suggested that the Festival afflatus had died:

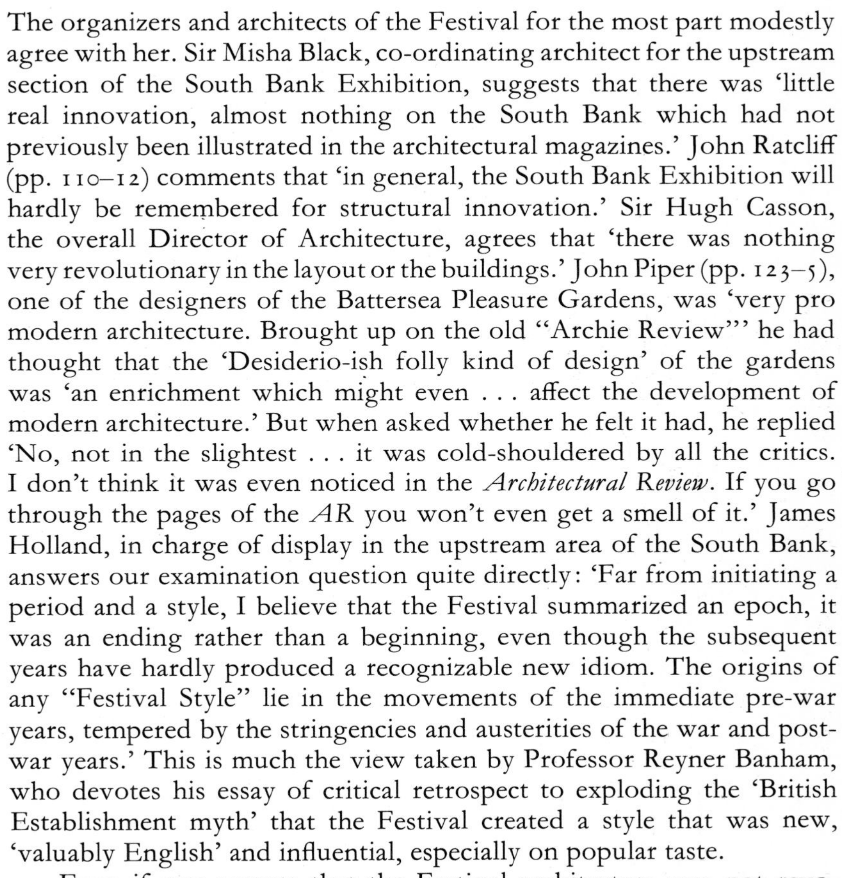
This time last year when our Festival was flaunting its pretty gaiety, we knew already that far from marking a rung on the ladder of progress this might be the furthest pinnacle we could reach. It was this underlying – this, as it seems now, all too surely founded – apprehension that gave our Festival such poignancy and strangely, such delight.

The organizers and architects of the Festival for the most part modestly agree with her. Sir Misha Black, co-ordinating architect for the upstream section of the South Bank Exhibition, suggests that there was 'little real innovation, almost nothing on the South Bank which had not previously been illustrated in the architectural magazines.' John Ratcliff (pp. 110–12) comments that 'in general, the South Bank Exhibition will hardly be remembered for structural innovation.' Sir Hugh Casson, the overall Director of Architecture, agrees that 'there was nothing very revolutionary in the layout or the buildings.' John Piper (pp. 123–5), one of the designers of the Battersea Pleasure Gardens, was 'very pro modern architecture. Brought up on the old "Archie Review"' he had thought that the 'Desiderio-ish folly kind of design' of the gardens was 'an enrichment which might even . . . affect the development of modern architecture.' But when asked whether he felt it had, he replied 'No, not in the slightest . . . it was cold-shouldered by all the critics. I don't think it was even noticed in the *Architectural Review*. If you go through the pages of the *AR* you won't even get a smell of it.' James Holland, in charge of display in the upstream area of the South Bank, answers our examination question quite directly: 'Far from initiating a period and a style, I believe that the Festival summarized an epoch, it was an ending rather than a beginning, even though the subsequent years have hardly produced a recognizable new idiom. The origins of any "Festival Style" lie in the movements of the immediate pre-war years, tempered by the stringencies and austerities of the war and post-war years.' This is much the view taken by Professor Reyner Banham, who devotes his essay of critical retrospect to exploding the 'British Establishment myth' that the Festival created a style that was new, 'valuably English' and influential, especially on popular taste.

Even if one accepts that the Festival architecture was not revolutionary, the fact that architects were able to impose it on the public after the Festival *was* revolutionary. This is a legacy which some of the Festival architects themselves deplore, as was shown by this passage of discussion tape-recorded at a dinner for Festival 'survivors' at the Royal College of Art in 1975:

JAMES GARDNER: I think architecturally it showed what we were going to be like for a bit.

SIR MISHA BLACK: I think that was why it was disastrous. I mean, I think that it was a curious mixture of exaltation mixed with disaster. I think that the results, in fact, were more harmful than useful.

RALPH TUBBS: But you could say that about Le Corbusier.

SIR MISHA BLACK: What it did, if I can just finish . . . it suddenly proved that Modern Architecture with a capital M was in fact acceptable. . . . Before the Festival, all the developers and all the get-rich-quick-on-the-

The Centenary pavilion – the 'little Crystal Palace building' at the foot of the Shot Tower, a token commemoration of the Great Exhibition of 1851.

maximum-amount-of-land-which-you-could-afford-to-buy characters believed that the only kind of architecture which was saleable was –

SIR HUGH CASSON: – National Farmers' Union.

SIR MISHA BLACK: . . . was National Farmers' Union. And suddenly after the South Bank they realized in fact that this kind of architecture was common currency, that people accepted the South Bank without cavil. And it released a flood of the worst kind of bastardized modern architecture which the country had ever seen, and from which we have been suffering ever since. And . . . I think that the harm which it did architecture was much greater than the good.

But even on this there can be two points of view. Brian Aldiss sees the Festival influence as delivering Britain from the horrors of Victorian architecture:

The cities of England 1951, not least its capital, were dominated by gloomy nineteenth-century buildings and bomb sites. Today, we may be fond of Victorian architecture because it no longer appears to dominate us with its funereal-and-marzipan pomposity; we have diluted it with beautiful structures like the Vickers Building and Centre Point. I'm sure a trip in a time machine to 1951 would re-awaken a hatred for the over-dressed pretensions of Victoriana. To it, and to the rat-infested ruins created by the war, the clarity of the South Bank in '51 came like a bite of lemon at half-time.

To its organizers, the Festival was neither a beginning nor an end, neither exclusively innovative nor exclusively nostalgic. Its ostensible purpose was to commemorate the centenary of the Great Exhibition of 1851. The idea of such a celebration had been first suggested to the Government by the Royal Society of Arts in 1943, and it was revived in the open letter which Gerald Barry addressed to Sir Stafford Cripps in the *News Chronicle* of 14 September 1945 which led to the Festival. But the centenary of 1851 was no more than a pretext – like the trivial *casus belli* that sparks off a war between two nations which have long been spoiling to scratch each others' eyes out. At the Royal College dinner, James Gardner recalled an embarrassing moment, at a late stage of designing the Festival, when it was suddenly realized that no provision had been made for an exhibit to recall 1851:

The funny thing is, do you know that building, that little Crystal Palace building that was at the bottom of the Shot Tower, was not in the original plans or layouts; and I did a doodle one evening and we showed it to Barry; he said 'Oh, it's marvellous' – it was just his cup of tea. Everyone had forgotten that we must have something, or we should have something, about 1851. So he said 'We must have that', but we said 'But there's no budget for it.' So he said, 'Oh, you go ahead with it.' And there was never any official budget for it, but somebody paid for it. And the joke is, it was the last thing demolished.

The Festival was originally conceived as an international exhibition with a strong emphasis on trade. We would demonstrate to the world our recovery from the war. Other nations would be invited to exhibit. But calculations based on using a Hyde Park site (as in 1851) showed that such a scheme would consume a third of the constructional labour of London for about three years, at a time when there was much war

damage to make good. So the ambitious plan was pared down to a British trade exhibition with an exhibition of the arts; but this plan too was radically altered when Herbert Morrison took over from Stafford Cripps as 'Lord Festival' and appointed the imaginative Gerald Barry as Director General. The nucleus of the Festival was to be an exhibition on the South Bank of the Thames, with Pleasure Gardens at Battersea. But from an early stage it was a policy decision that the whole of the United Kingdom should be involved in the Festival, with local celebrations, grants from the Arts Council for arts events and a 'Land Traveller' to carry the Festival message through the country, with a 'Festival ship', the *Campania*, to carry the same message round the coast. How far these local manifestations of 'the Festival spirit' were important in themselves, and how far they merely served as useful promotion for the London show, is debatable; but at least the Festival's organizers had a ready answer to anyone who suggested that the Festival was merely a London jamboree which the nation as a whole should not be expected to finance. The national character of the Festival was confirmed by the patronage and involvement of the Royal Family at every stage, from an address by the Princess Elizabeth at the Royal Society of Arts as early as May 1948, to the official opening and closing of the South Bank Exhibition.

The previous exhibition with which the Festival of Britain had most in common (always bearing in mind that it was in intention not just an 'exhibition' but a 'national enterprise') was the Philadelphia Exposition of 1876. This too had its pretext, its immediate *casus belli*: the centennial of American Independence, of which the bicentennial falls this year. There was special aptness in staging such a show in Philadelphia, for it was there that, on 4 July 1776, John Dixon gave the first public reading of the Declaration of Independence; and it was there that the new Constitution was framed, adopted and implemented for the first decade of the Republic's existence. But, as with the Festival of Britain, the real motive was to boost morale after a chronically debilitating war (in this case, the American Civil War), and to symbolize faith in the future, in the arrival of a new and happier era. Frank Anderson Trapp, Director of the Mead Art Gallery, Amherst College, Massachusetts, has written of the 1876 exhibition that its organizers wished 'to put the best possible face upon uncertain times and to call upon an idealistic vision of the past as the touchstone to the future'. The description serves for the Festival of Britain.

Significantly, both enterprises were led by war generals: in human terms, swords turned into ploughshares. General Joseph R. Hawley was president of the commission which supervised the Philadelphia Exposition; and General 'Pug' Ismay was Chairman of the Festival of Britain Council. The appointment of Ismay can be represented as a masterstroke of practical politics. Lord Beaverbrook's *Daily Express* and *Evening Standard* continually sniped at the Festival until it opened, partly from jealousy that the idea had been suggested by a rival newspaper, the *News Chronicle*, and partly because they associated the Festival with Herbert Morrison and the Labour party (though Morrison himself was insistent that the Festival should contain not a trace of party-political propaganda). Beaverbrook and his papers in turn influenced Churchill adversely, and the Lord President's office had great difficulty in preventing Churchill from coming out against the Festival overtly.

General Lord Ismay, Chairman of the Festival Council.

But 'Pug' Ismay, who had been Churchill's Chief of Staff in the war, could do no wrong in his eyes; and after he was appointed chairman, Churchill could not say publicly what he really thought.

A military strain ran throughout the Festival organization. Most of the organizers, the architects and designers, were young men, and being young, had served in the forces during the war. Military service had trained them in both long-term planning and the art of making *ad hoc* decisions; had taught them how imperative was clear communication throughout the organization; to know their exact rank and to do what they were told. Instant decision and instant obedience, perpetuated in Civvy Street by earnest young men with double-breasted suits, brigade ties and pipes, may make later generations smile or wince; but these qualities helped to bring the Festival to completion on schedule, within what must have seemed a nightmarishly short time.

That is the credit side; on the debit side, the employment of these young 'officers and gentlemen' did tend to give the Festival what Michael Frayn has called its 'herbivore' character. Barbara Dorf (p. 186), who spent the wartime years as a child in a north-west London suburb, writes:

The more one looked, the more one asked oneself: the Festival of *Britain*? . . . Whole vital areas of Britain were apparently ignored – the Midlands, the North – unless one counted some pleasing if prissy Wedgwood china as representing Midlands industry. . . . There was a fair amount of artwork, like mosaics and appliqué, the charm of which lay in its *lack* of professionalism and its Hampstead amateurishness. One assumed that this artwork was commissioned from friends of the organizers. . . . Very much of the Festival was alarmingly like a private club.

This is not entirely fair, since it takes no account of the many local exhibitions nationwide; and though the organizers did often commission works from, if not close friends, at any rate designers known to them, this was mainly, as Hugh Casson has explained, because there simply was not the time to put out most of the projects to public competition. But it does represent a fairly common criticism that the Festival was a paternalistic, 'Take It From Here' affair, a posh BBC-approved enterprise which did not draw sufficiently on the deep well-springs of British folk culture. There was a certain upper-drawerness about most of the Festival organizers, comically typified by Gerald Barry's casual remark in an account of a visit to see shot made in the old Shot Tower: 'Next time you are on the grouse moors remember Mephistopheles at the top of the Shot Tower.' At the Royal College dinner, Sir Hugh Casson accepted the 'Herbivore' label, and speculated as to what the Festival might have been like if 'Carnivores' had been appointed: for example, if Robert Maxwell, say, had been Director General, would he have made Noël Coward the caption writer instead of Laurie Lee?

If Ismay, as Chairman of the Festival Council, came from the most rigorously disciplined and 'Establishment' of all professions, Gerald Barry, as Director General, came from what is often regarded as the most irreverent and untrammelled of all: journalism. The journalistic strain ran as strongly through the Festival team as the military. Though

Casson was a qualified architect, he has made it clear that he got the job from Barry because he was a journalist: 'As an impecunious architect I'd moonlighted, doing journalism: I used to write "What to do with that cupboard under the stairs" . . . and I wrote for Gerald Barry in the *News Chronicle* on the future of architecture and all that sort of stuff.' Casson was a magnificent journalist – and still is: notice, in his contribution to this book, the deft pen-portraits of his Festival colleagues ('James Gardner . . . an imperturbable pipe-sucking and decisive figure, rather like an officer in an R. C. Sherriff play with a sharp sense of theatre'; 'James Holland – a relaxed replica of James Stewart') and his evocation of the Festival scene ('the National Anthem pomping through the intricacies of radar . . . the buildings, cockaded, groomed and patient like prize cattle'). Ralph Tubbs, too, advised the *Chronicle* on architecture, and Casson thinks Tubbs was appointed because he had written an excellent Penguin paperback on architecture. Soldiering and journalism have in common the necessity of keeping strictly to deadlines (which means quick decisions) and of communicating clearly. The journalistic habit of eliciting from an involved story a headline and captions was also valuable in making the complex narrative of the South Bank assimilable. And in an unpublished memoir kindly loaned by his son, Gerald Barry shows how integral to his thinking was the independence of 'editorial' matter from advertising which is axiomatic in good journalism:

A Festival souvenir tie from Battersea Park.

> An exhibition on this scale devised by the methods that we were adopting implied little short of a revolution. Always before, large-scale national exhibitions had been organized in trade sections, each displaying the accomplishments of an industry, a craft or even a particular firm. Space was sold to firms to display their own wares in their own way. This time we were going to dispense with all that. We were going to tell a consecutive story, not industry by industry, still less firm by firm, but the story of the British people and the land they live in and by. There was to be no space to let. No one would be able to have his goods on exhibit by paying to do so; they would get there by merit or not at all. There would be no Hall of Woollens or Pavilion of Sweetmeats or Garden of Horticulture; there would be no mammoth mounds of apples or effigies of Royalty in edible fats.

Gerald Barry was an expert and prodigal communicator. He personally kept up a barrage of Festival propaganda, through articles, broadcasts, addresses to the Royal Academy of Arts, speeches in the provinces with Huw Wheldon, and a lecture-tour in America, where he was relieved to find no resentment against the British junketings while America was fighting the war in Korea (though the Korean War drastically reduced the expected number of American tourists at the Festival).

Barry could always coin a golden phrase to catch the public imagination, even when the idea he had to put across was dispiriting or unpalatable. In the early stages of planning, it was thought the Festival would have to be housed in 'semi-rigid structures' (i.e. tents). The possibility of collapse under the weight of snow, and the difficulty of adequately fireproofing canvas, eventually ruled out this plan; but while it lasted, Barry presented it to his disgruntled architects as 'a twentieth-century Field of the Cloth of Gold'. He knew that the bright

Top, *a 'celestial omnibus' on its way to Europe.* Above, *Gerald Barry inspects the drivers before their departure (see pp. 170–1).*

colours of the Festival might be shocking to a nation schooled in drabness and camouflage grey; so in a broadcast he said of the South Bank design: 'We needed colour to make it sing.' When four London buses (pp. 170–1) drove off to spread the Festival gospel on the Continent, he compared them in a broadcast (27 July 1950) to E. M. Forster's 'Celestial Omnibus':

One of the greatest of living English novelists, E. M. Forster, once wrote a short story, which has become famous and found its way into all the anthologies, called *The Celestial Omnibus.* It was the story of a bus that broke the rules, that didn't keep to its itinerary and schedule. A few years ago I read a novel by John Steinbeck – *Grapes of Wrath* Steinbeck – called *The Wayward Bus,* which had something of the same theme. It would seem that there is a special fascination in the idea of something so ordered and circumspect in its movements as a public vehicle going, as it were, off the rails. It is a pleasant fantasy to play with, this notion of a bus-driver finding his normal routine intolerable and deciding to take another turning. Now on one day this week – on Tuesday morning to be precise – there were to be seen four brand new London buses of the latest type, shining in the familiar bright red paint, lined up on of all places the Horse Guards Parade in Whitehall – the Horse Guards Parade, sacred, as a rule, to the traditional ceremonial of the British army. . . . A most unwonted sight! In fact I suppose it was the first time that a London bus has ever penetrated this hallowed ground. . . . The fact was that these London buses were about to break the rules, to kick over the traces like the 'Celestial Omnibus' . . . and to take an entirely different turning. The Lord President of the Council, second only to the Prime Minister in seniority in the Cabinet, was there to inspect them. . . . These four buses, instead of running along the streets of London, were about to tour the roads of Europe. And the Lord President of the Council . . . had come to say good-bye and to wish them God-speed.

The image of the celestial omnibus, the inspired rule-breaker, was a parable basic to Barry's concept of the Festival. He knew that the British had been too busy making history for the last ten years to be in need of a gigantic, ponderous history-lesson. He knew that what they needed was a fling: the people who had been regimented so long by war and rationing must be allowed to kick over the traces. Again the right phrase sprang to his lips. The Festival would be 'a tonic to the nation'. The phrase was not wildly original, it could be easily digested; but it was not a cliché like 'shot in the arm' or 'breath of fresh air'. It was this vision of the Festival which made Barry such an ideal overlord. That he 'preferred fireworks to ballet', in Huw Wheldon's phrase, might make him the *bête noire* of Mary Glasgow at the Arts Council; but it also meant that the Festival was given appeal to the ordinary man; it was not allowed to sink into a bog of exegesis. Of course he knew that the Festival must have a serious *leitmotiv* if it were to be justified to the dour mandarins of Whitehall and the sniping Tory MPs. As Margaret Bean indicates in her recollections (pp. 183–4) and as Sir Misha Black admits with engaging candour in his, the educational side did sometimes get out of hand, and in the Dome of Discovery especially there was far too much to assimilate. But Dylan Thomas's astute poetic eye saw clearly that the Festival's main purpose was to be festive:

A Festival jumper on the Illustrated *cover of 5 May 1951.*

People who have come to the South Bank to study the growth and development of Britain from the Iron Age till now . . . will find no braying pageantry, no taxidermal museum of Culture, no cold and echoing inhuman hygienic barracks of technical information, no shoddily cajoling emporium of tasteless Empire wares, but something very odd indeed, magical and parochial: a parish-pump made of flying glass and thistledown gauze-thin steel, a rolypoly pudding full of luminous, melodious bells, wheels, coils, engines and organs, alembics and jorums in a palace in thunderland sizzling with scientific witches' brews, a place of trains, bones, planes, ships, sheep, shapes, snipe, mobiles, marbles, brass bands, and cheese, a place painted regardless, and by hand.

Perhaps you'll think I'm shovelling the colour on too thickly; that I am, as it were, speaking under the influence of strong pink. (And what a lot of pink – rose, raspberry, strawberry, peach, flesh, blush, lobster, salmon, tally-ho – there is, plastered and doodled all over this four-acre gay and soon-to-be-gone Festival City in sprawling London.) London: to many of us who live in the country, the Capital punishment. Perhaps you will go on a cool, dull day, sane as a biscuit, and find that the exhibition does, indeed, tell the story of 'British contributions to world civilization in the arts of peace'; that, and nothing else. But I'm pleased to doubt it. Of *course* it is instructive; of *course* there is behind it an articulate and comprehensive plan; it can show you, unless you are an expert, more about, say, mineralogy or the ionosphere than you may want to know. It's bursting its buttons, in an orderly manner, with knowledge. But what everyone I know, and have observed, seems to like most in it is the gay, absurd, irrelevant, delighting imagination that flies and booms and spurts and trickles out of the whole bright boiling; the small stone oddity that squints at you round a sharp, daubed corner; the sexless abstract sculptures serenely and secretly existing out of time in old cold worlds of their own in places that appear, but only for one struck second, inappropriate; the linked terra-cotta man and woman fly-defying gravity and elegantly hurrying up a w.c. wall; the sudden design of hands on another wall, as though the painter had said: 'Oh, to the daft devil with what I'm doing,' and just slap-slap-slapped all over the ochre his spread-out fingers and thumbs, ten blunt arrows, or as though large convict-birds, if there are any such, had waddled up the wall and webbed it as they went. You see people go along briskly down the wide white avenues towards the pavilion of their fancy – 'Our Humbert's dead keen on seeing the milk-separators' – and suddenly stop: another fancy swings or bubbles in front of their eyes. What is it they see? Indigo water waltzing to music. Row after row of rosy rolling balls spread on tall screens like the counting beads of Wellsian children fed on the food of the gods. Sheets of asbestos tied on to nowhere, by nothing, for nothing is anchored here and at the clap of hands the whole gallimaufry could take off to Sousa and zoom up the flagged sky. Small childbook-painted mobiles along the bridges that, at a flick of wind, become windmills and thrum round at night like rainbows with arms.

As counter to the passionate comedy of Dylan Thomas's account, we may end with the comment of tender melancholy which Ruari McLean, the designer, wrote in ink at the end of Marghanita Laski's *Observer* article in 1952: 'Personally, on that first morning when I first saw the Festival looking across the river from Charing Cross Station, it was so utterly beautiful and exciting that I wept; and later I loved it for other reasons as well.'

Right, *the Queen talks to workmen on the site of the* Royal Festival Hall, *2 May 1950*. Below, *a view of the Shot Tower (demolished in the early 1960s) which also shows some of the ground reclaimed from the Thames.*

Above, *the South Bank site in spring 1949.* Right, *Gerald Barry shows the King a model of the site.*

2 Recollections of the Festival

GERALD BARRY

Director General, Festival of Britain

1. A weekend of planning in the country

The more I thought about it the more I became impressed by the scope and above all the complexity of the project. . . . The first need of all – and it was urgent – was to rough-in a sketch of the whole picture, so that we could grasp its dimensions and know just what and how varied our task was to be. I therefore proposed that we should all spend as soon as possible a whole weekend in one another's company working continuously on this sketch. . . .

The response was immediate. We spent the first weekend in May at my house near Petworth, in West Sussex, all of us somehow packing in, and occupied the time in almost continuous session hammering out the shape of things to come. Weather and company were in their best form. In the daytime we sat round a table on the terrace with our sleeves rolled up, or paced the lawn in eloquent pairs, like walrus and carpenter, trying to grasp the immensity of our task and marshal the shoes and ships and sealing-wax into some sort of order and coherence. Below us the early summer landscape rolled away in succeeding folds of green and gold to the distant wave-crest of Chanctonbury, and the long, low horizon of the downs. In the middle distance stood the oaks of Bignor Park, dressed in the lime-green of their first foliage. Their beauty we inherit from an age of men that had such faith in the future of their country and so robust a sense of responsibility to their successors that they planted, not for themselves, but for their great-grandchildren. Here was our incentive.

2. A visit to the Shot Tower (December 1948)

Many people, myself included, at first thought that the Shot Tower should come down. It seemed to have little to say in terms of modern architecture and to be in danger of looking an anachronism. I was quite wrong. I reckoned without the sentiment of the Londoner and without the tower's possibilities. The ingenuity of Hugh Casson and Ian Cox, Science Director, turned it into one of the most attractive features of the South Bank Exhibition. The Londoner loved it because it was familiar, and its familiarity was given a new, exciting appeal by re-shaping its summit to accommodate a lighthouse and a radar telescope. The lighthouse had a special appositeness. Messrs. Chance Brothers, who supplied it, were celebrating in 1951 their centenary as lighthouse specialists; moreover it was they who manufactured the panes of glass for the Crystal Palace in 1851.

But whether it came down or stayed up, the work for which it was built must come to an end. . . . One day before it closed I climbed to the top to see how the job was done. It is often said that the shot for the troops at Waterloo was manufactured here. This is not so. This particular shot tower was built in 1826. There was at the time of the Napoleonic Wars another shot tower built in 1789 just the other

from 'Domes and Discoveries', an unpublished memoir, reproduced by kind permission of his son, Christopher Barry side of Waterloo Bridge, and it was in this that some of the ammunition for Wellington's army was made.

Visitors to the exhibition used to ask why they could not ascend the Shot Tower. If they had been allowed to try they would quickly have discovered the answer. The steps ascend in a wide spiral winding round the interior wall of the tower. There are 322 of them – I counted. One case of vertigo or exhaustion halfway up and the scene below can be imagined. . . .

The process had all the charm of the antique. At the top of the tower – or at a platform below if a smaller size shot was required – was a platform holding on which stood a large cauldron of molten metal, warmed from below by a glowing brazier. Beside it stood a vessel perforated at the base with a large number of holes almost too small for the naked eye to see. The scene was a John Piper burlesque. Over the cauldron loomed the gigantic figure of a man, sleeves rolled and forearms covered in long leather gloves, casting grotesque shadows up the wall who, armed with a ladle long enough for supping with the Devil, scooped up huge spoonfuls of leaden soup and emptied them into the monster colander. It was as primitive and domestic as that. Through the minute perforations of the colander the molten metal fell 120 ft into a large copper or hip bath at the base of the tower. As you stood below and looked upwards at it falling you were aware only (though it would have been different if you had put your head in the way) of a fine rapid rain. As the metal fell down the well of the tower it solidified, becoming first pear-shaped, then slightly concave and finally as it reached the hip bath a perfect sphere. . . . Next time you are on the grouse moors remember Mephistopheles at the top of the Shot Tower.

3. The opening ceremony

The morning of 3 May broke cold, misty – and *dry*. After a winter and spring of unparalleled rainfall, London had suddenly enjoyed six consecutive fine days: one raised the blinds on that Thursday morning hardly daring to hope for a seventh. It was an equivocal beginning, anything might be going to happen; but as we drove along to St Paul's hints of sunshine began to cast a pale promise through the mist. Crowds punctuated by police already lined the pavements, clutching Union Jacks and quizzing every passing motor. The grit spread over the empty carriage-way crunched like grapenuts under our sedate tyres.

Within the great cathedral the scene was supremely impressive. Here were assembled representatives from every corner of this island, the great and the unknown together: statesmen, diplomats, commanders, Members of both Houses of Parliament, Lord Mayors and Mayors in their robes and chains of office, leaders in the arts and the sciences, men and women of trades and professions, nurses, boys and girls – a rare gathering of the British people soon to be joined by their King and Queen and the whole of the Royal Family. Grouped in the aisles awaiting their resplendent part in the coming procession, or moving to their appointed places, were the Gentlemen-at-Arms, the Officers of Arms (Heralds), the King's Bodyguard of the Yeoman of the Guard, Yeomen Warders of the Tower, Trumpeters of the Household Cavalry – vivid pages of history in uniform.

Top, *dismantling the 'Lion of Hungerford' from the Red Lion Brewery, demolished to clear the site.* Above, *Gerald Barry and other Festival organizers with the smaller lion from the brewery gateway that faced Belvedere Road.*

With the Lord President, the Lord Privy Seal and Lord Ismay, I stood at the entrance to the portico to await the King and Queen. Opposite us stood the Archbishop, Bishop of London and Dean and Chapter of St Paul's, medieval in their copes. Over our heads stretched a blue and white canopy. Below us at the foot of the wide sweep of steps were drawn up a guard of honour of the Honourable Artillery Company, the band of the Welsh Guards, detachments of the Women's Royal Army Corps; in the centre, forming a circle round the railings of Queen Anne's statue, stood the Company of Pikemen of the HAC in their uniforms of the sixteenth century. In a vast arc facing the cathedral and all down Ludgate Hill an immense crowd surged and rippled under pressure from reinforcements behind and the restraining arms of the police in front. And here we stood at the top of the steps, a handful of men, privileged to occupy an almost empty grandstand to witness an instant of British history.

There was a lull, and some more arrivals. Up the steps came Winston Churchill, pausing above the first flight and turning with doffed silk hat and a broad smile to acknowledge the cheers of the throng. The Prime Minister, arriving immediately after, hurried shyly into the shadow of the portico almost as though alarmed by the applause: here was the contrast of two characters. Just then occurred the approved comic incident to break the mounting tension in classic style, like the porter scene in *Macbeth*. An incident perfectly suited, too, to the animal-loving English crowd: it was almost as though the thing had been 'planted' by an enterprising newspaper to provide a story and pictures. Next morning it was featured in the press almost as prominently as the pictures of the ceremony itself. A dog, escaped from goodness knows where and pursued by the affectionate derision of the multitude, scampered lankily up the empty roadway and tangled itself under the hoofs of the mounted police. Laughter, cheers and catcalls . . .

And now, from the furthermost reaches of Ludgate Hill was borne along the first seething intimation of the Royal approach. The crowds roared; the sun chose this instant to win its slow battle with the mist and sunlight glinted on helm and harness as the Household Cavalry jogged into view, escorting the Royal carriage. The King and Queen dismounted and climbed the steps, preceded by the Lord Mayor holding erect the Pearl Sword. It is a heavy sword and takes some holding. The Lord Mayor, who stands six feet four in his stockinged feet, held it as rigid as Cleopatra's Needle. So we greeted them, and they passed into the splendour within.

From my position next the centre aisle I could observe the procession at close quarters. The order of precedence in the programme reads almost like something from the age of chivalry. 'Portcullis Pursuivant, Bluemantle Pursuivant, Rouge Croix Pursuivant, Richmond Herald, Chester Herald, Lancaster Herald . . . the Archbishop preceded by his Chaplain bearing the Canterbury Cross . . . the Bishop of London . . . vergers . . . the Lord Mayor . . . the King and Queen, accompanied by nine members of the Royal Family.' The one incongruity in all this ceremonial was provided by two members of the Chapter known to me who as they came within eyeshot each gave me a prodigious wink. Surely, I thought, these of all people should have a more dignified sense of occasion, in their own place. But to them – I must suppose? –

St Paul's is simply what my office is to me, and this was just a rather more than ordinarily interesting piece of routine.

To anyone who had spent three years in helping to organize the Festival the service itself could not fail to be an experience deeply and richly moving. When it drew to its end and the congregation had joined in singing 'Jerusalem', those of us who felt constrained to join also in 'God Save The King' became quickly aware that this was not a setting written for the participation of ordinary mortals. From somewhere at the back of the cathedral trumpeters broke in with a descant that seemed to shiver the fabric of the building; so choir and organ brought the service to a tremendous close. The procession formed again, headed by the Gentlemen-at-Arms carrying their plumed hats in the crook of their arms. After them came the Heralds in square-cut, quartered tunics, black wands carried stiffly from the hip. So unfamiliar to the modern eye were these playing-card costumes they might have been clothing actors or puppets – until one perceived they covered men of sharply differing ages and shapes, one in particular so young, proud and handsome he might have been the prototype of all the heirs to English aristocracy, another so venerable the occasion was plainly an effort. Seeing these uniforms pass, one felt suddenly that St Paul's itself was too youthful a building for their presence. They demanded the antiquity of Gothic, not these renaissance rotundities.

4. Festival rock

My chief memory of the visit of Denmark's King and Queen to the South Bank is not one to be proud of. From the moment of their arrival at the Royal Pavilion the King set a smart pace, being an athlete and also no doubt having in mind engagements to come in a heavy programme. Being a sailor (he wore naval uniform) he went briskly through the Sea and Ships pavilion, then headed off at a trot past the Skylon towards the Seaside. Here there occurred a momentary check, the King pausing to see the Thames barge *Sara* dressed at her moorings off the river wall. I took the occasion to draw the Queen's attention to the stall where rock was being made and sold, and when she seemed interested I took a stick of it from one of the girl attendants and snapped it in half to show her that the words 'Festival Rock' ran right through the stick. (It was probably quite unnecessary, but it seemed a good thing at the time.) Would she, I asked, like a couple of sticks as mementos? Yes, she would, but she had three children – could she have three sticks? Handing me three, the girl said: 'That will be 2s 3d' (or whatever the price was). To avoid embarrassment I dived into my trouser pocket only to find I hadn't a penny of small change. 'I'll pay you later,' I hissed in what I hoped was an inaudible whisper; 'this is Her Majesty the Queen of Denmark.' She registered no interest except to repeat her request for payment. Queen Ingrid had by now begun to look in her own purse (but how should the Queen of Denmark on a State visit to England be carrying florins and sixpences?). A crowd stood about staring while, tension rising unbearably, I made another abortive attempt to penetrate the girl's defences. Mercifully at that instant the Science Director, standing at the Queen's left, came superbly to the rescue with the exact amount. But the crowning humiliation was to come. Accepting the money the girl next said: 'Can I have the coupons?'

Left, *perspective view by Hugh Casson of the television piazza, South Bank. The Television pavilion and Telecinema were designed by Wells Coates.*

Left *and* below, *drawings of the Skylon by day and night, by J. H. Moya, partner, Powell & Moya, architects, winners of the competition for a 'vertical feature'. This and the '51 Bar (see p. 105) were the only South Bank buildings put out to competition.*

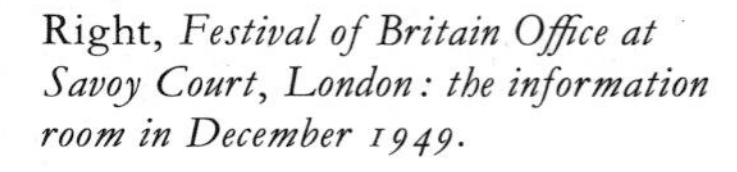

Right, *Festival of Britain Office at Savoy Court, London: the information room in December 1949.*

Right, *the Bailey Bridge decorations, designed by Misha Black. The river piling was designed by the chief engineer of the London County Council, and the bridge was built by the War Office.*

THE ARTS FESTIVALS
THE TRAVELLING EXHIBITIONS
THE SOUTH BANK
OF THE THAMES
The Site Today
South Bank Progress
SCOTLAND
WALES
NORTHERN IRELAND
The Concert Hall
This Month's Progress Chart

3 Festival Politics

ADRIAN FORTY

'THE FESTIVAL', said Archbishop Fisher at the closing ceremony in October 1951, 'has been a good thing for all of us: it has been a real family party.' The Primate's bland words spoke for the nation, in the way that Primates could in 1951 but can no more, and came close to expressing in the cosily domestic prose of the time what almost everyone must have felt about the Festival of Britain. The Festival had been fun, fun of a dimension rarely encountered in Britain at times other than major victories, and fun sustained throughout the summer (a wet one at that) of 1951. It is not easy for us now to appreciate the scale of the nationalized euphoria in 1951, when every paper produced a Festival issue, turnstiles jammed and queues formed to see the greatest show for at least twelve years, the exhibition of the 'British achievement in arts, sciences and industrial design'. The success of the Festival is undeniable: what needs more exploration is what the Festival meant in terms of contemporary politics, for fun, just as much as disaster, can have a political significance, especially when the fun occurs, as the Festival did, at a time of crisis. The epithet 'A Tonic to the Nation', coined apparently by Gerald Barry, the Director General of the Festival, expressed the establishment's view of the function of the Festival; but seen in the light of contemporary politics, and also with the hindsight of the way in which the relative affluence of the fifties was used to delude the population into believing that Britain's economic health was sound, it might be more appropriate to describe the Festival as 'A Narcotic to the Nation'.

Tonics are for patients who are past the worst. Although it was hoped that this would be true of Britain in 1951, ironically the Festival came too late to be a tonic, and by 1951 was an anachronism. The original plans for the Festival were laid in the last years of the war, and the preparations were begun in 1947, when the affairs of the world, and of Britain, looked as if they were starting to improve. By 1951, when the Festival was ready, Britain's economy was no better than it had been three years before (while the real truth of its inherent shakiness was beginning to be recognized), and the world situation was deteriorating: these were not the indications for a tonic, though because of the build-up given to the Festival, that was how it had to be presented. The Festival provided the illusion that Britain was recovering, which was very much what people wanted to believe, but in reality the Festival concealed the fact that the patient was suffering a relapse. It is the contradictions, between the situation for which the Festival was intended and the situation in which it emerged, and between the advertised purposes of the Festival and its actual effects, that deserve our attention now.

The first suggestion for a national Festival was made in 1943 by the Royal Society of Arts, which proposed a commemoration of the 1851 Great Exhibition; the idea was followed up by Gerald Barry, then editor of the *News Chronicle*, in an open letter in 1945 to Sir Stafford

Cripps, the President of the Board of Trade. Barry's idea was for an international exhibition, and this was the proposal examined by a departmental committee set up under the chairmanship of Lord Ramsden to look into the prospects of regular trade fairs. The Ramsden Committee reported in favour of a 1951 Festival, which was still envisaged as an international exhibition. The proposal seems to have slumbered awhile in the offices of the Board of Trade, and when it re-emerged one major revision had been made to it, that it should not, because of the expense, any longer be an international Festival, but simply a national one costing about one-sixth of the sum. Cripps was not interested in the revised proposal, and passed the matter to Herbert Morrison, Lord President of the Council, who presented the scheme to the House of Commons on the 7 December 1947. He explained that the plans for a trade fair had been dropped, but went on:

'Lord Festival': Herbert Morrison, Lord President of the Council.

Nevertheless the Government feel that it would not be right on this account to abandon the celebration of the centenary, and we therefore propose to mark it by a national display illustrating the British contribution to civilization, past, present and future, in arts, in science and technology, and in industrial design.

The decision to drop the international trade fair aspect of the exhibition was taken on economic grounds, but it is worth asking why the Government believed that an international exhibition would not have been worth the expense. In the first place, trading possibilities with a decimated Europe were clearly limited. But, in addition, British interest in collaboration with the European states had cooled after the flush of victory in 1945. In the years after 1945 the two alternative British strategies that were considered worth pursuing were either that Britain should establish herself as a third independent power to keep the balance between the US and the USSR, or that she should align herself closely with the US on the pattern of the 'association of friendship' discussed by Churchill in his speech at Fulton in 1946. The formation of a European alliance was not yet widely considered to be a sensible alternative, partly because of Europe's exhausted condition, and partly because of the British Government's suspicion of the politics of the European states, especially those of France and Italy, both of which had powerful communist parties. The willingness of Ernest Bevin, the Labour Foreign Secretary, to involve Britain in European politics was limited to co-operation on defence, under the terms agreed on the basis of the Brussels Treaty of 1948. Very reluctantly Bevin took part in the formation of the Council of Europe, but he was not prepared to extend British involvement as far as political or economic partnership. The majority of the British public was even less interested in European unity than Bevin, and in the circumstances it was not surprising that the Government showed no desire to pay for an international trade fair, which would almost certainly have raised the unwelcome question of European economic co-operation.

Once the international trade fair scheme had been dropped, Cripps decided that he did not want the Board of Trade to be concerned with the revised plan for a national exhibition to commemorate 1851. Nor, apparently, was any other minister much interested in it, so it was handed on to Morrison, who was the only senior minister without departmental responsibilities. Morrison's main job was to organize economic planning and co-operation between departments, and his own small staff consisted mainly of economic experts: not at first sight the obvious choice of department to organize a national Festival. However, if Morrison's colleagues were not interested in the Festival, Morrison himself was enthusiastic about it from the start. Donoughue and Jones in their recent biography of Morrison say that he really cared about the Festival and came to regard it as a pet project; and Max Nicholson, who was Morrison's permanent secretary, said that in his opinion Morrison attached even more importance to the Festival in his work than Donoughue and Jones suggest.[1] Part of the reason why Morrison cared so much about the Festival (he was nicknamed 'Lord Festival') may have been that it was one of the few aspects of his work as Lord President which had any direct and tangible product, since most of the rest of his administrative activities only achieved their results through the work of other departments. But whatever Morrison's reasons for wanting the Festival, there is no doubt that it was through his patronage that the Festival was a success. Had he not been willing to take it on the plans might well have been quietly dropped, or at least cut down substantially more than they were.

Morrison's first task was to overcome the indifference of the other ministers and the Civil Service to the Festival. He succeeded, according to Max Nicholson, by a little gentle arm-twisting that he was able to exercise through his position of influence in drawing up Cabinet agendas. The co-operation of the departments seems to have been won fairly swiftly, and once he had confirmed that the Festival would have a share of the budget (the original total estimate was for £12,000,000), Morrison went ahead to set up a Festival Council which was to be responsible for the major decisions and appointments. The significance of the council was that it removed the Festival from direct ministerial control and demonstrated that it was not a party political event, a point which Morrison insisted on and defended throughout the Festival's gestation period and life. He saw the Festival as a national enterprise, and this intention was reflected in the appointments to the council, amongst whom were to be found a number of reliably apolitical British establishment names, such as Sir Kenneth Clark, John Gielgud, Sir Malcolm Sargent and Sir Alan Herbert, as well as two leading Conservatives, R. A. Butler and Colonel Walter Elliot. Although the Festival Council occupied only an honorary and advisory position, and the main work of organizing the Festival was carried out by the Festival Office, the council did take some decisions. The most important of these was its choice of the South Bank as the site for the national centrepiece of the Festival, in preference to the alternatives that were suggested, such as Osterley and Battersea Park.

Was Morrison's belief that the Festival was not a political event correct, or was this simply artful naïvety on his part? Taken literally, he was right that it was not a partisan event. Attitudes towards the Festival did not fall into party divisions, but were drawn along the boundary of the two groups which Michael Frayn has described in his excellent essay on the Festival as the 'Herbivores' and the 'Carnivores'.[2] The Festival was the triumph of the Herbivores, who, according to Michael Frayn, were

1. The sources of information about Morrison's career are limited because he destroyed many of his own papers, and his official papers are not yet available. The biography by Bernard Donoughue and G. W. Jones, *Herbert Morrison: Portrait of a Politician* (London 1973), is based heavily on interviews with people who knew Morrison. In this chapter I have drawn from Donoughue and Jones's biography; I also interviewed Max Nicholson, who provided me with information about the official organization of the Festival. The main printed source of information about the Festival is the booklet published by the Festival Office in 1952, called *The Story of the Festival of Britain 1951*.

All the quotations in this chapter, unless otherwise attributed, are from *Hansard*.

2. Michael Frayn: 'Festival', in Michael Sissons and Philip French (eds), *Age of Austerity* (London 1963).

A Low cartoon from the Evening Standard *of 21 November 1950.*

the radical middle-classes – the do-gooders; the readers of the *News Chronicle*, the *Guardian*, and the *Observer*; the signers of petitions; the backbone of the BBC. In short, the Herbivores, or gentle ruminants, who look out from the lush green pastures which are their natural station in life with eyes full of sorrow for less fortunate creatures, guiltily conscious of their advantages, though not usually ceasing to eat the grass.

The Carnivores consisted of an unusual alliance, not to be seen again until the Common Market debates, of right-wingers who despised every action of the Labour Government, the Evelyn Waughs and the readers of the *Daily Express*; and of a small number of puritan left-wingers, who, not without good reason, saw the Festival as an example of middle-class social democracy in action, with no opportunity whatever for the participation of the working class, the 'People', in whose name the Festival was created. The Carnivore combination kept up continuous abuse and criticism of the Festival from its inception in 1947 until its opening in 1951, whereupon they were silenced by the self-evident popularity of it.

The greatest Carnivore of all was Churchill, who, embittered by his defeat in 1945, consistently attacked most of the work of the Labour Government, but picked the Festival as the particular target on which to concentrate his most vituperative criticisms of its domestic policy. Given Churchill's reputation, this was embarrassing for Morrison (especially since he deeply admired Churchill), and it was to silence Churchill that Lord Ismay was appointed Chairman of the Festival Council. This was a most unlikely appointment, and surprised even Ismay himself, though he took it, out of relief at not having been offered something even more unpalatable. Ismay had been Churchill's wartime Chief of Staff, and was a friend of his, a relationship which made it impossible for Churchill to continue to attack the Festival in public, though it did not stop him from continuing to encourage Beaverbrook to employ all the powers of abuse of the *Daily Express* and *Evening Standard* on the Festival.

With the exception of the Battersea Funfair, which aroused the sabbatarian, anti-hedonist lobby into more violent attacks than were made on any other part of the Festival, most of the criticism of the Festival was made not of the content of the exhibitions, but of what they stood for. As for appreciation of the quality of the design, whatever the organizers might have hoped, that was limited to a few *cognoscenti*, whose attitudes are discussed in Reyner Banham's chapter. For the crowd, it was enough for the contents of the Festival to be new and unusual. What mattered much more was firstly that there was to be a publicly financed exhibition at all, and secondly that it was to take place in the draughty economic climate of post-war Britain: both points are vital for understanding the kinds of criticism that were made of the Festival, and also its ultimate success.

Post-war Britain was a land of shortages of a variety of kinds. Perhaps the most serious, because it affected many other commodities, was the shortage of foreign exchange currency, the result of running down the reserves during the war and of having had to resort to extensive borrowing. The exchange crisis was endemic, but it reared its head higher than usual on three occasions during the Labour administration. The first was in 1947, when full convertibility between sterling and dollars had just been restored, and there was a sudden rush of speculation against sterling, which, at $4·03 to the pound, was overvalued. The convertibility crisis was not resolved until, after a second epidemic of speculation in 1949, the pound was devalued to $2·80 in the autumn of that year. Although this temporarily stopped the drain of foreign currency, it had the undesirable side effect of raising the cost of imports. The third epidemic occurred at the very end of the Labour administration, in the third quarter of 1951, when there was a further rise of import prices, this time the result of the inflation of world commodity prices due to the Korean War.

The significance of these crises for the Festival was that they both provided ammunition for the opponents of the Festival, and also directly interfered with construction on the South Bank. The currency shortages put periodic squeezes on the supply of imported building materials, for which there was already a pressing demand for reconstruction purposes, for building new houses, schools, hospitals and factories, and for repairing war damage. Although the Festival only represented a tiny proportion of the national demand for building materials, the Festival's critics raised the question of whether it was right that any building materials at all should be spared for the frivolous purposes of the Festival when many people were without even a house.

In addition to the shortages of imported materials, there were domestic shortages, of which those of coal, steel and of skilled labour were the most serious. The coal shortage was an uncomfortably real experience for everybody in the winter of 1946–47, but the inability of the mines to meet the national demand affected industry as well, and in particular the steel industry, though the real problem here was a history of under-investment and insufficient productive capacity. The third problem, the shortage of skilled labour, was particularly acute in the building industry, and it was in its demand for skilled building

A Low cartoon from the Evening Standard *of 6 April 1951.*

tradesmen that the Festival was most guilty by using more than its share of the London labour supply, though this was not an aspect of the Festival's economy that was picked on by its critics.

Apart from their political implications for the Festival, the shortages of steel, wood and labour also interrupted construction work. Sir Hugh Casson, Director of Architecture on the South Bank, found that many of the designs for the pavilions had to be revised when he was told that little or no wood would be available following devaluation in 1949. Similarly, as a result of the steel famine, the Festival Hall had to be substantially redesigned with much less structural steel. But it was not only through the shortages of the particular commodities of which the Festival was a consumer that the opponents of the Festival found fuel for their attacks, but also in the fact that most consumer goods continued to be rationed until the early 1950s just as severely as they had been during the war, and in some cases even more severely (bread, for example, which had never been rationed during the war, was rationed briefly in 1946). That the Government was prepared to spend £12,000,000 on an event which seemed far from necessary when most people were forced to do without things that no doubt seemed to them, as individuals, very necessary, struck some as a sign of the Government's inability to get its priorities right.

Morrison handled all these criticisms both skilfully and successfully. To those, like the arch-Tory Sir Waldron Smithers, who asked trying questions, like how many houses could be built with the materials allocated to the Festival, and did the Lord President realize that there were still 2,300 people in Orpington waiting for a home?, Morrison's customary and effective reply was that the Festival had been agreed to by all parties, and that if the opponents of the Festival did not like it, they could attack it openly on grounds of principle, but not by sniping criticisms of this kind. On the occasions when the principles were criticized, Morrison always succeeded in convincing the House of Commons that Britain needed the Festival. In a full debate on the

A cartoon from the News Chronicle *of 24 November 1949.*

economic situation in October 1949, when all public expenditure was cut, and the Festival survived its darkest hour with a reduction of only £1,000,000, Morrison argued that to abandon the Festival because of the crisis would be like going into mourning. 'Is that the way', he asked rhetorically, 'to buck ourselves up when we are in difficulties? I do not think it is.' The Festival came in for renewed criticism at the end of 1950 and in early 1951, by which time the Korean crisis had taken on a menacing aspect. Morrison was asked a number of times whether he would defer or cancel the Festival in view of the war. It would not have been worth stopping the Festival at such a late stage, but Morrison preferred to defend it in the same kind of way as he had before:

> I quite agree that there is plenty to be anxious about in the state of the world, but we do not know how long this anxiety without large scale war is going on . . . and . . . in this situation, which may continue, it is profoundly important that we should keep the self-respect and morale of the British people on a high level.

The Korean War precipitated the Labour Government's worst internal crisis, around the contentious issue of the introduction of National Health Service teeth and spectacle charges. In the budget of April 1951, Hugh Gaitskell, the Chancellor of the Exchequer, was forced to reduce domestic expenditure to pay for the military commitment in Korea that the Americans had asked for, and that Attlee had agreed to provide. The domestic cuts affected all the social services, including the NHS. Gaitskell insisted that charges for teeth and spectacles be introduced as part of the saving, but Aneurin Bevan, who, although he was no longer Minister of Health, had been principally responsible for the creation of the NHS, had promised that he would not allow charges to be introduced as long as he was a member of the Government. The situation was made worse by the mutual dislike of Bevan and Gaitskell, and also by the absence of Attlee, who was ill at the time. Gaitskell, backed up by Morrison, refused to give way, and Bevan resigned, taking with him Harold Wilson, the President of the Board of Trade. Bevan's departure attracted much attention in the press and in the country as a whole, and gave the Government a lot of unwanted publicity. On the 3 May, two weeks after Bevan's resignation, the Festival opened; not only were the words of Bevan's last ministerial speech still fresh in people's minds, but the papers were full of the recent British casualties in Korea; within two weeks they were to report the defections of Burgess and Maclean. May 1951 was not an auspicious month for the Government, and, combined with the cold wet weather, it might have seemed an inauspicious month for the Festival too.

In its role as a foreign currency earner, the Festival was also a victim of the Korean War, because fewer Americans than had been expected came across the Atlantic to see it. One of the counter-arguments that had been used to defend the Festival against those critics who accused it of consuming expensive imports was that it might earn foreign currency, and especially dollars, from tourists. As things turned out 14 per cent more tourists did visit Britain in 1951 than in 1950, but Americans, who had been put off foreign travel by the war scare, did not figure largely among the increase. Unless it was to distract the public's attention, the summer of 1951, when we seemed to be on the brink of another world war, was not a time that any politician would have picked as an occasion for a major national exhibition celebrating the end of the previous war.

Yet in spite of this calendar of setbacks, disaster and deprivation, the Festival was a great success with the public, and in a contrary sort of way the accumulation of adversity may have contributed to the popularity. In the first place, the Festival was a unique event, so unusual that it distracted people's attention from other events, and, in the particular circumstances of 1951, it acted as a strong and popular narcotic, which is probably what Morrison had hoped. Secondly, because of that peculiar trait in the English psyche which makes people more willing to enjoy themselves when they have had to sacrifice something first, the Festival, which appeared to have survived the economic crises at the cost of many individual sacrifices of benefits like housing and petrol, was more rather than less popular for taking place at a time of austerity. The sacrifice, in view of the actual cost of the exhibition, was more imagined than real, but it may nevertheless have helped people to feel that it was 'their show'.

Whatever the facts about the Festival's popularity in 1951, there is no doubt that it would have been much more timely if it had taken place about three years earlier. By 1951, in a deteriorating world situation, and in the expiring breaths of the Labour administration, the Government's great achievements were long past. Most of the reforming zeal of the Labour Government was exhausted by the end of 1947, when all the great social and economic reforms, the National Health Service, National Insurance, the New Towns, the Town and Country Planning Act, had been established, and all the main plans for nationalization, with the exception of steel, had been completed. The last three years of the Labour administration were taken up with coping with a succession of crises, and no very radical reforms were either proposed or attempted.

The cautiousness of the Labour party in these years was one of the main reasons for Bevan's disagreement with the rest of the Government, and in particular with Morrison, who believed that there was no need for any further reforms, and that the Government's task should be simply to tidy up the organization of those industries which had been nationalized. In addition, the leadership of the party suffered from serious exhaustion after 1947, affecting the party both mentally and physically (Attlee and Morrison were seriously ill, and both Bevin and Cripps died). The Festival, which was initiated in 1947, at the peak of the Government's activity, would have been much more effective from a political point of view if it had occurred within a year of its birth; but because of the time taken to plan, organize and build, the Festival was not ready until the heroic period of the Government's administration was over, and not before there was a thickening atmosphere of national gloom. It was with good reason that an MP could ask what there was to celebrate in 1951.

The question of what the Festival was celebrating came up from time to time, and the answer was not as obvious as Morrison often made it seem. Officially, the purpose of the exhibitions was to illustrate the British contribution to civilization since 1851, in the arts, in science and technology, and in industrial design. A literal reading of the exhibition catalogues confirms that this was indeed what the Festival was about, and the visitor was frequently reminded that the discovery of the atom and the invention of radar were British achievements. However, some more perceptive critics did realize that the Festival might be interpreted as a celebration of the achievements of the Labour Government. Morrison himself refuted any such suggestion, and turned down the requests of some of the left-wing members of the Labour party for more attention to be drawn to the Government's achievements since 1945. In the exhibition as it opened there was indeed nothing, except in the Schools pavilion on the South Bank, that referred to recent reforms, and even there Morrison intervened to remove all mention of the politically hot subject of free school meals.

Nevertheless, if we step back from the contents of the exhibitions, it was clear that at least some of the success of the Festival was generated by the popularity of the social reforms. Even the Ramsden Committee, which had seen the purpose of the Festival as a celebration of the peace (which it was partly, a kind of Triumphal Parade of the Arts of Civilization, though not so blatantly so as the Paris Exhibition of 1925 had been), made one important condition to their recommendation:

To justify the heavy expenditure of money and the large allocation of labour necessary to make an international exhibition a success, it is essential that in the meanwhile there must have been adequate progress made in the provision of dwelling houses, schools and other public institutions already promised, and in addition sufficient industrial buildings of all classes provided to enable industry to function efficiently.

The Ramsden Committee carefully avoided all mention of social reform, but nevertheless their meaning was clear, that the Festival would be neither justifiable nor a success unless the Government could demonstrate a successful reconstruction programme. As reconstruction and social reform were not distinguished in the Labour party programme, the Festival could not fail to be a celebration of both, and that was how it was understood by the majority of visitors. The South Bank was above all something real that people could see and enjoy, a more vivid experience than such worthwhile but unglamorous moments as the citizen might find, NHS card in hand, sitting in a doctor's waiting room.

Although this was how many visitors interpreted the exhibition for themselves, and it may explain much of the enthusiasm for the Festival, the exhibitions themselves told a very different story. Story it was too, because all the exhibitions, following the pattern of Ministry of Information wartime exhibitions, were designed round narrative themes. The South Bank Exhibition was planned by Ian Cox, a former member of the Ministry of Information, round the theme of the Land and the People. The guidebook informed the visitor that

The belief that Britain will continue to have contributions to make in the future, is founded on two factors from which, in combination, British achievements, past and present, have arisen. Those two factors are the people of Britain and the Land of Britain. . . . The land, endowed with scenery, climate and resources more various than any other country of comparable size, has nurtured and challenged and stimulated the people. The people, endowed with not one single characteristic that is peculiar to themselves, nevertheless, when taken together could not be mistaken for any other nation in the world.

The exhibition was designed to show the ingenuity of the British people in using the resources available to them, and to this extent, though not in any overt political way, it was a highly nationalist affair. The exhibition was meant to be, and was, an affirmation of faith, not only in British resourcefulness, but also in the British way of life; or, as the Archbishop of Canterbury put it:

> the chief and governing purpose of the Festival is to declare our belief in the British way of life, not with any boastful self-confidence nor with any aggressive self-advertisement, but with sober and humble trust that by holding fast to that which is good and rejecting from our midst that which is evil we may continue to be a nation at unity in itself and of service to the world. It is good at a time like the present so to strengthen, and in part to recover our hold on all that is best in our national life.

Archbishop Fisher's sermon at the opening ceremony of the Festival betrays something of the nationalist character of the Festival, now, twenty-five years later, its most embarrassing aspect. We can understand the British need to recover national morale in the late 1940s because of the way in which Britain's position as a world power had been suddenly, dramatically and permanently eclipsed in the closing years of the war. What is not so easy to understand is why this had to be done by such a studious censorship of everything foreign (a severe case of this was the decision to ban foreign foodstuffs from the South Bank restaurants and cafeterias).

Britain's withdrawal from European politics after 1945 has already been mentioned; at much the same time the argument was developed that Britain could act as an independent power, a 'third force' between the US and the USSR. The determination to take an independent course, expressed by Attlee's decision to develop the British atom bomb, encouraged politicians to ignore what was later to have a major effect on the British economy, the formation of the European Economic Community. The Organization for European Economic Co-operation had been set up in 1947 to handle the distribution of Marshall Aid among the European states, and in 1949 M. Schumann the French Finance Minister introduced his proposals for a European Coal and Steel Community.

Remarkably, these discussions in Europe received almost no attention in the House of Commons; nor did the early stages of the formation of NATO get much more parliamentary time, though because European defence was the one aspect of foreign policy that the Government took seriously, it did get rather more ministerial attention. Significantly, though, neither the European Coal and Steel Community nor NATO occupied anything like as much parliamentary time in 1951 as did the Festival of Britain, in spite of the subsequent importance of the former to Britain's internal as well as external condition. The Festival, in its nationalist aspect, seems to have been a symptom of the British isolationism of the late 1940s; and, in a more direct way, the enormous coverage that it was given in the British media may have helped distract attention from the developments that were taking place across the Channel.

Morrison's insistence that the Festival was not a political venture was, taken at face value, sincere. As he said on one occasion, 'the last thing in the world I would wish would be that this should turn into – or was ever contemplated as – a political venture.' On the other hand, Morrison's preferred political technique was to avoid direct confrontations and, while keeping the people happy, to carry out efficient behind-the-scenes management. Within this scheme, the Festival had an important part to play, and especially for Morrison, for the centre of his political empire was London; the Festival was heavily weighted in London's favour, and particularly South London's, where Morrison's main connections and his constituency were. Morrison's own remarks reveal how much importance he attached to the Festival as a means of keeping the nation docile and contented, as for example when he wrote at the opening, 'I want everyone in Britain to see it, to take part in it, to enjoy it. I want to see the people happy. I want to hear the people sing.' While these were laudable hopes and would have been approved of by almost everyone at the time, organizers and visitors alike, what is astonishing is the extent to which Morrison believed that he was capable of manipulating the emotions of the British people.

The state-organized fun was not, we should remember, restricted to the South Bank, but was carried into the provinces and villages of Britain: 'Spontaneous expressions of citizenship', said the Festival guide, 'will flower in the smallest communities as in the greatest.' The local festivals, which received no central government aid, took the form either of civic improvements, tidying-up and restoring historic buildings, or exhibitions of crafts, or pageants, concerts or plays. They helped overcome, in a small way, the provinces' cultural dependence on London, and to some extent counteracted the autocracy of the organization of the rest of the Festival. The local festivals were apparently a success, and in many cases, such as the reconstruction of the Colston Hall in Bristol, or the restoration of the Walker Art Gallery in Liverpool, or, on a smaller scale, a children's playground, seats and litter bins in the village of Abinger in Surrey, provided lasting improvements. But the real triumph was that eight and a half million visitors were drawn to the South Bank in the five months that the Festival was open. Twenty-five years later what is surprising is not only that so many people should have visited and enjoyed the Festival, but also that the Government should have been prepared to put it on, and that the public were so willing to join in and respond to the state-directed fun. Ten years of war, rationing and controls had established a tradition of bureaucracy in Britain; queues had become a habit (so much so that visitors to the Festival were found sometimes forming queues to nothing), and by 1951 people were thoroughly tractable in their willingness to enjoy a show which had been organized for them, but not by them.

Morrison's policy of planned fun was in the short run highly successful, in that so many people so obviously enjoyed themselves at the Festival, but did it affect the way people voted? In spite of Morrison's denials that it had any political significance, the Government was well aware that the Festival might influence the electorate. When Attlee wrote to Morrison about the best time to call an election in 1951, he justified in his letter his decision to delay until the autumn with three reasons. One was that the Festival, which would close at about that time, would have had the maximum opportunity to collect as much popularity for the Government as it could. Ultimately, though, the Festival probably made little difference to the outcome of the election (Labour lost, but won more votes than the Conservatives), since it failed to distract attention from the issues on which the election was fought, the crisis caused by the Persian nationalization of the Anglo-Iranian Oil Company, and the Korean War.

Although it is hard to put any precise value on the political effects of the Festival, it did represent an important step in the policy of state support for the arts. In 1940 the Government had set up the ponderously titled Council for the Encouragement of Music and the Arts (CEMA) to organize concerts and exhibitions round the country and help break London's monopoly of artistic activity. After the war CEMA changed its name to the Arts Council and carried on the same kind of work, while a new organization, the Council of Industrial Design was set up to promote good taste in product design.

The decision of the Labour Government to finance these two bodies indicates that there was a strong belief in some quarters that the arts in Britain both deserved and needed official support in peacetime as much as in wartime, if they were to survive and grow in modern society. The Festival itself was the apogee of this policy, since it provided the money and the occasion for architects, composers, painters and sculptors to work on a scale much larger than was normally possible. Morrison, whose approach to management was always rational and efficient, decided that while the organization of the Festival as a whole should be the work of the specially created Festival Office, the artistic and design contributions should be managed by temporarily increasing the budgets of the existing Arts Council and CoID, rather than by forming any new temporary bodies. In this way both the Arts Council and the CoID increased their reputations, while the Festival gave the CoID the opportunity to tighten its grasp on British taste, a monopoly it held for most of the rest of the decade.

The other aspect of the management of the Festival that is interesting, and particularly so in the light of the other work of the Lord President's office, was the decision that so far as possible the organizers of the Festival should be professional architects, designers, engineers, etc., and not professional administrators. The Festival was in part an early experiment in technocracy, a principle that was being encouraged in other fields by Morrison's office, particularly in scientific development, where Max Nicholson, an enthusiast for technocracy, was responsible, and also, though not successfully, in the management of the newly nationalized industries.

Why was the Festival so popular? What brought eight and a half million people to the South Bank, and sometimes over a hundred thousand on a single day – the equivalent of more than a month's visitors nowadays to the Festival Hall, the Queen Elizabeth Hall, the Purcell Room and the Hayward Gallery put together? What urged people to go there by night and dance in their overcoats to Geraldo's Embassy Orchestra? What could have made them enjoy the self-indulgence of the exhibits so uncritically, to marvel at tractors rising and falling on hydraulic plinths in the Countryside pavilion, and smirk at a plaster cast of the White Knight, there to symbolize British eccentricity? The Festival was a knockout because for the first time for ten years, people saw freshly applied coloured paint, saw new furniture that was not utility, saw buildings that were both new and also very different to anything constructed on these shores before, and had fun that was, in austerity jargon, 'off the ration'. It was the first sign that the life of shortages and controls was not far from ending, and that the future might be more colourful and more enjoyable than anything known before; it was an image of what Britain might be like with full employment and a welfare state.

While this was true, and certainly was how people appreciated the Festival at the time, we should not forget that the image was illusory and partly false. The Festival was the work of an élite, the Herbivores, and whatever ideals they might have had for the Festival, its most powerful popular effect was to create a chimerical vision of a world of plenty that seemed almost within reach. When the end of rationing and a general upturn in the economy in the mid-1950s put the chance of owning a fair range of consumer durables within the grasp of the majority of the population, the Government still sustained the belief in the chimera, though it described it as fulfilled. Harold MacMillan's memorable slogan, 'You've Never Had It So Good', was designed to persuade people that the dream had come true, and to veil other shortcomings from sight. Understood in this light, the Festival was partly responsible for introducing the particularly 1950s brand of political millenarianism that persuaded people not only that if times were rough they would soon be better, but also that happiness could be found through material possessions and plenty of shiny paint.

In 1951, though, the Festival basked in its own success, and the only disappointing part about it was its closing. Morrison had deliberately not made an early decision about when the South Bank should close, and had preferred to wait and see how the exhibition went. He seems not to have wanted to allow it to continue into 1952, as a number of people requested, since he probably thought that much of its impact would be lost if it dragged into a second season; and in any case he wanted the South Bank cleared so that the next stage of the Festival Hall development could go ahead. The buildings themselves were only temporary structures, which had not been intended to last more than a year, and would no doubt soon have started to look shabby if they had been left up for longer.

Although Morrison saw the Festival close at the end of September while he was still in office (by this time as Foreign Secretary), he never had the opportunity to decide the future of the Festival. Labour lost the general election in the autumn of 1951, and it was the new Minister of Works, David Eccles, who gave the order for immediate demolition on the South Bank. 'I am unwilling,' he said, 'to become the caretaker of empty and deteriorating structures.' He explained the haste with which he sent in the demolition contractors by his wish to have the site levelled and made into a garden in time to be used the following year for the Coronation celebrations, an appropriate Tory version of the public spectacular to succeed the socialist Festival of Britain.

Opposite, *the Sea and Ships pavilion, South Bank, under construction, architect Basil Spence, 18 June 1950.*

4 *Festival Star*

WILLIAM FEAVER

DETLING PARISH COUNCIL decided to do something about the Festival of Britain. A landmark seemed appropriate. So they took the official Festival symbol and removed the head and bunting which left them with a simple triangulated star, easy enough to peg out on the steep North Downs, directly behind the village. There were Nissen huts near by, still full of squatters, slit trenches in the woods, stray bomb craters from 1940 and, over the brow of the hill, the empty and already decaying runways of Detling aerodrome. It was only a day's work to slice off the turf laying bare the chalk. Then the Festival Star shone across mid-Kent. Detling had done its bit.

Abram Games's symbol was designed to go everywhere, on Downs, on flowerbeds, on the side of the exhibition ship *Campania* and on a variety of objects all more or less approved by the Festival Souvenir Committee. It appeared on ashtrays, horse brasses, on the Wilmot Breedon Festival paperweight with plastic wavelets lapping all around, on pencil sharpeners, commemorative soap and novelty Slipper-sox.

Cover of the Festival issue of Punch, *30 April 1951.*

The symbol proved wonderfully adaptable, incorporating as it did all the essentials of what came to be recognized as Festival Style – part romantic, part utility, part plain-sailing. It served as the Festival call-sign, as the design equivalent of the caption writers' catchwords 'Festival Spirit' and 'Festival Mood'.

Firstly it was jaunty, like Mr Therm. Hark the Heraldic. Then it was patriotic, though not stridently so: Britannia ruling the roost, looking forward sideways in Rank Charm School profile. Britannia resurgent stuck like a golf tee into the map of England, pinpointing and pirouetting with a subliminal suggestion of St Paul's looming through the war clouds, the phoenix arising and taking it on the chin. Flags fluttering, red, white and blue. Regatta rather than naval review.

On the exhibition guides the motif went whirligig, like a recycled swastika scything thin air. And, inevitably, it was parodied. Fougasse drew a special version for the cover of the *Punch* Festival number, the serene lady transformed into a frisky Mr Punch and the star wilted into banana skins. But the implications of the original symbol remained clear, a three-line chorus, 'Britain can take it' (in Crown Film Unit terms), 'Britain can make it' (as selected by the Council of Industrial Design) and 'Britain can be fun'. Margery E. Thomas wrote a poem about it for a *Festival of Britain* anthology published privately in Ilfracombe:

> *Her form is gaunt and steadfast,*
> *Her chin is lifted high,*
> *Optimism is her motto –*
> *And she will ne'er say die*

Clearly, despite her brand new look, the Festival Britannia was a matriarch at heart. She only had to lower her neoclassical visor and drop the bunting to revert to hard-pressed normality. For the time being,

COLOUR PLATE I: *an official Festival poster, bearing the symbol designed by Abram Games.*

Colour plate captions continued on p. 49.

FESTIVAL OF BRITAIN

II

IV

V

III

VI

◁ VII

VIII

IX

X

XI ▷

4'3"
1'0"
3 0"
6'5"
6'6"
10"
3'9"
Festival Gardens, Battersea
John Piper
1950

THE ILLUSTRATED
LONDON NEWS
FESTIVAL OF BRITAIN
1951

COLOUR PLATE II: *the Transport pavilion, South Bank, architect Arcon.* III: *the Fairway, South Bank, showing, at right, coloured canvas screen to York Road by Architects' Co-operative Partnership; in the background, the Rocket Restaurant, architect Gordon Tait.*
IV: *outside wall of the Homes and Gardens pavilion, architects Katz and Vaughan.*
V: *decorative wall treatment, South Bank.*
VI: *the space between two pavilions; in the background, 'abacus' screen, designer Edward Mills; right, the Homes and Gardens pavilion; foreground, sculpture* Youth Advances *by Jacob Epstein. The South Bank designers placed great emphasis on the landscaping of the spaces between buildings.*
VII: *a new source of decorative patterns was found in crystallography and developed by the Festival Pattern Group: top left, wallpaper by John Line & Sons, based on a crystal-structure diagram of mica; middle left, decoration for pottery by Peter Wall, then of the Royal College of Art, based on the crystal-structure diagram of haemoglobin; right, dress prints by British Celanese, based on the diagram of afwillite; foreground, PVC sheeting by Mary A. Harper for the Dunlop Rubber Company, based on the diagram of insulin.*
VIII: *detail from the embroidered relief mural 'The Country Wife', designed by Constance Howard and made by her students and members of the Women's Institute. It was exhibited in the Country pavilion, South Bank (Crown copyright; photograph taken by Peter Macdonald, Victoria and Albert Museum) (see p. 107).*
IX: *design drawing by Bruce Angrave for the Dragon, Tree Walk, Battersea Pleasure Gardens (see pp. 128–9).*
X: *paper model of the Emett locomotive* Nellie, *from a Puffin cut-out book by R. Emett and R. Keeling, published in 1951, shown here in made-up state (see pp. 125–7).*
XI: *design drawing by John Piper for towers in the Grand Vista, Battersea Pleasure Gardens (see pp. 123–5).*
XII: *cover of* The Illustrated London News *by Terence Cuneo, 1951.*

however, she epitomized the Festival's lightsome mood, carefully posed between highly serious and merely knees-up.

The names given to the South Bank pavilions (Minerals of the Island, Land and People, The Living World and Power and Production) struck a similar benign yet firm BBC For Schools note and were a far cry from the lordly titles (The Great Circle, Drake's Way and Aussie's Way) Kipling had thought up in 1924 for the Empire Exhibition at Wembley. But then circumstances had changed, and the wartime morale-boosters of the previous decade – Ministry of Information display stands and poster-campaigns, and Crown Film Unit documentaries – no longer fitted either. In his Festival film *Family Portrait*, for example, Humphrey Jennings redeployed his trusty nationhood imagery, everything bar Spitfires doing victory rolls over cornfields. But Beachy Head, Household Cavalry, Penicillin, Captain Cook, throb of Industry and all, it somehow failed to amount to a convincing national likeness.

Similarly, when the Arts Council, acting in something of a Post-War Artists Advisory Committee capacity, commissioned sixty painters and twelve sculptors to 'make their contribution' to the Festival the results were rather too worthy. Fifty-four out of the sixty paintings materialized at the RBA galleries in an exhibition called '60 Paintings for '51'. Large by the standards of the time, being a prescribed minimum of 45 × 60 in, their titles were symptomatic. They included *Hop-picking, Rye*, *Intruders in a Wood*, *Industrial Landscape* and '*As I wend to the shores I know not,/As I list to the dirge, the voices of men and women wrecked*'; in other words a medium wavelength range of specialities, from Braque-ish Cornish headlands to Lowry Lancs., from Josef Herman's mountainous miners to faun-like neo-Romantics alarmed by trees. All the artists had their costs paid and a jury picked five paintings for the Arts Council to buy. Of these only Lucien Freud's *Interior near Paddington*, with a rain-coated Soho character blinking in unaccustomed daylight beside a Triffid house plant, and Robert Medley's *Bicyclists against a blue background*, a huddle of Picasso-esque figures comparing Raleighs, appear to reflect any sort of Festival style or period-mood.

Besides getting Arts Council commissions several painters were also asked to do murals for the South Bank, among them John Minton, Ben Nicholson, Josef Herman and Keith Vaughan, whose outstandingly inappropriate *At the Beginning of Time* in the Dome of Discovery showed a batch of lads striking poses beside a mastodon skull. In best British Restaurant tradition many of the other murals consisted of cheery folk – Staffordshire figures crossed with S. G. Hulme Beaman's *Toytown* troupe – at work and play.

John Piper's stagestruck architectural panorama on the back of Homes and Gardens and Graham Sutherland's *Origins of the Land*, a pterodactyl-infested gravel pit, were at least characterful and different. But the most positive contribution by a painter to the South Bank was undoubtedly Victor Pasmore's ceramic mural outside the Regatta Restaurant. Pasmore had not long abandoned his misty Chiswick river-bank idiom for decisive and increasingly constructivist abstraction. Both the mural and his *Snowstorm: Spiral Motif in Black and White*, in the Arts Council exhibition, emerged as key Festival motifs: roughcast textures with cosmic overtones.

The main Festival sculpture exhibition was held by the LCC in Battersea Park. The mobiles there caused a bit of a stir and Marino

Mural by John Piper, Homes and Gardens pavilion, South Bank.

Lucien Freud, Interior near Paddington *from the catalogue of the Arts Council Exhibition '60 Paintings for '51'.*

Marini's customary horseman of the year was much admired. One piece was deemed so ugly by the head keeper he kept it hidden; in case it rained, and the plaster melted, he explained. The Arts Council provided a Henry Moore, *Reclining Figure*, a fine specimen with braced, Ercolion legs, for the South Bank; also Jacob Epstein's wide-eyed *Youth Advances* and Barbara Hepworth's *Contrapuntal Forms*, two limestone figures set high on a plinth beside the Dome of Discovery. These aroused interest, but the majority of the classified works of art on show proved not so much dull exactly as unnoticeable. If it was to suit the South Bank and look any good at all, art had to be mixed freely with the other exhibits. But then, as it turned out, everything conspired to upstage the sculpture, even the wiry chairs and conical flowerpots. The sculptures lay marooned, for safety's sake, in the middle of barrier ponds or were just things that stood around mute as you ate your sandwiches.

There were one or two exceptions: Reg Butler's *Bird Cage*, a paeon of spikiness, and Eduardo Paolozzi's wall fountain, an arrangement of cups and basins on a scaffolding which succeeded in hinting simultaneously at both Giacometti and Heath Robinson. Richard Huws, one of whose previous triumphs had been a talking Mechanical Man for the Fitter Britain Hall in the 1938 Empire Exhibition in Glasgow, made a 43-foot bucketing Water Sculpture which tantalized crowds for so long as it took to complete one of its teetering splash-downs: and so won more attention than all the other sculptures put together.

There were further magical effects which fell on the other side of the tacit demarcation line between art and exhibit: the gas flames hissing in the fountain at the end of the Fairway. These were especially dramatic at night: 'Flowers of Fire That Bloom When The Moon Rises', the *Picture Post* caption writer reckoned. And while Siegfried Charoux' *The Islanders*, a statue of a couple and child, was a sheer enormity, the great screens which separated everyday London from the South Bank world, one strung with balls like an atomic structure line-up, the other a mass of canvas panels, could be regarded as a novel and functional sort of sculpture. The Skylon, turbines and propellers, the coal-faced tetrahedron sheltering Minerals of the Island, the highly strung observation platforms beside the river: every major feature or exhibit seized attention and left the Fine Art looking prim and out of sorts.

The most calculated of all the bids to contrive a Festival style, and, eventually, its greatest cliché, was officially fostered by the Council of Industrial Design which, not content with presenting a photographic index of 25,000 approved products in the arches under Waterloo Bridge and selecting the manufactured exhibits, also decided to sponsor patterning. In 1949 Hartland Thomas, its chief industrial officer, had heard it mentioned that crystallography might provide intriguing and absolutely modern motifs. A Festival Pattern Group was established to make arrangements among fourteen manufacturers for the promotion during the celebrations of designs based on the crystal-structure diagrams or atom maps of felspar, china clay, aluminium hydroxide, insulin and haemoglobin. Misha Black's posh Regatta Restaurant was chosen as the launch spot with molecular and crystalline motifs on furnishings and tableware. John Tunnard did a globule painting on the walls and Pasmore's mural outside more or less harmonized with the overall scheme. Man-size atomic structures and snowflakes were ranged along the gallery and dress circle in the Dome of Discovery (which also contained a model atomic pile). 'Everything is made of atoms', Basil Taylor explained in the Official Book of the Festival.

Cover of Future Books, *volume II, edited by Marjorie Bruce Milne.*

On the cover of *Future Books*, vol II, 1946, there was a collage by G. A. Adams of a hole in a brick wall through which appeared a shining, peaceful, atomic-age city. Corbusier-designed, perhaps, more likely a mirage. It was one of a thousand reconstruction images of an England of super-highways, ivory tower blocks, unlimited concert halls, branch libraries and swimming pools at a time when reality, as often as not, meant hoardings to mark bomb sites with prefabs for the fairly lucky, Nissen huts still for a few unfortunates.

In 1951 the forseeable future, in terms of housing, was put on show in the architecture exhibition at Poplar. The South Bank, on the other hand, was a *Future Books* dream, a new Jerusalem, a Laputa, of White Knight, atomic piles, totem poles and Skylon, and one of W. G. Grace's cricket bats, of trees laden with red and white lights and of the possibility of a stereoscopic film-trip down the Thames in the Telecinema.

In the months leading up to the Festival the public was given two views of the South Bank: the site itself, all mud and scaffolding and industrial disputes, and the ideal, scale model. J. D. M. Harvey painted an official bird's-eye view from somewhere above Big Ben with the whole of South London sunk in typical post-war gloom apart from the festive spot basking in Persil-bright sunshine, perfect in every detail. Terence Cuneo made an even more affirmative picture for the cover of *The Illustrated London News: Exhibition Opening – Special Number*, with Britannia perched in the foreground checking her position on a globe, and a bronzed chap next to her gazing down with a quiet, minor public school smile on what the magazine described as 'a scene of remarkable architectural beauty in the modern manner', the Dome shining like a Trojan shield, the Thames true blue, the Skylon poised.

Cover of Patons and Baldwins Festival Knitting Book, 1951.

One day soon after the opening, Sir Gerald Barry made an ascent in the Festival balloon so as to experience this ideal view at first hand. As he rose and drifted towards Dartford the South Bank dwindled once again to model scale and the blemishes vanished. 'It was one of the most pleasant experiences of my life,' he said. Judging from aerial photographs, however, it appears that the actual place didn't quite match up to the picture forecasts; not so much in detail as in tone. The Dome looked flatter. The railway obtruded and the rest of London seemed not so different, not so bad after all. 'This exhibition needs sunshine', J. B. Priestley told Home Service listeners.

But then autopsy views are always bleak and, for the ordinary earthbound visitor ('Book your tickets in advance. 5/– all days except Tuesdays. 10/– Tuesdays. Make sure of getting in') crossing the Thames by Bailey Bridge, spurred on by Richard Huws's flickering ornamental spinners, was like time-travelling. On the far side lay the gleaming perspectives of tomorrow. The South Bank had an air of touchdown, the Dome a flying saucer, the Skylon on its zigzag supports ready to be catapulted to the stars, the Main Concourse imbedded with a criss-cross pattern of landing lights, the line-up of fountains at the near end splashing a welcome. Then you noticed the precinct sound: no traffic, just people's feet traipsing up, down and around, swarming through the installations, Lowry figures, crowd-scene extras from *Metropolis* or *Things To Come*.

Here, beyond doubt, was the Township of the Future, the sort of place Dan Dare strove to defend in 1999 from the appalling Treens of the Red Moon, masterminded by the tiny green-headed Mekon. But for those who knew a bit about the standard ingredients of world fairs the surprises were relatively few. The Dome, to them, was a streamlined version of the usual Grand Palais or stadium. The Skylon was the traditional vertical feature; if not an Eiffel Tower exactly, it was comparable to the Trylon at the New York World Fair in 1939.

And true, once the special effects had worn off – the scale and newness and tulip and fondant colours – the Festival sensation dulled a little. Follow the dotted line along the floors, stick to the Recommended Circulation and you were soon obliged to queue, never quite knowing whether it would be worth it in the end. For many of the buildings were deceptive. Indeed, one or two of the more Marks and Spencer entrances led to surprises. Inside the Lion and the Unicorn pavilion, for instance, there was a beguiling rush of 208 plaster doves way above the ground floor drollery. And the Land of Britain, which was decidedly banal at the start, suddenly turned into the Natural Scene where F. H. K. Henrion's great white artificial oak took over, a stream trickling round its base, ivy scrabbling along its branches. It was a splendid fantasy object, not unlike Enid Blyton's 'Faraway Tree' or the one the Swiss Family Robinson used as a house.

There were plenty of other superlatives: the tallest unstayed mast in Great Britain (a present from British Columbia), the largest-ever sheet of plate glass. The art of display being half the secret of Surrealism, the exhibition abounded in Dali, Magritte and Ernst effects. A biscuit-making plant operated next to a hypodermic needle manufactory. The Post Office Railway shuttled the mail along a brief track entirely automatically. Historic aircraft were tethered in mid-flight. Rear portions of an oil tanker, a passenger liner and a whale factory-ship stuck out of the Sea and Ships pavilion, just as Nash or Wadsworth might have imagined them. In the base of the Shot Tower kaleidoscopic views of London twinkled, while on top a radio telescope made soundings in outer space. As the shadows lengthened courtyards and concourses became de Chirico piazzas. Screens accentuated the effects, rockeries were provided in odd corners for neo-Romantic tastes and, wherever possible, windows, entrances and walkways were so arranged as to frame vistas, making them appear fresh off the screen or page. Everywhere scenes were composed in Ashley Havinden, Beverley Pick, Games, Henrion and Lewitt-Him graphic terms. So, bringing style to the fore, the South Bank reflected the marketing devices of Daks, Kia-Ora, BOAC, Mr Cube and Mr Therm. The World As Advertised.

It became difficult to tell where the 'Export or Die' goods ended and fantasy took over. The South Bank generated fictions. It was used as a backdrop for sci-fi and fashion photography, and the climax of *The Little Red Engine Goes to Town* came in the Transport pavilion. Leslie Wood (who had taken over the illustration of the series from the Lewitt-Him partnership) represented the Fairway in living-room terms with buildings like radiograms on tapered legs and the Dome an ultra-modern electric heater.

Up-river at the Festival Pleasure Gardens fantasy was the rule. Rowland Emett's Far Tottering and Oyster Creek Railway chugged 500 yards and back again, so deliberately whimsical as to be almost beyond a joke. The Lewitt-Him Guinness Clock performed remarkably and the John Piper/Osbert Lancaster collaboration (neo-Romantic/Architectural Review) resulted in some nice pastiche Regency and Fanny by Gaslight era effects. In the funfair proper private enterprise flourished. 'Moggo the Largest Cat Alive' may not have lived up to the claim, but people loved the flying saucer sensation of the Rotor, which pinned them to its walls as it spun.

Yet, for all this, the whole Battersea complex was overcast with

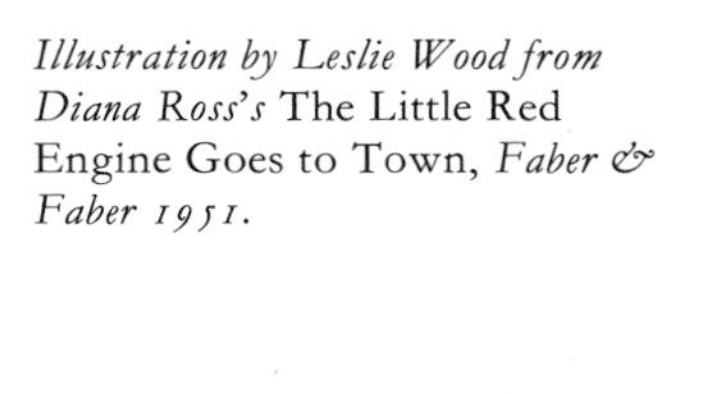

Illustration by Leslie Wood from Diana Ross's The Little Red Engine Goes to Town, *Faber & Faber 1951.*

municipal good cheer. It was as though Fonthill Abbey and Southend Pier had been taken over by the authorities, cleaned up and issued with a 'U' certificate. Worst of all, as it turned out, the Pleasure Gardens were neither cleared away at the end of the season nor properly maintained. While the new Conservative Government reduced the South Bank to a ground plan in 1952, the gardens were left to stagger on, decline and rot for the next twenty-five years.

But enshrined in memory the South Bank remained the popularly accepted idea of 'modern' for a whole generation. Braced legs, indoor plants, colour-rinse concrete, lily-of-the-valley splays of light bulbs, canework, aluminium lattices, Cotswold-type walling with picture windows, flying staircases, blond wood, the thorn, the spike, the molecule: all these became the Festival Style.

Style merges with jargon: and the Festival Style, which never achieved grandeur, was more remarkable for its conventions than for any masterpieces. An ode to petrol, entitled 'The Festival Spirit', may help explain why the South Bank became so quickly regarded as a period piece:

Let's be gay, goodbye to sorrow,
POOL today, but SHELL tomorrow.

For, while its futurism ensured its survival as a feast of modernity for some years, the dawn of what Beaverbrook Newspapers proclaimed as 'The New Elizabethan Age' brought with it fresh market forces. Brand names returned and multiplied. The Dome disappeared. The imbedded Fairway lights were smashed into little mudholes. The South Bank degenerated into National Car Park, Shell Centre and culture bunkers.

Meanwhile, however, the South Bank idiom spread. As Heathrow grew through the Comet years, adding observation decks and ever-increasing departure lounges, Festival mannerisms kept reappearing. In the New Towns carillon towers, token sculptures, malls and concourses paraded Festival airs. At Peterlee in County Durham Victor Pasmore contributed styling to an entire housing estate: Festival townscape persisted.

Coventry became the Mecca of the Festival Style. The Godiva shopping precinct with its fountains, flower tubs and raised walkways, its cosified scale and impression of not quite coming to terms with the brash methods of supermarketeering, is a perpetual South Bank. And Coventry Cathedral marks the apotheosis of the Festival.

Basil Spence won the competition for the cathedral design in 1951 and the building was consecrated in 1962. There, today, South Bank memories are enshrined. Enter through the bomb-site leftovers of the old cathedral, go down the steps and into the new. On the vast glass entrance screen John Hutton engraved a host of ascending Mintons. On a side wall, Epstein's St Michael strikes down the Devil: both have the same ravaged bronze eyes as the 'Advancing Youth' beside the Homes and Gardens pavilion. John Piper's stained glass flushes into incandescence behind the rough-hewn boulder font. The jutting choir stalls, the hi-fi ceiling, the pillars made to appear barely to touch the floor, the inscriptions round the walls, the wrought iron thorns in the Gethsemane Chapel where a gingerbread angel kneels with crystallographic motifs on its tunic and fern wings, the Recommended Circulation: the building, its furnishings and fittings amount to a total recall.

In pride of place behind the altar is Sutherland's 'Christ in Majesty' tapestry. This, the prize exhibit, a craft masterpiece, nevertheless looks uneasy: too poster-like and blown-up. Abram Games's Festival symbol would have been more appropriate there, the helmet doffed of course and replaced with a fifties orbital halo.

A quarry ate into the North Downs near Detling and covered the hillside in white dust. The Detling bypass cut through the woods. In 1954 myxomatosis killed off the rabbits so the thorns grew unchecked and smothered the Festival Star.

Interior of Coventry Cathedral, opened 1962, architect Sir Basil Spence, tapestry altarpiece by Graham Sutherland.

Artists at work: top left, *Henry Moore;* top right, *Barbara Hepworth;* left, *Jacob Epstein;* above, *Feliks Topolski;* opposite, *Graham Sutherland.*

5 The Role of the Design Council

BEFORE, DURING AND AFTER THE FESTIVAL OF BRITAIN

PAUL REILLY
Director, Design Council

IT IS VERY APPROPRIATE for the Design Council – or the Council of Industrial Design, as it used to be called – that an exhibition to commemorate the Festival of Britain should be held at the Victoria and Albert Museum, for the CoID's claim to play its prominent role in the 1951 Festival had been well and truly laid five years earlier at the V & A itself. Indeed, almost the first instruction received in 1945 by the newly formed CoID was to start planning a National Exhibition of Industrial Design to open in September 1946, a project that was publicly launched at a luncheon on 2 November 1945, at which the then President of the Board of Trade, Mr Hugh Dalton, addressed an audience of some three hundred rather sceptical manufacturers, designers and journalists. Some people and some industries felt the whole idea to be premature in view of the continuing effects of the war on their production, but the offer of space in many of the still vacant galleries of the V & A was not to be resisted.

After two or three months, however, the general attitude was clearly that, even if the work of preparation was a nuisance, it was a nuisance that in the end would be well worthwhile. Some manufacturers even told the CoID that it was very good to be set a target and deadline to speed their development of post-war designs and prototypes. The challenge of organizing such a national exhibition, later to be called 'Britain can make it' (a title which attracted enormous publicity and some ridicule), also served the infant CoID well, for, as was stated in the Council's first report to Parliament, it provided a 'crammer's course' in the practical problems of design. The exhibition also served the further valuable purpose of trying out and breaking in many clever young designers, who five years later were to win national and even international acclaim on the South Bank. Most prominent among these were James Gardner, the chief designer of 'Britain can make it' and later of the Festival Gardens in Battersea Park, and Misha Black, who in 1951 was responsible, together with Hugh Casson, for the layout of the South Bank.

'Britain can make it' did two further things for the CoID: it proved beyond a shadow of doubt first that the much maligned British public would respond to good design when shown it (nearly a million and a half visitors queued and paid to see the exhibition at the V & A); and secondly, that British manufacturers, however suspicious of outside advice or criticism, *would* submit to competitive selection, if the bait was big enough. Had this latter point not been established in 1946, it is doubtful whether the 1951 Festival could have been carried through as eventually conceived, for, although it was planned to mark the centenary of the Great Exhibition of 1851, it was above all to be a selective exhibition, the selection to be done by fully independent judges, subject to no commercial pressures.

Furthermore, the machinery of selection set up for 'Britain can make it', comprising as it did not only independent juries, but also many industrial advisory committees and technical assessors to help sift the 1,300 exhibitors from the 3,500 candidates, was to prove exceedingly useful when it came to tackling the far larger challenge of the Festival of Britain. Indeed, the CoID was quite correct to suggest in its first annual report that the particulars of the many firms, products and policies, filed as a result of 'Britain can make it', 'should have considerable long-term value to the Council when the Exhibition is over'; for there were to be three logical steps following that early filing system: the first was the 1951 Stock List, the second, Design Review on the South Bank and the third, Design Index, as now maintained in the Haymarket, Glasgow and Liverpool Design Centres.

Thus the CoID was not really surprised when, on 5 December 1947, Mr Herbert Morrison, in announcing that the Government had decided to hold another exhibition in 1951, stressed that a considerable part of the work would fall on the CoID. In those days the thinking was that there should be several separate Festival exhibitions each on a different theme, one of which should be 'a first-rate design display, which will include consumer goods, civil transport, certain classes of capital goods and some handicraft production'. It was, however, the CoID itself, led by its Director, Mr – later Sir – Gordon Russell, which argued against this in favour of industrial design being seen, not as a separate subject on its own, but as an essential part of the quality of life itself. The Council's role was therefore changed, with Government approval, to embrace the selection and collection of all those industrially produced exhibits, together with certain handicrafts, which would be needed to illustrate all the themes in the many 1951 Festival exhibitions – for it should not be thought that the South Bank was the only show; it was only the centrepiece of the whole Festival of Britain, which included half a dozen or more large official exhibitions, both static and mobile, for all of which the CoID had to find exhibits.

This decision not only helped to unify the Festival and its administration, but it brought industrial design much nearer to the centre of things, as an equal partner with the other main interests, such as science, art and entertainment. The CoID was in fact represented in the central planning of the Festival at all levels. It was perhaps largely thanks to this pervasive influence or constant interference of the CoID that the Festival came to be widely praised for its attention to design in its every detail.

The main work of selection and collection of exhibits fell on the Council's Industrial Division, led by Mark Hartland Thomas, a distinguished architect who was later to found the Modular Society. He built up a team of specialist industrial liaison and development officers whose duty was two-fold: firstly, to survey British industry in order to find the best products and the most interesting developments for exhibition; and secondly, to stimulate adequate supplies of well-designed objects, particularly from the more sluggish and less imaginative industries. For ease of survey British industry was divided into fifteen categories, ranging from the craft based to the technologically advanced. The industrial officers concerned with each group were responsible for ensuring that all firms in their categories were aware of the needs and aims of the Festival, while the more senior of these industrial officers were given the further responsibility of working out the detailed themes to be presented in the various South Bank pavilions and in the other official Festival exhibitions. These key figures were given the title of Theme Conveners. Thus the CoID became responsible not only for electing all the exhibits, but also for writing much of the script and for ensuring that the designers of each section were fully briefed.

Building on its earlier experience of the 'Britain can make it' exhibition, the Council was careful to work closely with the many industrial trade associations concerned with the overall theme of British achievement, and invited them to join with the CoID in organizing a great number of Discussion Groups at which the hopes for the Festival were explained in a good deal of detail. These Discussion Groups were also used to publicize the other important tool of the CoID – the 1951 Stock List – for it had soon become apparent that a survey of British industry would be of little value without means of recording the findings. So a pictorial card index of all products – eventually over 20,000 of them – that were considered exhibition-worthy was built up, though only half could actually be shown. The CoID did, however, persuade the Festival organizers to find room for the whole of the 1951 Stock List, by then renamed Design Review, to be shown on the South Bank. In its Fourth Annual Report for 1948–49 the Council suggested that this Design Review might well become a permanent feature of the Council's work; this suggestion was vigorously supported after the close of the Festival, particularly in a *Times* leader which argued that this pioneer index of British design should not be dismantled, but should be constantly weeded and kept up to date, a challenge that the Design Council is still doing its best to meet.

While the survey of British industry was thus being conducted and recorded, Mark Hartland Thomas turned his attention to the other aspect of his problem: namely, the stimulation of new design thinking so that fresh products might be ready by 1951. For this he devised two further tools, the 'M'-Service and the Festival Pattern Group. The former was a scheme for bringing good new designs to prototype stage, so that they could be presented more realistically to potential manufacturers. The Council believed, perhaps a bit over-optimistically, that many interesting designs were lying untested as sketches and drawings in designers' bottom drawers, and therefore it undertook in a limited number of cases to advance the cost of model making and to assist in bringing such ideas to the attention of likely manufacturers. However, only a handful of new products resulted from this well-intentioned initiative.

The Festival Pattern Group was a rather more encouraging story, though its influence was short lived. It arose through Mark Hartland Thomas having attended in May 1949 a weekend course at Ashridge, organized by the Society of Industrial Artists, the purpose of which was to show to an audience of designers visual material from other arts and sciences in order to broaden minds and introduce new ideas. Among the papers read was one by Professor Kathleen Lonsdale on crystallography, a subject in which at that time Britain led the world. She threw out the suggestion that some crystal-structure diagrams might make good textile designs. Hartland Thomas followed this up at once by writing to Dr Helen Megaw of Cambridge who had already drawn out some of these diagrams as a basis for decoration. On seeing the drawings he decided that the patterns should not be confined to textiles, but offered more widely to many industries concerned with decoration, but only to one firm in each industry. Eventually twenty-eight manufacturers joined the scheme, representing industries as widely different as textiles, cutlery, pottery, plastics, paper and glass, while the patterns themselves derived from sources such as insulin, afwillite, china clay, haemoglobin and resorcinol.

Hartland Thomas wrote at the time:

I had it in mind that we are at a stage in the history of industrial design when both the public and leading designers have a feeling for more richness in style and decoration, but are somewhat at a loss for inspiration. Traditional patterns that have come down to us from ancient Greece and elsewhere had lost much of their sparkle by now; and the fashionable alternative of a doodle on a piece of paper, folded for symmetry, could hardly lay the foundations for a new school of design. But these crystal-structure diagrams had the discipline of exact repetitive symmetry; they were above all very pretty and were full of rich variety, yet with a remarkable family likeness; they were essentially modern because the technique that constructed them was quite recent, and yet, like all successful decorations of the past, they derived from nature – although it was nature at a submicroscopic scale not previously revealed.

It was a nice, ingenious argument, but the crystal-structure diagrams, although widely used by the designers of the various Festival displays and particularly by Misha Black in his South Bank Regatta Restaurant, can hardly be said to have laid the foundations for a new school of design – indeed they barely survived the Festival year, though in a strange way they seemed to symbolize for many people the Festival of Britain Style. The real achievement, though, was not in the patterns themselves, but in the bringing together of so many leading manufacturers from so many different industries to collaborate on such a project, for there was then and, alas, still is far too little conversation on design between the many industries that furnish a home or even between those few that lay a table.

The CoID's work for the Festival did not come to a full stop on the opening day but continued throughout the year: not only through the manning of many South Bank information points; the policing of the souvenirs being sold from the kiosks, for only such as had been successful in a competition organized by the CoID were eligible for sale on the South Bank; the organizing of the first ever International Design Congress, the forerunner of all the subsequent congresses organized by the International Council of Societies of Industrial Design – but also through the laborious but essential job of returning every one of the ten thousand odd exhibits to their lenders. That this task was completed without a hitch was largely due to the Council's good fortune in having recruited to its staff retired Major General J. M. Benoy, who had been one of the army's logistical experts; and five years later it was also thanks in large measure to the administrative skills of the same Major General that the CoID was able so smoothly to open in the Haymarket its first permanent, constantly changing, selective exhibition of modern British design. But, above all, it was thanks to the Festival of Britain, to the fillip it had given to British industry, to the interest in design that it had aroused and to the confidence it had created in the practical, commonsensical approach of the CoID, that the Council was able on 26 April 1956 to invite the Duke of Edinburgh to open the world's first Design Centre.

6 Three Years a-Growing

RECOLLECTIONS OF THE FESTIVAL BEFORE THE TURNSTILES OPENED

IAN COX
Director, Science and Technology

THE FESTIVAL OF BRITAIN was nothing if not a visual affair and it should be easy enough to recall one or another of its components through photographs, film or visiting the final home of exhibits initially assembled or designed for a five months showing. Such a piecemeal retrospective cannot, however, convey the overall effect created by the totality of these components when they were fully articulated one with another. For it was on this spatial relationship between exhibit and exhibit, section and section, building and building and, even, exhibition and exhibition (coupled with a persuasive route of circulation – a 'way to go round') that the Festival largely depended for the conveyance of its theme.

For a theme to be developed visually, however, by not a few architects and display designers, each contributing his own chapter to the narrative, there must perforce be some pre-existing plan in written form – indeed, not only a plan but a sound supporting structure of ideas and physical facilities. But when the lights go up and the turnstiles open these, of course, are no more in evidence than the builders' scaffolding – or, better, the bone beneath the skin. 'Better' because the Festival's ontogeny was something of an organic process, all parts of the body growing more or less simultaneously with the supporting skeleton not all that much ahead. This was forced on us by lack of time which made impossible a more logical sequence of processes, as ideally it might be: purpose decided, site secured, thematic plan, narrative planning for component sections, architectural master plan and then architectural plans for individual buildings and display design for each section proceeding simultaneously.

In starting, though, with observations on exhibitions I am in danger of perpetuating the misconception that the Festival of Britain consisted only of such things – or even of just one on the South Bank of the Thames. In fact, of course, it was much more than this. There were many and varied Festivals of the Arts, gardens of National Trust houses were brought into first-class condition, the learned societies and institutions put on special programmes of symposia, lectures and displays, while at village level there was tree planting and other commemorative acts – down to the presentation of a Festival Cup to be played for annually by the Bowls Club. That said, it may be permissible now to concentrate one's recollections mostly upon those three years of planning and creation that preceded the opening of the South Bank Exhibition, for it is this in particular that has remained in the public mind as the symbol of the Festival.

Basic to the organization of this Festival was the intention that it should be brought into being as far as possible through existing bodies which already carried national authority. These were known as the Constituent Bodies and included the Arts Council, the Council of Industrial Design, the National Book League, the British Film Institute and, for the implementation of the exhibitions, the Central Office of

Information. For science and architecture there were no comparable bodies in existence so special councils for each were created – the one for science in May 1948. By intention, both were advisory rather than supervisory. Their executive officers were appointed Directors of Science and Architecture respectively in the Festival of Britain Office, which was a temporary government department under the Lord President of the Council.

Fundamental to all our work of planning and implementation was one peculiar fact which distinguished the Festival from all other large operational undertakings of which I (and I believe all my senior colleagues) had had previous experience: months before it had a plan, staff or funds, it had an inescapable target date – the centenary of the Great Exhibition. As I have already implied, every method and procedure for planning, obtaining briefing material and converting ideas into visible reality had from the beginning to pivot on this hard fact.

Although, as I have said, the initial proposals for the Festival envisaged several specialist exhibitions, one of which was to display science and technology, the Executive Committee, when I joined it in June 1948, was already considering an additional so-called Combined Exhibition; this would provide a centrepiece for the whole Festival, each Constituent Body contributing the elements appropriate to its own particular interests. The realization of such an exhibition in London depended upon a suitable site being found and a guarantee in advance that either pre-existing accommodation or building materials would be available – and it took some months for these problems to be worried out. In the meantime, however, there was no doubt that this exhibition's scope and theme would have to be declared pretty well at once if the scientific or any other content was to be properly chosen and worked out in visual terms in time for the opening, whatever shape and size it eventually assumed.

At this moment it was a long way from being clear what exactly the exhibition would contain, for no Constituent Body was yet organized to make proposals for content. Thus, the immediate requirement was for an intellectual plan (as distinct from an architectural one) capable of execution on any scale, and one that should offer logical placing for a wide range of subject matter in such a way that displays of great diversity would together tell a coherent story of British achievement. It was to the preparation of such a plan that I addressed myself particularly during those early months (I couldn't get to work as Director, Science without one). The outcome – what was to be the basic scheme from which the South Bank Exhibition developed – was accepted by the Executive Committee in August (1948) and by the Festival Council (our supreme body) in September.

The requirements were met by working out a theme that in reality answered the following questions: What is it that gives the British character and British achievement such diversity? What is the link between the past and the present that gives us such faith in the future? What provides the spark for British initiative? The answer to all seemed to lie in the great variety and diverse natural resources of the island of Britain, a mixed race of people and an innate curiosity within these people which urged them to explore and discover in every sphere. Interactions between these factors, which are permanent, provide the continuity between past, present and future.

Transferred to a physical site, such a theme naturally resolved itself into two main sequences: on the one hand, the Land and what the People have achieved in the course of developing its resources; on the other, the way of life evolved as the People have progressively resolved the diversity of their characteristics and have fitted themselves to their environment. Between these two 'horns', as one visualized them, and intercommunicating with them through a number of radii, had to be a central area displaying the activities and achievements of the People through exploration and discovery in their widest senses – the People's projection of themselves outside their own immediate surroundings to discover and develop overseas territories, yes, but also through intellect and the aids of science they themselves had devised to bring back knowledge from all spheres of the universe.

But more than such an outline was soon called for by the architects and display designers, and it was elaborated in a fifty-one-page document – 'a provisional indication of sectional treatment' – by the following April. By now, the Upstream and the Downstream sequences (my 'horns') and the Dome of Discovery were already specified by name. At this stage, it should be recalled, we still had no certain knowledge of what the precise content of any one section would be although there was no doubt as to the part of the story it would tell. For such a situation as this, our theme had a number of advantages. First, because it was based on reality, it offered a logical place for any item of subject matter that might be proposed. At the same time, since it adhered strictly to the Minister's definition of intentions, it facilitated selection of material by providing no place for subject matter outside the terms of reference. This was of great importance at a later stage when proposals began to come in from all quarters: the existence of an approved theme provided clear grounds for the rejection of irrelevant ideas.

The second advantage of the theme was that it gave maximum freedom to the architectural planners while providing them with a clear intellectual plan to interpret and one from which they were able to estimate the relative spatial requirements and character of the various components. This was done by presenting the outline plan, not as a series of ready-made sections, but as three narrative sequences, each telling a progressive story. These 'stories', however, all consisted of a number of 'chapters' which offered a variety of alternatives against the time when the sequences would have to be segmented off into separate pavilions, each with its own atmosphere. This was done shortly before the elaboration of the theme to which I have just referred. It was essential, however, that the order of 'chapters' – that is, the narrative – should be preserved if the exhibition's story were to remain intelligible. I believe, in fact, that the South Bank was the first multi-pavilioned exhibition to use such a narrative form.

Two cases of pay-off for internal flexibility in a thematic plan with a rigid exterior come to mind when recalling the early history of the South Bank Exhibition. The first is that, although a central display area (Discovery) was an essential part of the original conception, its projected content had to be resorbed into the Land and People sequences when the South Bank became available as a site and the railway viaduct bisecting it made a central feature impracticable. Before long, however, a dome of novel construction was conceived and it became possible to restore the third component of the exhibition to its original status. The second case is the Lion and the Unicorn pavilion which may be remembered as having particular appeal. A suggested placing for the part of the story it displayed was on the original thematic plan. It was not, though, something envisaged in our terms of reference nor was there any staff to work it up; consequently, it was absent from the site plan in its intermediate stage. However, when eventually all agreed that there must be some such display in a 'combined' exhibition, there was no doubt as to its logical place.

Another advantage of internal flexibility relates to the subtraction of subject matter. When the South Bank plan was first put on paper it was assumed that all Constituent Bodies would contribute to the exhibition's content. This proved not to be the case. By September 1948 the provision of thematic material and the briefing of display designers was left solely to the Science Council and the Council of Industrial Design, both acting through their executive representatives. Nevertheless, the thematic plan was not altered as a result of this. We could still achieve what we set out to do, but we had to make the qualification that the theme would be illustrated almost entirely by examples taken from science (in its widest sense), technology and industrial design.

Yet a fourth example of the flexibility of the theme was its adaptability to the much reduced display space in the Festival ship *Campania*. It was also used as a basis for the 'Tours of Britain' scheme which could have told the same story but 'on the ground' if we finally failed to get an adequate site or accommodation for the Combined Exhibition. Indeed, the plan was pursued even after a site was secured until it became clear that we would not get enough backing from the coach operators.

Of the two bodies primarily concerned with the content of the South Bank Exhibition the Science Council had much the greater involvement in the thematic story: it was by means of this that the achievements of science would be presented to the public as something of real and lasting importance in their history and in their daily lives. Further, the narrative form made it possible to demonstrate how technological development follows on the discovery of scientific principles. The Council of Industrial Design, on the other hand, was naturally concerned first that the exhibition should provide a vehicle for the display of the widest range of British manufactured goods. So, as soon as it was satisfied that the thematic plan offered the necessary opportunities, it had then to organize its approach to industry so that a sufficiency of exhibits of the requisite standard would be assured for showing in 1951. It was the Science Directorate, therefore, that provided the narrative element and most of the briefing on what should be displayed (not 'how') for the architect/designer/theme convener teams appointed for each section. This was true also for the Festival ship and, of course, for the Science Exhibition in South Kensington.

Over the years 1949–51 the Science staff never numbered more than eleven. Their job was first to arrive at a shortlist of British contributions to civilization in science and technology, apportion these to their appropriate sections in the thematic layout and then provide authoritative written briefs to enable the display designers to bring them to life in visual terms. So that the selection of these British contributions should be as representative as possible of the best-informed

opinions in the country, my council agreed to the formation of eighteen specialist panels representing the principal branches of science, pure and applied, to advise on this and ultimately to remark on the proposals for display – that is, the designers' interpretations of the written briefs supplied to them for all topics selected. These panels had a total membership of 156 top-ranking scientists and technologists, and none so far as I remember had need to meet more than three times. This advisory panel system worked admirably, both for the South Bank and for the Science Exhibition, and contributed a greater corpus of high-level professional advice than, I guess, can ever have been made available in comparable circumstances before. So far as science was concerned, it really did make the Festival a national affair and I still recall the co-operation that was so freely given with a feeling of particular warmth.

But, meanwhile, what about the Science Exhibition my council was created to sponsor and I was appointed to direct? The site originally proposed for this was Earls Court; before long, though, it was discovered that, on account of other bookings, it could not open there until July 1951, three months after the Festival itself. This was not considered acceptable. Then it was hoped that a large enough site would be obtained for the Combined Exhibition to render a separate Science Exhibition unnecessary. This was not realized and my council finally recommended that an additional exhibition was still required for the display of the more fundamental aspects of science that might either spoil the balance of the Combined Exhibition (it wasn't yet called the South Bank) or be excluded on grounds of space. By the end of the year our worries about a site were assuaged by the Ministry of Works undertaking an early completion of the basement and ground floor of a new 'centre section' destined for the Science Museum in South Kensington – though at all times the exhibition would be quite separate from the Museum.

Planning then began for the theme and content of this exhibition for which £750,000 had been allocated. After six months, however, in July 1949 the ceiling figure for the whole Festival was greatly reduced by the Chancellor of the Exchequer and the Science Exhibition's share was cut to £400,000 – £100,000 of this having been earmarked for the 'Newtonian House', of which more later. Such a reduction did not permit even condensation of the comprehensive plan on which we were working, so we had to find a more limited theme, and without delay. After assessing the expected coverage of science on the South Bank we saw that the subjects most in need of additional treatment were physics, chemistry, metallurgy, physiology and medicine. To demonstrate what was new in these sciences within a single compass we adopted the brief of 'advances in the understanding of the structure of matter, living and dead, special attention being given to the application of such knowledge to human and technological problems'. With these terms of reference we began, at the end of July 1949, to plan a second Science Exhibition – the one the public actually saw.

In deciding upon the degree of specialization we should allow ourselves, we assumed a public that had a predisposition to interest in science which we could stimulate and increase. This assumption appeared justified by the relatively constant attendance figures obtained as soon as the exhibition began to make its own publicity. Our method was to use, as far as finances would allow, moving display techniques that told

Screen at the entrance to the Science Museum Exhibition, based on the carbon atom, designer Brian Peake. The hexagonal aluminium units were designed by Gordon Andrew, in pale blue and yellow with arrow motifs in brilliant red; ball motifs, copper on black stand.

their story without the necessity for lengthy written descriptions, which are always an obstacle to the popular understanding of science. To this we added a few items of immediate human appeal such as the mechanical 'tortoises' that were made to steer themselves automatically towards light, and a prototype calculating machine that could play the game of NIM. We arranged the circulation so that on either side of the main gangway through the exhibition a narrative story was told in its simplest form; bays leading off this gangway contained contributory displays for those members of the public who wished to satisfy their interest further. A factor that contributed very largely to the success of this exhibition was our determination that it should be gay and attractive in appearance, giving the lie to the notion that science is sombre or grim. This appealed particularly to our visitors from abroad.

Soon after the Festival opened, someone with an interest in these things observed that, having found new and exciting ways of presenting science on the South Bank, we put them out-of-date even before opening by what was then devised for the exhibition in South Kensington. This, of course, was intended as a compliment, and it is true that, even within the few months difference in starting dates, the science staff and display designers had learned a lot about the most productive way to work together and, indeed, about new idioms that might be employed for the interpretation of science. But the publics we envisaged for the two exhibitions, and the time and degree of attention they were likely to devote to each display, were so different that I am still doubtful if much, or anything, that was produced for South Kensington would have been really appropriate to, say, the Dome of Discovery.

Finally, when the exhibition turnstiles had spun for the last time, what happened to everything? Furniture and the like aside, it had always been recognized that the Festival would be a great opportunity for the enrichment of the national collections, for it caused the creation of many objects and displays of permanent value. With this in mind, the Science Council approved that a panel should be set up (and serviced by my Directorate) to advise on the most suitable recipients for such material as would ultimately become available – notably the national collections and government institutions at home and in the Commonwealth, public collections and teaching establishments (all allocations to be free of charge) and, in a few instances, public bodies operating for profit who would be required to pay. The thoroughness with which this was done, exhibit by exhibit, is demonstrated by the length of the panel's final recommendations – 117 pages. These covered the South Bank, the Science Exhibition, *Campania* and the Kelvin Hall Exhibition in Glasgow.

But as well as all this, one recalls certain projects that never materialized, wondering, perhaps, why someone hasn't attempted them since. The 'Tours of Britain' I have already mentioned. All that survived of this scheme was a series of guidebooks that made use of the approach we had worked out for the tours themselves. The 'Newtonian House', which had very distinguished scientific backing, was to consist of a place (in fact a huge kind of bowl) in which the laws of gravity would appear to have been modified sufficiently to introduce visitors to an enchanted world where people stood or sat, not on a flat floor, but on a curved wall. Their apparent weight would change as they walked about and objects thrown or rolled on the floor would travel in peculiar trajectories. This device was not a mere stunt. It offered immediately an opportunity for carrying out experiments which otherwise could only be envisaged ideally within the matrix of the Theory of Relativity. Planning and experiment went quite some distance, but it was stopped when the Director of the Science Museum (who was to have inherited it) decided it was more of an entertainment for spectators than a means of scientific experiment and so would be unsuitable as a permanent feature among his collections. Much exploratory work also went into the possibility of constructing a new planetarium. This project was dropped when it became clear that it could not be completed by 1951.

I was glad to hear only this summer, however, of a relatively ambitious project of ours that is still in permanent use. This is the radio telescope that was operated from the Dome of Discovery, with its 'dish' aerial mounted on the top of the Shot Tower. This was beamed on the moon and visitors could see on a cathode ray tube signals being transmitted there and their reflection back about two and a half seconds later. Radio signals from much deeper in outer space were also on show. In a sense this was a prototype for the great radio telescope at Jodrell Bank where, I learn, it is still part of the operating equipment.

Ten years later, and for ten years after that, I was again able (from a room in the Shell Tower) to look down over the South Bank site, but by then the only visible reminder of what stood there in 1951 was the circular outline of the Dome of Discovery persisting on the car park that had come to lie between me and the river wall.

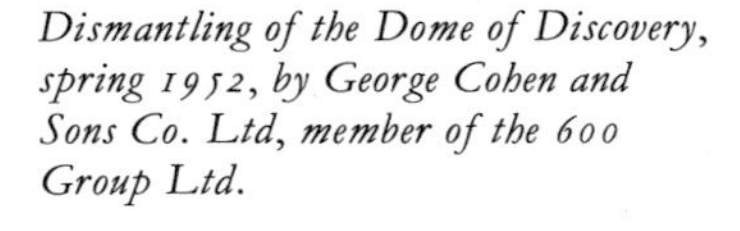

Dismantling of the Dome of Discovery, spring 1952, by George Cohen and Sons Co. Ltd, member of the 600 Group Ltd.

7 A NATIONAL ENTERPRISE

Introduction

MARY BANHAM

It is significant that the Festival of Britain *was* a national enterprise. It is so often forgotten that it was a genuinely national event and not confined to the South Bank and Battersea Pleasure Gardens, as Londoners often seem to think. There were two major Festival exhibitions outside London's South Bank, Lansbury, Battersea, Science Museum and other shows: the Industrial Power Exhibition at Kelvin Hall, Glasgow, and the Farm and Factory Exhibition in Belfast. In addition, the Festival ship *Campania* travelled round the coast, visiting many ports, and the Land Traveller Exhibition took the themes developed at the South Bank exhibitions to four major provincial towns.

Nearly every town and village marked the occasion of the Festival in some way. Those places which would have normally held a nationally known event, like a music festival or a pageant, staged a special one on the occasion of the Festival. Trowell, in Buckinghamshire, was chosen as *the* Festival village, slightly to its surprise, not for its great beauty or tidiest gardens, but because it was deemed to be the typical, thriving English village and as near the middle of England, geographically, as could be managed.

The Festival was also meant to be a celebration of peace. As things turned out, by the summer of 1951, it was primarily a cheer-up effort, as Adrian Forty points out in his essay. The Festival encouraged cultural contributions; many special works, some of which were new departures in the theatre, in music and in the visual arts, were commissioned or supported by the Arts Council. The Royal Festival Hall, which was intended as a permanent structure on the South Bank, was a London County Council project which would have been built, Festival or no Festival, though it may have been given a different name. It was inaugurated at the same time as the exhibition because this was convenient and it made good sense.

Fountain by Richard Huws.

Finally, the Festival also aimed to attract international interest. This was achieved, to a certain extent, through its personnel based abroad. To publicize the Festival buses travelled round Europe. Information desks for foreign visitors were set up at points of entry into Britain, the main one being at Southampton, where the 'Queens' arrived regularly from the USA. But although the Festival hoped to attract an international audience, it did not in itself aspire or pretend to be an international event. Looking at what was created at the South Bank, and talking to the people who were responsible for it, one becomes aware of a fascinating synthesis of imported and home-grown ideas. At least, 'synthesis' is an accurate description when it refers to the work of skilled designers like F. H. K. Henrion, Misha Black, Maxwell Fry and Jane Drew, who used artists from many backgrounds in the realization of their designs. But, apart from the buildings, the word does not accurately apply to the whole of the South Bank.

It is interesting to note in the sections which follow that the 'makers' of the Festival, those same architects and designers who have been

UPSTREAM CIRCUIT
1 The Natural Scene
2 The Land of Britain
3 The Country
4 Minerals of the Island
5 Power and Production
6 Sea and Ships
7 Transport
8 Dome of Discovery
DOWNSTREAM CIRCUIT
9 The People of Britain
10 The Lion and the Unicorn
11 Homes and Gardens
12 The New Schools
13 Health
14 Sport
15 Seaside
OTHER DISPLAYS
16 Television
17 Telecinema
18 1851 Centenary pavilion
19 Shot Tower
20 Design Review
21 Skylon
22 Royal Festival Hall

claimed as innovators, did not believe even then that they were breaking any very new ground. To many, the work carried out for the Festival represented a consolidation of already widely held beliefs and to others a tying-up of pre-war threads before embarking on post-war challenges. In Sir Hugh Casson's words, the men with 'shavings in their hair' and 'concrete on their boots' were finally realizing ideas that had been saved up during the war years. 'It was everyone's pent-up fifth-year scheme!'

Certainly some structural innovations did come out of the Festival: the Dome of Discovery by Ralph Tubbs, described here by Sir Ralph Freeman; Skylon by the architects Powell and Moya and engineered by Felix Samuely; and much of the work designed by Maxwell Fry and Jane Drew and engineered by Ove Arup in the downstream section on the South Bank. Some of the designers interviewed for this book feel that new ground was broken, however, in the field of translating the two-dimensional drawing into a three-dimensional working object, for example the Emett railway at Battersea.

There is no doubt that the Festival was an astonishing achievement given the difficulties of the time; it involved the concerted effort of a great many people in the kind of collaboration which is difficult to achieve today. It also provided the first real chance for almost a whole younger generation which had emerged from the war, keen and anxious

Flag message flown by SS Campania *as she entered Southampton to prepare for her Festival Exhibition stay.*

Below, *winners of the vertical feature competition: left to right, Michael Powell, Philip Powell and Hidalgo Moya.* Right, *the 300-foot Skylon under construction. It was said that 'like Britain it has no visible means of support'.*

to get going in their own field. Reputations were established, and even if work did not follow fast and furious, new capabilities and skills were discovered by this younger generation whose potential was stretched by the demands of the Festival. It is easy to see why, to them, the period leading up to the summer of 1951 is remembered as an exciting, fast-moving time, never to be repeated.

Yet those among our contributors who were already established before the war, and those whose earlier years were spent outside England, saw the Festival as only one manifestation in an ongoing process.

The significance of the Festival for us today is not so much that it made a particularly important stylistic statement in design but that it was a genuinely national popular public event of amazing proportions, unexpectedly successful and still remembered more than any other event of this kind.

The overall intention of the Festival of Britain was that, through its diversity, the people who visited its various manifestations should not only be entertained but also educated; people were in fact encouraged to come *expecting* to be educated. In addition, the Festival provided colour (after the drabness of the war), light (after the darkness of the blackout) and fun in the traditional fairground sense. But the Festival organizing team would not have been seen to have done their job unless visiting families went away feeling instructed and, in some undefined way, improved.

The British public did seem to take note, and approve of, the planning, buildings and landscaping at the South Bank and at Lansbury, and it is probably this that led them to demand similar standards in their own post-war environment. The environment aspect was spelled out in detail in the Homes and Gardens pavilion on the South Bank, with its specially furnished rooms, and at Lansbury (for which Sir Frederick Gibberd was the architect of Chrisp Street market) in the show flat, where the interested members of the public were offered advice as to where the furniture could be purchased. Harlow New Town was designed by the same men, some of it in the years before the Festival, as was Lansbury.

In the sections which follow, fairly detailed accounts are provided by virtually all the protagonists in projects related to the Festival, in and out of London. However, some gaps occur where those responsible have died in the meantime, among them Wells Coates, architect of the Television cinema and pavilion on the South Bank which contained much new and exciting material. The national and thematic scope of the manifestations presented in the context of the Festival needs no further evidence than a look at the sections which follow: the South Bank, Battersea, Lansbury, the Science Exhibition, the Land Travelling Exhibition, the *Campania* floating exhibition, Glasgow and Ulster.

THE STORY

THE EXHIBITION TELLS

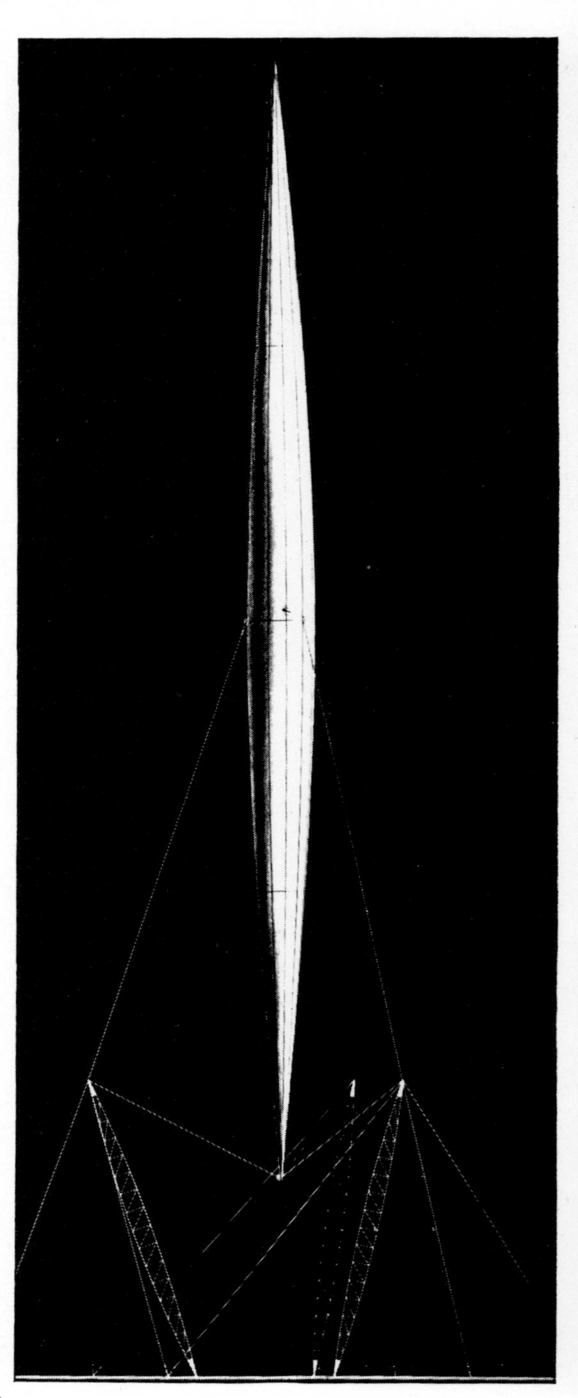

What the visitor will see on the South Bank is an attempt at something new in exhibitions—a series of sequences of things to look at, arranged in a particular order so as to tell one continuous, interwoven story. The order is important. For the South Bank Exhibition is neither a museum of British culture nor a trade show of British wares; it tells the story of British contributions to world civilisation in the arts of peace. That story has a beginning, a middle, and an end—even if that end consists of nothing more final than fingerposts into the future.

The Pavilions of the Exhibition are placed in a certain deliberate sequence on the ground as chapters are placed in a certain deliberate sequence in a book. And, within each Pavilion, the displays are arranged in a certain order, as paragraphs are arranged in a certain order within each chapter of a book. This is a free country; and any visitors who, from habit or inclination, feel impelled to start with the last chapter of the whole narrative and then zig-zag their way backwards to the first chapter, will be as welcome as anyone else. But such visitors may find that some of the chapters will appear mystifying and inconsequent.

The story—as any visitor whose feet follow the intended circulation will observe—begins with the past, continues with the present, and ends with a preview of the continuing future. The belief that Britain will continue to have contributions to make in the future, is founded on two factors from which, in combination, British achievements, past and present, have arisen. Those two factors are the People of Britain and the Land of Britain. And those two factors continue.

This, then, is the theme of the interwoven serial story which is embodied in the South Bank Exhibition: the Land and the People. The land, endowed with scenery, climate and resources more various than any other country of comparable size, has nurtured and challenged

8

Two pages from the guide to the South Bank Exhibition.

and stimulated the people. The people, endowed with not one single characteristic that is peculiar to themselves, nevertheless, when taken together, could not be mistaken for any other nation in the world.

So, throughout the length of the Exhibition, there will be unfolded the tale of the continuous impact that this particular land has made on this particular people, and of the achievements that this people has continued to derive from its relationship with this land. The South Bank, then, contains a new sort of narrative about Britain: an Exhibition designed to tell a story mainly through the medium, not of words, but of tangible things.

The South Bank site is divided by the Hungerford Railway Bridge, which has been used in the layout of the Exhibition as the inner binding that separates the narrative into its two main volumes. The circuit of Pavilions that lie, in a rough semicircle, upstream from Hungerford Bridge, tells the story of the Land of Britain and of the things that the British have derived from their land; the circuit of Pavilions that lie, in a rough semicircle, downstream from Hungerford Bridge, relates the story of the People of Britain in the context of their more domestic life and leisure.

But even the whole two volumes of the Land and the People, taken together, must give an incomplete idea of the distinctive British contribution, unless a third volume is added: a memorandum on the pre-eminent achievements of British men and women in mapping and charting the globe, in exploring the heavens, and in investigating the structure and nature of the universe. These discoveries, together with some of the practical developments, are reviewed in the Dome of Discovery, which lies within the body of the Upstream, or Land Circuit.

Both the first chapter of the Land story and the first chapter of the People story open on the Fairway. It is from either of these starting points that visitors are invited to begin their tour of the Exhibition.

The architecture and the display, which embody the theme, were planned under the responsible direction of the Festival Office's Exhibition Presentation Panel, which has the following membership:

GERALD BARRY, *Director-General, Chairman*

CECIL COOKE, *Director, Exhibitions, Deputy Chairman*

MISHA BLACK, O.B.E.

G. A. CAMPBELL
Director, Finance and Establishments

HUGH CASSON
Director, Architecture

IAN COX
Director, Science and Technology

A. D. HIPPISLEY COXE
Council of Industrial Design

JAMES GARDNER, O.B.E.

JAMES HOLLAND

M. HARTLAND THOMAS
Council of Industrial Design

RALPH TUBBS

PETER KNEEBONE, *Secretary*

The theme of the Exhibition was devised by IAN COX

The Editor of the captions that accompany the displays was LIONEL BIRCH.

The list of eminent men and women who have contributed to the Exhibition, either by advice or active planning of individual displays, is too long to be contained within this Guide. Their help has made the Exhibition a truly national undertaking. Acknowledgements are made by name in the Exhibition Catalogue which is published separately.

¶ A narrative Exhibition, such as this, develops its theme by means of things you can see and believe. Each of them is clearly captioned, so a written description of the displays exhibit by exhibit is unnecessary. What may help the visitor, however, is a summary of this theme as it is revealed, section by section, in the Exhibition. This is the purpose of the pages that follow.

Period Piece

HUGH CASSON

Director, Architecture, South Bank

SOMETIMES it is easier to remember an end rather than a beginning. For me the start of the Festival was elusive and fragmentary. People and events, ideas and places skitter about like blobs of mercury over the polished board of those early months of 1948 and are hard now to recapture and imprison. The end of the South Bank Exhibition, on the other hand, was hard-edged and immediate.

I remember it well. It was a weekend in September. Saturday began early . . . a clean misty pale-coloured morning sharp and thin to the nose . . . a deathbed repentance it seemed after three years and six months of bad weather. It was 8.30 a.m. On the empty Fairway a knot of cleaners were listening to Geraldo – dark glasses and belted overcoat – rehearsing his band below a dew-dripping canvas canopy. In the distance the Lord Privy Seal – carnationed and cheerful – was making his last inspection. Twelve crowded hours later the crowd was boiling and singing on the Fairway, carved horizontally by the violet slicing knives of arc lamps. Up in the control tower the manager – a Calvinistic-eyed Scotsman called MacDermott, a tense silhouette with a telephone at each ear – kept an eye on the dancing. By 11 p.m. it was Gracie Fields and 'Wish me luck' – should it have been Vera Lynn I wonder? – and fainting bodies handed over the pink adoring faces . . . sleep-struck tots, middle-aged marrieds, couples hand-in-love, a few determined drunks. Midnight. Warm, starry, magical. Exit turnstiles clicking and champagne corks popping in the VIP pavilion. Autograph hunters besiege Gracie's car outside. Within, Ministers listen unlistening to everybody's ideas about what to do with the site.

Sunday sees a drop in the temperature of celebration. A farewell service, conducted in the Royal Festival Hall by the Archbishop of Canterbury, a farewell cocktail party at the Science Exhibition in South Kensington – the National Anthem pomping through the intricacies of radar – the Brigade of Guards wheeling and circling on the Fairway of the South Bank in the chill evening breeze. The Festival flags are lowered to a roll of drums. By midnight the lights are still on, the metal and glass still wink and glitter in the glare, the fountains crash, but the place is empty except for cleaners and security men. The buildings, cockaded, groomed and patient like prize cattle, await the humane killer of official policy. It was over.

Now the Festival of Britain of course – as we never tired of saying or being told to say – was more than the South Bank Exhibition. But the South Bank Exhibition was the true star of the show and it is the South Bank surely by which the Festival is remembered. It didn't look that way in the autumn of 1948 when I was rung up by Gerald Barry (whom I'd never met). We met in his office in Savoy Court. He was a plump, quick-moving man, fair-haired and friendly with an enthusiastic manner and a sharp uplifted nose that seemed to truffle for ideas and jokes. He explained the administrative set-up – a General Advisory Council under Lord Ismay, a series of specialist advisory Committees (Architecture chaired by Howard Lobb) and a new temporary government office under his own directorship. 'I am sorry to tell you,' he said, 'there's not likely to be any building to do – it's just keeping an architectural eye on things. But it looks like being fun.'

The job was full-time and the salary was £1,000 p.a. If possible, I was to start at once. I accepted immediately. I was interviewed again, by Max Nicholson of Herbert Morrison's office. He had, he said, already found me the best secretary in London, Kate Harris. He had indeed.

I was a latecomer to the team of Herbivores – as Michael Frayn was to term us – collected by Gerald Barry to devise and run the show, among them Huw Wheldon (Art), Ian Cox (Science), Paul Wright (PR), Cecil Cooke (Exhibitions), George Campbell (Finance). The deputy chairman was Bernard Sendall (Admin). During the summer weekends in his Sussex cottage – a real Herbivore ploy – an outline programme had already been drafted and a Presentation Panel set up to give it three-dimensional form. A sub-committee – known as the Design Group – of which I was, to begin with, to be chairman was being appointed at the same time. It consisted of two old friends and two strangers. The architects Ralph Tubbs and Misha Black – one of the most experienced exhibition designers in Europe – I had known and worked with for many years. James Gardner, co-ordinating designer of the fantastically successful 'Britain can make it' Exhibition (1948), I had seen in the distance during the installation of our tiny contribution – an imperturbable pipe-sucking and decisive figure, rather like an officer in an R. C. Sherriff play, with a sharp sense of theatre and a genius for instant improvization and lightning draughtsmanship. All three were part-time only.

The only other full-time designer besides myself was ex-COI designer James Holland – a relaxed replica of James Stewart with a gently sardonic manner and a weary experience of mounting wartime exhibitions in unlikely places and difficult circumstances. We were to work closely together (meeting almost daily at the end) for three years in a state, even when exhausted, of almost continual elation and mutual confidence.

We met first in our temporary base – an unheated office in Cadogan Gardens. The Festival Council had decided to mount a central exhibition in London but was still looking for a site. Hyde Park, the Kensington Museums and Battersea had been looked at and for one reason or another discarded. Meanwhile we worked on the theme, 'Britain's contribution to civilization – past, present and future', seen against the background of a working world. A total area of 400,000 square feet was to be aimed at (it turned out to be 344,000 in the end) and the story broken down into separate chapters – or pavilions. One day we were summoned from our attic to have a look at the South Bank site, which had been suggested in 1946 by Misha Black. On paper it looked marvellous – centrally placed, with good communications and within sight of Big Ben and Trafalgar Square. Too good to be true, we said. It was. To start with, it was tiny (only 27 acres). Next it was cut in half by a public right of way and by Charing Cross railway bridge, beneath which were a number of snugly housed tenants with unexpired leases and right of access. Most of the upstream half was dominated by a mountain of bomb rubble, the downstream by site clearance operations for the new Festival Hall. Along the full river frontage, work was to begin on a new river wall and contractors' working areas had already been set aside. As there was no survey of the site available nobody knew what or where services existed and there was only one tree. (It's still there.) 'Just the job', we said at once. 'Never mind the complications, just look at the view.' The Council agreed. The LCC was keen. Herbert Morrison (Lord Festival, as he was later to be called) gave it all a push. Within a few weeks the confusion had cleared. The right of way to Waterloo could be piped overhead, the arch tenants decently displaced, the contractors' working areas made more restricted, the rubble removed. Landing stage pontoons were agreed with the PLA, a tube station extension with London Transport, site entrances with the police. A site survey was started and the Shot Tower reprieved.

Meanwhile, confident that all would be sorted out in time, the Design Group sat on in Cadogan Gardens

Sir Hugh Casson, Director, Architecture.

James Holland, Chief Exhibitions Designer, South Bank.

James Gardner, member of the Design Panel, South Bank, and Chief Designer, Battersea Pleasure Gardens.

with tracing paper piling up round our knees trying to produce a Master Plan. The problem was frankly a nightmare. The brief demanded a narrative exhibition, a story – yet to be written, of course – to be told in proper sequence chapter by chapter, pavilion by pavilion. Tradition demanded that there had to be a central feature as memorable and dramatic if possible as the Eiffel Tower. Most important of all, the whole place, however varied in detail, had to be given a visual personality which, we hoped, would be the fruit of a common design philosophy. Inevitably we aimed too high to start with. Ralph Tubbs arrived one morning with a proposal for roofing over Trafalgar Square to provide a platform main entrance, to carry from there a raised catwalk over Northumberland Avenue to join a new footbridge over the Thames. (The Bailey Bridge built for us by the REs was the only survivor of that idea.) Somebody – experienced in exhibition delays – suggested a standardized modular structural system over the whole site – a sort of vast jungle-gym – into which any sort of story could later be fitted. A third proposal was to enlarge the site by floating some of the exhibition on rafts. But urgency is a wonderful concentrator and within a week or so the main decisions had been made because they had to be. They were four in number:

1. The site was divided in half. So, by good luck, was the theme. Upstream would be given to the Land of Britain, downstream to the People of Britain.
2. The South Bank site must be linked physically and visually to the North Bank.
3. The central and dominating structure was to be a saucer dome – which (as far as we could discover) had not been used before – and of course it must be the largest dome in the world, i.e. more, it seemed, than 300 ft in diameter.
4. Since the site was so small, any grand-manner layout was impossible. Impressive vistas and monumental effects were out of place in an area which could be crossed on foot in a few minutes or comprehended at a glance.

Nervously the first lines went down on paper to be tidily drawn out by our two assistants, Leslie Gooday and Wycliffe Noble. Practicalities again limited our choices. The new footbridge and new tube station extension – our principal public entrances – determined our main arena or fairway where the story was to start. There was only one area large enough for the dome – which we had decided had to be 365 ft across . . . why not? Gradually it began to fall into place: the Origins of the Land, Agriculture, Mining, Industry all grouped round the shining cranium – as we saw it – of invention. (Hence the Dome of Discovery.) The Origins of the People through and under the bridge to Education, the English at Home, their character and recreations, the Arts and the Seaside (again naturally by the river) all grouped round the Festival Hall, still to be built.

By December 1948 the Master Plan was ready to be presented to the Festival Council and to be sent for comments and approval to all the interested authorities. The Design Group meanwhile had moved on to the next stage. How was it to be designed and built? Eventually three recommendations were made and agreed to:

1. Each zone should be designed by a different architect and different display designer under the general Design Group's co-ordination.
2. Some zones should be subject to competition.
3. Every attempt should be made to find and commission young and untried talent.

Each of the Design Group could – if he wished – have a building of his own. Ralph chose the Dome, Misha a restaurant and the Bailey Bridge. I chose the Shot Tower zone.

Not all these aims were achieved, though the Skylon, won by Powell and Moya, was the fabulously successful result of a competition. Some of the younger architects considered could not meet the hair-raising timetable. There were other considerations too. Time was short but tempers must not be. It was like casting a film in which everybody had to be a star and given the best lines. The final choice, though not an easy one, was free from rancour or log-rolling. In the end – on the South Bank or elsewhere – some fifty architects whose work and attitudes we admired were commissioned. We chose them for their honesty of aim and sympathy of viewpoint; they all spoke the same language but each with enough variety of intonation to make it interesting. They were young – all under forty-five – and because of the interruption of war largely untried. (No member of the Design Group had built anything larger than a house.) I record this, not to indulge in the characteristically British pursuit of cultivating the amateur, but to pay tribute twenty-five years later to all those – in particular Herbert Morrison, Gerald Barry and members of the Architecture Council – who stood by us through it all and only came to the rescue when we cried for it, to the consultant engineers who never raised an eyebrow at architectural antics but patiently helped us to get them built, and lastly to the quality, efficiency and energy of the builders.

By 1 February the South Bank list had been drawn up and approved. By 1 March each architect had been given his brief, his building line and his budget, and the Festival Office could turn to other matters. First of these, for us at least, was the organization of the building programme. In February Freeman, Fox & Partners, direct descendants as it happened of the firm who had carried out similar tasks in 1851, had been appointed consulting engineers for the Dome. Ralph Tubbs and I, after one or two discouraging visits elsewhere, had been to see Sir Ralph Freeman – a tiny white-haired man with piercing blue eyes – in his Victoria Street office. 'Could it be built?' we said; 'or rather, could it be built in the time?' 'No trouble' was the implication of the answer, if not the exact words. (In fact the design and wind tunnel tests were completed and competitive tenders received between May and August 1949.)

Having got so energetic and experienced a firm on the books it seemed wise – and how wise it proved – to extend their responsibilities,* later to be shared with R. T. James & Partners, to the administration of all the building work on the South Bank as well as the co-ordination of all structural and foundation work (services had been gallantly undertaken by the LCC). Here again quick decisions were needed. Foundations, because of the variable condition of the site, were to be kept shallow. Steel, although controlled, was chosen for speedy erection and dismantling, pre-cast concrete units preferred to the complications of shuttering. Wood, the most useful and versatile of materials, was desperately short and had, alas, to be avoided as far as possible.

The Design Group – by now we had deserted our attic for Savoy Court – were busy on other tasks. The Treasury (why is its hand always called 'dead'?) were pressing for estimates. Those for building, the engineer's task, were comparatively easy because orthodox. But what of displays, at that stage still undecided? What would be the cost of finding, transporting, insuring and feeding husky dogs for the Polar Display, or battery hens in the Pavilion of Agriculture? What was a fair price for a full-sized statue of the White Knight or a model of a tanker's rudder? And what of the oddments? Drinking fountains and ice-cream kiosks, litter bins and signposts, trees, fireworks, toilet paper? How many or how much were needed? What would they cost? The list was endless but it had to be made and it had to be priced. There were negotiations, too, with the War Office over the Bailey Bridge, with the Admiralty over the loan of waterbus pontoons, with caterers and bus companies and floodlight experts, with the Raw Materials Commissions (building was still controlled by licence), the Royal Fine Arts Commission and the Metropolitan Water Board. Some were helpful, while others seemed 'armed invincibly', as Thomas Spratt once put it, 'against the enchantments of enthusiasm'.

By 1 May the first architects' sketches were in. Although in some early enthusiasm they had outrun practicability, the budget or even the building line, there were no disappointments. A few weeks passed while the designs were examined and checked. Estimates had to be made, structural systems agreed, alternatives and cuts suggested. It quickly became clear that we were going to overspend our budget which, to make matters worse, was cut in June by £1,500,000. There were a few more weeks of painful adjustment but on 26 July 1949 – a great day for all of us, and almost exactly to the day a century since the start of the 1851 exhibition – work started on the South Bank site.

Ralph Tubbs, architect, Dome of Discovery.

The agenda of the Design Group remained as crowded as ever. (By now we met also in the evenings, breaking off at 9 p.m. for cannelloni in a nearby Italian caff.) Here are some of the items from the August minutes: helicopters, site passes, experimental canvas, cleaners' uniforms, coloured asphalt, contractors' hoardings, visual symbolism, balloons, baby slings and fireworks. It was Festival policy, of course, that everything had to be of a high visual standard, and in those days that often meant specially commissioned designs. This was our particular worry. Costs, contracts and supply programmes were dealt with by others, equally hard-pressed, in the Festival Office.

By this time the theme and content experts were needing display designers to work with. Where were they to be found? The handful of experienced designers was already fully stretched. There were no design schools in those days pouring out their annual quota of talent in textiles, graphics, ceramics or industrial design. The net had to be cast wide and in unlikely places. Painters, window dressers and illustrators, poster designers and sculptors, cartoonists and weavers were looked for and interviewed. Lists were made, applications invited. Almost every Design Group meeting involved looking at and appraising half-a-dozen submitted portfolios. Those fortunate

**See* Sir Ralph Freeman's recollections, pp. 91–3.

enough to get a commission, on the South Bank or elsewhere, usually faced a design problem that was as unfamiliar to them as it was challenging. A graphic artist, perhaps, who had never in his life designed anything in three dimensions, would find himself with a hangar to fill with a complicated scientific story and a nightmare list of exhibits of all shapes and sizes. He would have to find his own experts to make, say, replicas of Celtic jewellery, a diorama of what Birmingham looked like two million years ago, a tapestry depicting the four seasons, the bust of a famous physicist. He would have to cost it too. One more cow in the Agricultural pavilion, for instance, would mean a reassessment of the costs of feeding, carting manure, veterinary fees – even perhaps an extra gully and run of drain.

We in the Design Group were frankly awed by the unruffled competence and professionalism shown by these designers bumping around in such previously uncharted seas. But inevitably such matters took time to think up and the buildings began to run ahead of their contents, not very fast though and certainly not fast enough. The winter was wet, tempers frayed, strikes frequent, materials in short supply and drawings delayed so that of the 6,000 or so working drawings issued only 830 had reached the contractors by 31 December.

It was a dispiriting time in the Festival Office. All glorious projects – it has been said – grow stale as they grind on to completion and 1951 seemed too far away at times. The Establishment, suspecting the Festival to be a radical middle-class racket, had always tried to ignore it. The press had been almost totally hostile. The international situation – the Berlin Blockade and in 1950 the Korean War – was as usual disturbing. Sir Thomas Beecham described it as a monumental piece of imbecility. The President of the Royal Academy said the South Bank would be a death-trap through overcrowding. Evelyn Waugh was horrified, Noël Coward facetious. Even the switchboard girl – so my friends alleged – used to reply 'Festering Britain here'. England, reduced by now to smaller rations than at the worst period of the war (8d a week for meat), sucked its teeth and waited. To those not directly concerned with concrete mixers and site meetings, it was not an encouraging time. We had as well our personal disasters. The Bailey Bridge fell into the river when launched. A water main burst. The gun mounting to take the radar service on the top of the Shot Tower fell from the top, causing the tower to jump off its foundations – but luckily also to jump back. The rain continued to fall, the progress charts looked more and more improbable.

By now our office had greatly expanded, and responsibilities were devolved. Misha Black took the site meetings upstream, I took the downstream ones. James Holland chased the upstream displays, James Gardner those downstream, and Ralph Tubbs concentrated on the Dome. Painters and sculptors – again chosen from our lists – were interviewed and recommended for thematic or decorative work. The Arts Council had commissioned four special works by Henry Moore, Barbara Hepworth, Frank Dobson and Jacob Epstein. (The last was once turned away from my office by the doorman on the grounds that he was a drunken-looking bum.) The commissioning procedure was simple. Once the artist was agreed the papers would drop into the gearbox of the Contracts Department and the artist would emerge with his brief – always in two parts: first the production of sketch or maquette (at which point, if necessary, relations could be broken off on payment of an appropriate fee), and then the completion and delivery of the work. Some, like John Piper and Graham Sutherland, worked in their studios; others, like Feliks Topolski and Kenneth Rowntree, worked on the site. Similar commissions were arranged for all other officially sponsored enterprises. On Sundays I would drag my protesting children around the half-built chaos, listing things to be done.

In mid-1950 Howard Lobb, assisted by the brisk and orderly Jack Ratcliff, was appointed Controller of Construction to help speed progress. Together one day of desperate worry we went to see Herbert Morrison in Downing Street. He listened, swivel-eyed and whistling under his breath, to our wail – delayed deliveries, strikes, official indecisions, budget cuts – one eye on Lobb, the other focused disconcertingly on the ceiling. He was as always loyal, helpful and marvellously cheerful, and we emerged encouraged into the rain.

Inexorably the weeks went by with their daily quota of problems or happy chances. The Royal Daimler got stuck in the mud by Waterloo Bridge. Southern Railway train drivers complained they were dangerously blinded by the reflections from the surface of the Dome. Rats gnawed through the cables. An old barge dock, unexpectedly disclosed by an excavator, was filled with water and used as a display for sailing dinghies and model boats. The foreman rigger erecting the Skylon descended from his spidery eyrie, tripped on a manhole cover and complained of dangerous working conditions at ground level. A mouse's nest appeared in the giant straw figures of the Lion and Unicorn. The site became a popular attraction to visiting VIPs – each visit logging up its quota of lost working hours.

As soon as a building was finished – or at least roofed – it was taken over for storage or for contractors' offices until needed for display. Ornamental lakes, once built, were filled with stacks of bricks or temporarily roofed to serve as carpenters' shops. Lorry routes had to be charted in advance to avoid the network of trenches being dug for services: sewers and gas, water and electricity, crowd control lines and television cables. Cranes and concrete mixers, canteens and first-aid huts, dumps of sand, lavatory basins, reinforcing rods had to be placed where they would be least in the way. Trees had to be brought in, propped up and protected until they had taken root. The General Manager and his immediate staff were in residence and busy recruiting cleaners and attendants, booking bands and events, and organizing security and maintenance. (There was something like half a million square feet of glass to clean.) Nearly 20,000 exhibits had to be installed. Whether a telescope, a cricket bat or a pedigree bull, a railway engine or a sofa cushion, it had to be labelled, catalogued, insured and placed in position, and special arrangements made (so easily forgotten, this) for the quick clearance of the mountains of crates and packing paper.

In Belfast, Glasgow and Poplar the buildings nourished their own crop of difficulties and disappointments – being dealt with, thank goodness, largely by others. Battersea looked like Passchendaele. On the South Bank, landscape architects had now taken over the spaces between buildings, floodlighting was under test and the site was thrown open for a day – a great success this – to the wives and families of those working there. Like charwomen scrubbing a floor, the contractors' huts and dumps gradually withdrew to final pockets of resistance – an unused flat roof or a piece of waste ground on the perimeter.

Suddenly it was finished. From a pigeon-proof dais in front of St Paul's, requested, designed, made, installed and tested within three days (thanks to Leslie Gooday and a smart contractor), King George declared the Festival open. I nipped into my office to find only one letter – a Roneo'd notice of dismissal. A few hours later, top-hatted against a steady drizzle, we huddled under the Dome while awaiting the Royal inauguration. 'Is it like what you expected?' asked the Queen. The only answer was 'Yes' – but it wasn't. It was much, much better. It was serious and irreverent, gay, bright coloured and, if you agree with Bertrand Russell's description of intelligence as 'the role of finding a means for realizing an end determined by passion', it was also an *intelligent* exhibition. For six months it was the most exciting place in London. Moreover it had opened to time and within the budget – thanks to the army of architects and engineers, technicians and building workers, script writers and sculptors, scientists, painters and canteen cooks, typists, lorry drivers and gardeners who between them had miraculously transformed 27 acres of battered buildings and neglected mudflats into a new world.

For five months it was open. Eight million people visited it. There was dancing on the Fairway at night – often in hats, overcoats and drizzling rain. Miss Matto, a French film actress, wore a Dome of Discovery hat in Hyde Park. The foundation stone (Mark II) of the National Theatre was laid outside the Festival Hall. Wynford Vaughan-Thomas broadcast from the top of the Skylon and Charles Elleano crossed the Thames on a tightrope (after forgetting his balancing pole).

At the end of it all there was an auction (the chairs and the plaster doves from the Lion and Unicorn pavilion were best sellers); the Fine Art works were distributed by the Arts Council; the exhibits returned to their owners, the site left deserted and windswept. In November the LCC commissioned a report from their Chief Architect and Chief Officer of Parks and myself on the next step. We drew attention to the newly disclosed panorama of the North Bank – 'marching', as James Bone put it, 'as majestically as a policeman to its proper climax at Scotland Yard' – to the newly appreciated use of the river, to the pedestrianized, informally scaled exhibition layout which had proved so popular and so workable, to the importance of attention to detail, to the legacy of good will for the area left by the exhibition. We recommended the temporary retention of certain buildings and facilities (including the Shot Tower and Boat Pier), and the maintenance of public access. Some of this was done, some not. The area is dominated today by a banal office block. The Dome site is still a car park, and nobody dances there any more. All is not lost but most of it is.

Was it all worth it? Was nothing left but a deserted, beaten-up building site, a tatty funfair in Battersea Park, a well-meant piece of redevelopment in Poplar and a decorative style to be expressed in artefacts that were too spindly, too multi-coloured, too overwrought? It would be easy to think so. Easy and wrong. It made a sizeable and much-needed dent in what Huw Wheldon called 'the national dinge'. It was a magnificent exercise in patronage. (Apart from the South Bank, the lift given to all the arts was tremendous.) Architecture in its fullest sense – i.e. places not buildings – so long the Cinderella of the arts, became the true Princess of the Festival. Important as was the content, it was the packaging that everyone remembered. Although there was nothing very revolutionary in the layout or the buildings, there was plenty of serious thinking under the funny hats; many ideas worth passing on were to be adopted by the designers of our environment. Designers were able to shake a leg to show what they were capable of when challenged. The nation was alerted to possibilities and opportunities hitherto undreamed of. But the real achievement of the South Bank was that it made people want things to be better, and to believe that they could be. It was noticeably unboastful and nobody was taught to hate anyone. Beneath the flags and the fireworks it had, in retrospect, a spiritual quality which is good to remember.

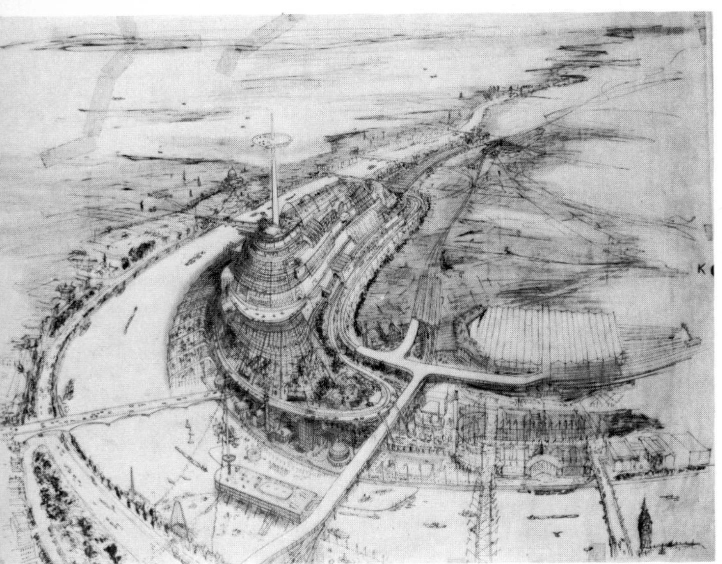

Top, *a celebration at the Royal Festival Hall Restaurant: left to right: Jack Godfrey-Gilbert, Misha Black, Richard Miles (Deputy to Misha Black), Hugh Casson, Howard Lobb and John Ratcliff.* Above, *the first concept for the use of the South Bank as the site of the Festival of Britain, designer Misha Black, drawing by Hilton Wright. Published in* The Ambassador, *August 1946.*

Architecture, Art and Design in Unison

MISHA BLACK

Member of the Festival Presentation Panel and Design Group; co-ordinating architect for the upstream section of the South Bank Exhibition; co-ordinating designer for the Dome of Discovery; co-architect for the Regatta Restaurant and the Bailey Bridge

WE WERE very serious. If the South Bank Exhibition was to exude gaiety the architectural clowns who provided it would themselves be morosely and professionally dedicated to the task. Those of us who were responsible for the design of the exhibition set ourselves two objectives. The first was to demonstrate the quality of modern architecture and town planning; the second to show that painters and sculptors could work with architects, landscape architects and exhibition designers to produce an aesthetic unity.

On these two counts our success was complete. We failed to achieve many peripheral objectives and thus dulled the bloom of our basic achievements, but we did produce a contemporary enclave on the South Bank and vanquished, at least for the time being, those who claimed that modern architecture (as we were then content to describe it) was unacceptable to the tradition-conscious British and could not be welded satisfactorily into the fabric of an ancient city. The South Bank also proved that informal town planning could give character and a sense of place to a small area, that majestic avenues were not the only recipe for urban pleasure.

This being conceded, however, as I feel sure it must be by those who visited the exhibition, it remains true that there was little real innovation, almost nothing on the South Bank which had not previously been illustrated in the architectural magazines. Geodesic domes, random stone walling, laminated timber trusses, stretched canvas and glazed façades were already, in 1948, accepted design idioms, the subjects of study and argument in all architectural schools. Though the Skylon was brand new, the rest was the British issue of international architectural currency; but what had previously been the private pleasure of the cognoscenti suddenly, virtually overnight, achieved enthusiastic public acclaim.

Architecturally the South Bank Exhibition was a milestone; it is sad that many imagined it to be a signpost to be used later to justify the commercial buildings which over the past quarter century have more often degraded than improved our cities. But it also set the stage for those architects who could profit from the new climate of perception and acceptance. That architects with the requisite creativity and sensitivity proved to be thin on the ground in the later fifties and sixties was not the fault of the South Bank team; that civic and commercial developers were quicker to accept the fashionable quirks of the exhibition rather than its fundamental concepts was more a saddening social comment than grounds for criticism of Festival architecture. But for the moment, the five months long moment, the air was rich with applause. Only those of us who had been simultaneously fathers and midwives to the South Bank birth were conscious of the ailments of the child who fortunately was destined only for a short if exuberant life.

I shall later adumbrate our basic misconceptions, but let me first describe our one unquestionable success. From the earliest planning exercises, the Festival Design Group were determined to celebrate the talents of Britain's artists simultaneously with those of its architects and designers. We sought the collaboration both of the famous and of those who were not yet renowned and this collaboration was enthusiastically provided. Henry Moore, Jacob Epstein, Barbara Hepworth, Keith Vaughan, Victor Pasmore, Ben Nicholson, John Minton, Feliks Topolski, Frank Dobson, Graham Sutherland, John Piper, Reg Butler and some twenty other artists carved, modelled and painted in complete unison with the architects who ensured that walls were available for murals and plinths for sculpture. Practically every concourse was designed to contain a major work; each building was a sanctuary for important works of art.

It was odd that this raised little comment from the eight and a half million visitors or the press. Only a few years previously Epstein's *Rima* in Hyde Park had been tarred and feathered for reasons which were explicit only to barbarians, but on the South Bank, Epstein seemed barely noticed, Hepworth was accepted with a shrug, while the magnificent Henry Moore attracted less attention than the huge boulders which brought to the site a whiff of the Forest of Dean. The reason for this nonchalant reaction was partly *embarras de richesse*. When there was so much to see and experience, when the Skylon soared to the sky and the Dome of Discovery spanned the days of the year, it is not surprising that a carved block of stone only eight feet high should seem, to most, of little importance. But for those who were willing to shorten their sights, to seek for quality rather than scale, the contribution of the artists was a special pleasure.

Each of the co-ordinating architects awarded himself one building which he himself designed; it was the lifeline to sanity, a specific job to compensate for the tasks of co-ordination which demanded diplomacy and persuasion as much as perception. I chose the Regatta Restaurant and the decoration of the Bailey Bridge across the Thames. In this South

Looking at the Dome of Discovery, 2 May 1950: left to right, Anthony Eden, Group Captain Peter Townshend, then Equerry to King George VI, and Misha Black.

Bank corner my colleague Alexander Gibson and I set out to show how a building could be a neutral ambiance for the work of artists, how vision could be satiated while stomachs were repleted and that purpose need not be sacrificed to architectural quality. When visitors approached the restaurant over the Bailey Bridge they were assailed by the whirling abstraction of a tiled mural by Victor Pasmore; for the garden Lynn Chadwick built a delicate construct; the lower vestibule was graced by a mural by John Tunnard, the inside of the restaurant by a painting by Laurence Scarfe. The door handles were bronze hands modelled by Mitzi Cunliffe, which Barbara Hepworth refused to touch as she associated them with amputation. In all it was a visual feast of a higher order than the food, but it was accepted without controversy. Few seemed to be aware of what had been attempted, but for myself and a few others it was a private joy which compensated, or at least so I like to believe, for our errors of architectural detail.

It is regrettable that no careful analysis was made of the failure, in terms of public interest, of the brave attempt to unify art with architecture which characterized the whole South Bank concept. It is probable that the fault resided in our lack of sufficient appreciation of the problem of scale. We, and the artists, were too timid and inexperienced. It may be that we would have done better with fewer and bigger pieces of sculpture and even larger murals. But the one gigantic bas-relief by Siegfried Charoux in the Sea and Ships pavilion designed by Basil Spence had, in fact, less impact than the more modest Epstein. This may be because the latter was the more important work, as it was for me until my young son (as he then was) looked at the figure poised on tip toe with hands outstretched and asked 'where is the bicycle?' I could never again contemplate Epstein's *Youth Advances* with unassociative aesthetic pleasure.

The moral of this art/architectural activity was, I now feel sure, that art only has impact on large sections of the community when its subject is deeply emotive and when it is at the same time of such aesthetic consequence that no one can contemplate it without empathic involvement. I fear that few of the works of our artist colleagues simultaneously met both criteria. But for those of us who knew every nook and cranny of the South Bank, the works of art were a recurring joy, a compensation for mental anguish and physical exhaustion.

The work of the landscape architects, Maria Shephard, H. F. Clark, Peter Shepheard and G. P. Youngman, was also accepted as though there was no surprise in five hundred trees springing to immediate leaf-laden life in what, only a few months previously, had been a building contractors' desert. The tens of thousands of tulips (changed overnight into summer flowers), the turf, rocks, streams and waterfalls were all accepted as normality while I remained amazed that nature could be harnessed by our command into instantaneous activity.

Associating the artists with the architects presented no problems. Each accepted the authority, wisdom and skills of the other; the task of the co-ordinating architects was the simple one of bringing together those of like mind and intention. Co-ordination of building with interior exhibition design was more difficult. Complete harmony existed only when the designer was responsible both for structure and content. This was so in the Lion and the Unicorn pavilion, designed by Robert Goodden and R. D. Russell, and the Homes and Gardens building, designed by Bronek Katz and Reginald Vaughan. Both groups of architects produced unassertive structures, concentrating their energies and interest on the contents. The Homes and Gardens pavilion was professionally competent and economic, the Lion and Unicorn a delicious romp which succeeded in demonstrating with humour and slightly wry tolerance what the official catalogue described as 'two of the main qualities of the national character: realism and strength on the one hand and, on the other, independence and imagination'. Those were heroic days! But where the interior designers and the architects were different teams, and equally self-opinionated, the co-ordinating architects and designers spent time which they could ill afford and patience which was in short supply to achieve at least the semblance of co-operation.

The cause of this strain was an initial misconception of what the exhibition as a whole could achieve. All of us who were responsible for the initial concept of the South Bank Exhibition fell cheerfully and willingly into the same trap. The exhibition should, we planned, tell the whole story of British history and achievement. Everything that could be said would be said: there would be brown owls and flatfish, a locomotive and aircraft, Anglo Saxons and Romans, chemistry, biology, physics and nuclear science, telescopes, agriculture and Darwin, all the Nobel Prize winners and Polar dogs, public health and the White Knight. All of Britain past and present was to be crammed into the 27 acres of the South Bank site. It was to be a *narrative* exhibition, based on the assumption that visitors would take the scheduled route and absorb much, if not all, of what was displayed and captioned. The script was edited by Lionel Birch and Laurie Lee, tens of thousands of descriptive words were carefully, and sometimes brilliantly, written and edited. Only a fraction of this verbosity was read. The theme conveners, who were responsible for the content of the exhibition, were determined that everything should be shown and explained; the interior exhibition designers tried to cram their gallon of exhibits into the pint pot of the buildings; the architects screamed with righteous indignation as the mass of exhibits and display devices threatened to destroy the spatial quality of their buildings. There were exceptions: the exhibits designed by James Gardner enhanced Cadbury Brown's elegant 'People of Britain' building, but more often structure and exhibits were at odds.

The problem was most acute in the Dome of Discovery. The ten theme conveners were determined that nothing should be omitted which did credit to Britain; the team of exhibition designers filled the Dome solid; the architect protested but packing-it-in continued. Eventually so much was displayed as to make comprehension impossible. Only a general memory of creditable British exploration, invention and industrial capacity remained in the mind of even the most devoted caption reader and exhibit viewer. The magnificent awe-inspiring interior space, designed with great sensitivity by Ralph Tubbs, was diminished to no useful purpose by the interior display. I should know as the interior was one of my special responsibilities.

The catalogue proclaimed that 'the exhibition tells a continuous story' but it is doubtful whether more than a single sentence lingered in the mind of even those visitors who returned many times. The magic of the exhibition was that of place, of a mirage seen from the North Bank which became a reality once the turnstile had clicked. It was the total experience which was remembered and cherished: the Dome lying on the ground as though it had newly arrived from Mars, entering into its crypt and then up to be encompassed by a metallic sky; the Skylon poised for take-off; the fountains designed by H. T. Cadbury Brown which rose and fell over flaring gas; Richard Huws's great gusher of a water sculpture which cascaded a thousand gallons of water – when it was not choked by orange peel; the interior of the Shot Tower vanishing upwards into mystery; the night view across the river to the illuminated fairy palace Whitehall Court with its pinnacles embellished by a host of flags; lights bedded into the Fairway to become glow-worms for dancing over. Amidst such marvels the wording of a caption, the meticulous positioning of a Design Council selected tea service took second place.

The narrative served its essential purpose in providing an armature for planning and a route for meticulous map readers. The mass of exhibits satisfied those who felt that this gave them their money's worth. But the exhibition would have been better than it was if the number of exhibits had been decimated, if a few could have symbolized the multitude, if the interiors of the buildings had been less cluttered with intellectual bric-à-brac.

The Dome of Discovery was at its most dramatic when empty, when on a bitterly cold evening in the winter of 1950 all the workmen on the site were invited to a celebratory meal, the roofs having been finally battened down on all the buildings. A few naked bulbs gave illumination, the dark areas were greater than the lit, braziers glowed with minimal warmth. The speeches of exhortation to greater effort and fewer trade-union disputes were dreary and misconceived. The atmosphere became as frigid as the night when suddenly one man sent his paper plate (food eaten) whizzing across the void. In a moment a thousand plates were spinning, until the whole volume of the Dome was alive with white discs, as though invaded by flying fish. This was a magical moment which all the skills of the exhibition designers could not emulate.

It is axiomatic that an exhibition must contain exhibits; many of them, on the South Bank, were splendid, many of the display devices ingenious, designed with exemplary professional skill and sometimes beautiful – but much of the effort which was harnessed to the narrative chariot was misconceived. I remember only the big things: the 74-inch reflecting telescope in the Dome, the steam locomotive, sailing boats, the cows (regularly milked), the husky dogs mushing on salt simulating snow. But this may well be a personal failing – a preference for image over idea – as all I remember of Wembley in 1924 is the Prince of Wales in butter, unsure whether the sculptor's refrigerated material came from Australia or New Zealand.

For the co-ordinating architects and designers the two years preceding the opening days were continuous anguish and anxiety. There was peace only during the weekly evening meetings of the Design Group when the sense of common purpose and mutual understanding made the length of our agenda tolerable. It was a battle against time, against the weather which turned the South Bank into a frozen girder-strewn lunar landscape, against labour disputes, against budget cuts, against bitter newspaper criticism, against the pundits (Professor A. E. Richardson in particular) who predicted that the number of expected visitors would inevitably cause panic and disaster, that London's traffic would grind to a halt. I had a recurring dream in which the Design Group had been transmogrified into mice nibbling away at a ballroom-sized biscuit: the biscuit was the project and somehow or other we had to consume it before 4 May 1951. But we did, more or less, manage to eat the cookie.

By the night before the opening day I had been without sleep for thirty-six hours. At 4 a.m. we decided it was time to remove the contractors' huts which were then still in the main gangway of the Dome of Discovery. As the walls came down and the floor panels were lifted rats scattered in all directions to be chased by joiners and painters, their physical exhaustion extinguished by the excitement of the hunt. By morning the rats were dead, the gangway swept and the carpet laid to receive the Royal Family.

On the opening day it poured with rain but inside the pavilions all, on the surface, was serene. The Royal Family rode the escalators in the Dome in solemn procession. The air was aflutter with congratulations. The Beaverbrook press switched from condemnation to adulation. I managed to keep awake during a thanksgiving lunch in the Regatta Restaurant and sleepwalked over the Bailey Bridge to bed.

On 30 September the massed bands of the Brigade of Guards beat the Retreat, the dancers on the Fairway linked arms and sang 'Auld Lang Syne', and euphoria was diminished only when the cleaners arrived to sweep up the daily rubbish mountain. The next day I walked round the exhibition for the last time. It had already assumed the air of a ghost town. Exhibits were being removed, the valuable objects were being packed, and the demolishing gangs were mustering. A public sale was held on the site, and South Bank aficionados struggled to the Underground clutching plaster doves, Race chairs, light fittings and butterflies immortalized in plastic cubes. The Treasury had spent too long quibbling about a fair price for the Dome and the Skylon and the earlier enthusiasm of potential buyers had evaporated, so they also were demolished and sold for scrap. Soon the Festival Hall was marooned in a sea of exhibition debris.

The carnival was over.

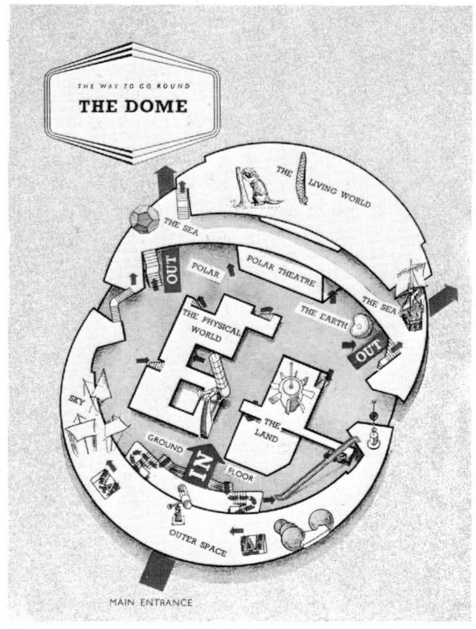

The Dome of Discovery

Architect Ralph Tubbs; *engineers* Freeman Fox & Partners *(see pp. 91–3); display designers* Design Research Unit; *co-ordinating designer* Misha Black *(see pp. 82–5)*. Above, *interior view*. Left, *plan from the South Bank guide*. Opposite above, *view from the People of Britain pavilion*. Opposite below, *model of Charles Darwin beside the skeleton of a megatherium. Section designers:* Stirling Craig, Austin Frazer.

CHARLES DARWIN SAW THAT MANY
ANIMALS, like oysters, produce millions
of eggs, or young, most of which perish

'I enjoyed it more than anything in my life'

ANTONY D. HIPPISLEY COXE

Features editor, News Chronicle*; representative of the CoID in the Festival Office; member of the Presentation Panel; Theme Convener of the Homes and Gardens section and the Seaside section of the Festival Exhibition; responsible for River Spectacles*

ON THE MORNING of 5 May 1951, I received a letter from Gordon Russell, Director of the Council of Industrial Design, which started, 'Now that the really astonishing thing has happened and the South Bank Exhibition has actually opened after all . . .'; it ended, 'The peculiar and highly improbable background to the whole operation must, I verily believe, have given it an atmosphere very congenial to one who savours the bizarre and macabre with such relish. Indeed, you gave me the impression, which I found very comforting, of scanning new terrors and new depths of chaos with pleasure, even with delight.'

Although I am proud of that letter, I quote it with more humility than pride, because it sums up much more neatly than I can what working on the Festival was like. It *was* astonishing that the South Bank Exhibition opened on time. The background to the whole operation was *indeed* peculiar. New depths of chaos occurred with rather terrifying frequency. And I enjoyed it more than anything in my life.

Gerald Barry, as editor of the *News Chronicle*, had, in 1945, called for 'a great Trade and Cultural Exhibition, to be held in London during the centenary year of the Great Exhibition of 1951'. He had also given me my first post-war job as features editor on his newspaper. When he asked me if I would like to join him as the representative of the Council of Industrial Design in the Festival Office, I jumped at the opportunity. All sorts of other jobs came my way. They could roughly be divided into the serious and the light-hearted, which occasionally overlapped. Even representing the Council had its absurd moments – when, for instance, 'urgently required, most important industrial exhibits', turned out to be six paper hats.

I served on the Presentation Panel, which was responsible for all the visual and many non-visual aspects of all the official exhibitions, from choosing the architects and designers, to naming the restaurants. Gerald Barry was chairman, and most members were architects, designers, writers or radio men. The chairman's experience of working to a deadline was very useful when time was squandered in debating whether 'pantechnicon' and 'telecinema' should or should not be spelt with a 'k'. He also had a meticulous eye for detail, which, coupled with an enquiring mind, prevented a lot that was insufficiently considered from just slipping through.

Many members of the Panel had a healthy horror of red tape, but the civil servants who were appointed to the Festival were not always able to cut themselves free from its entanglement. When Bernard Sendall joined us as Controller, he was able to mediate between the volatile and sometimes impulsive creative element and those whose job it was to ensure that the correct machinery was brought into operation.

In holding the whole organization together, one of the most important ties, I think, was Gerald Barry's sense of humour. This could sometimes have been called black, but he could find humour in practically any situation. There were many times in the Festival Office when his sense of the absurd relieved a deep sense of frustration.

As Theme Convener of the Homes and Gardens section, I tried to get the designers to do more than display the best that Britain had to offer. They were encouraged to make a new contribution to the post-war world by solving some of the problems that faced us. One square yard of the South Bank, if offered as a part of a building site, was, even in those days, worth £40 and the value would obviously increase. The economic use of space in the home was, therefore, at the root of many problems. Dual-purpose rooms such as bed-sitters and kitchen-diners could help. The designers were asked to produce a paper analysing the problem they had to tackle before they went anywhere near their drawing-boards. I think this approach was successful; it produced quite a few new ideas, such as furniture that grows up with the child. The one thing I deeply regret was my total failure to cope with the gardens. Here I missed a wonderful opportunity.

I was also Theme Convener of the Seaside section, where the serious and the light-hearted met. This was a battle-ground over which I was constantly skirmishing. It had always been the first to be threatened with a cut in times of financial strain. Consequently it was the last section to be finished. The designers, whose brilliant, aesthetic approach was as sharp and clean as a sea breeze, were not always in sympathy with the displays, some of which I wanted to be 'vulgar' in its true sense of 'belonging to the crowd'. I felt that our visitors' feet and powers of concentration might well give out at this point, as it came at the end of a pretty long trek round a thematic exhibition. So this was a place where one could relax and perhaps smile a little at our rather strange – but very national – seaside customs. How *do* those letters get inside the sticks of rock? What *was* it that the Butler Saw? And while the fisherman on the end of the pier may be an universal figure, donkey rides and Donald McGill postcards are essentially English.

Rock caused a fearful flutter in the Concessions Co-ordinating Committee. Reading their memoranda one gets a picture of pursed lips, shaking heads and frowns. 'The consideration of the merit as a display feature of the making of Rock is not, of course, within the terms of reference of this Committee . . . but the Presentation Panel are aware that the Catering Committee have expressed an opinion that the sale of sweetmeats should be strictly confined to pre-packed sweets such as chocolate, and that even ice-cream should only be sold in pre-packed form as experience has shown that the sale of non-pre-packed sweetmeats is one of the chief causes of unsightly litter.'

I still cannot understand why something that is wrapped before it reaches the shop should cause less litter than that which is wrapped at the point of sale or not wrapped at all. Back and forth the memos flowed until it was actually referred to the Executive Committee, who brusquely informed the Concessions Co-ordinating Committee that Festival Rock was to be manufactured in the Seaside section and sold there as well as at other kiosks.

The civil servants were not the only ones to suck their teeth at the Seaside section. The Association of Health and Holiday Resorts were most perturbed to think that we might intend to reveal ourselves as a nation of eccentrics. They gave me the impression that Bournemouth had never heard of Blackpool. Grave doubts were also expressed about the peep-shows, and the Lord Privy Seal actually came in person to check that 'What the Butler Saw' was not pornographic. Then I had more difficulties over the donkey rides. And so it went on.

Yet all these features got remarkable press coverage, from fourth leaders in *The Times* to editorials in *Home Chat*. A million people are said to have enquired about the fisherman on the end of the pier, and one enterprising reporter calculated that 250 miles of Festival Rock would have been sucked away by the end of the exhibition.

Not all the battles were won. Amongst other things, I had picked up the responsibility for River Spectacles and Fireworks. But my plans had to be abandoned in one of the financial crises. Sometimes projects very nearly came unstuck. I wanted a narrow boat from the canals to share the South Bank moorings with *Sara*, the Thames topsail barge. The Inland Waterways Association located one and I went to see her set off down the Grand Union Canal on her journey south. Fortunately I noticed that canvas along the sides was laced in such a way that it looked as if it was hiding something. It was. An enterprising advertising man had realized that the side of a boat moored off the South Bank would make a splendid poster hoarding to plug a well-known make of bicycle.

Once the exhibition opened most of us hoped we could relax a little. But no sooner had one thing been accomplished than another landed in one's lap. One of these was a file which bristled with so many 'Any Comments?', 'Over to you', 'Noted' and other non-committal remarks that it had obviously been passed around for quite a while. Someone had pointed out that the persons to whom the file referred should not be treated as royalty. This stung me into action, because the file contained a very civil request to visit the South Bank Exhibition from the Pearly King and Queen of Lambeth.

Seaside section, South Bank, architects and designers Eric Brown and Peter Chamberlin.

It so happened that the Evening Activities Sub-committee (another committee on which I sat) had proposed inviting the Pearly Kings and Queens. This had been turned down because the Festival Gardens were considered more suitable. So there was little chance of getting an official visit organized. I suggested to the *News Chronicle* that they should sponsor a levee of Pearlies to elect a Festival King and Queen and the editor agreed. Twenty boroughs from Acton to Woolwich were represented. We breakfasted off whelks, cockles and a mixed grill, washed down with Guinness. After a tour of the South Bank, we boarded a steamer for the Pleasure Gardens, and it was 'Knees Up Mother Brown' all the way.

This turned out to be a greater success than I had anticipated. That day a number of French journalists had been invited to visit the South Bank. Delighted as they were with their reception and the exhibition they were looking for some original news peg on which to hang their story.

I believe it was this event that persuaded Gerald Barry to stage more stunts. Anyhow, Jack Triggs of the Publicity Department and I were given a special assignment to organize such events. The first stunt I did was to make a balloon ascent from the South Bank. Ballooning had not then returned to popularity and there were less than half-a-dozen men in England with an aeronaut's licence. (This allows the holder to pilot a lighter-than-air vehicle, whereas an aviator's licence is for a heavier-than-air machine.) I was fortunate in finding George Long, an aeronaut of nearly forty years experience, and, accompanied by a BBC commentator, we made our ascent. Once I had overcome my initial fright I found it an almost sublime experience. Up there in the silent air each noise could immediately be traced to its source. It was as if one could see sound. The only hitch occurred when George Long discovered that the sand carried as ballast had not been sifted and contained large stones. Directly below us were the glass-houses of the Lee Valley.

I paid £5 to insure my life for £5,000 for that one journey, and I was not allowed to claim the premium as an expense. (The rules governing expenses were very peculiar. I still have a memo which says that if a journey is made by taxi-meter cab, a receipt for the fare should be obtained from the driver.) But the trip was well worth the premium, and I persuaded Gerald Barry to make an ascent a few days later.

It was from Jack Triggs that I learnt the fundamental rule that publicists should never attract publicity to themselves because this distracts from whatever they are trying to publicize. So from then on we remained fairly anonymous, Jack using his excellent contacts to get the stars of stage, screen and sport to make evening appearances. Amongst them were Gracie Fields, Richard Murdoch, Arthur Askey, Kenneth Horne and Diana Dors. Meanwhile I set out to get someone to cross the Thames on a tightrope.

Finding the man was easy. Elleano agreed to do it straight away. Getting the wire was much more difficult, and it took considerably longer than expected to rig. Then there was the question of permission: permission from the PLA, permission from the Metropolitan Police, permission from the River Police and permission from the LCC. Eventually, Elleano was allowed to make his attempt 'between 1300 and 1400 hours on September 22'. That was at slack water, low tide, before the river traffic came up on the flood.

Adjustments were still being made to the wire long after 2 p.m. At 3 p.m. the crowd began to get restless; and there was a record attendance that day. The gates were closed at 2 p.m. for two and a half hours with 83,000 visitors inside the exhibition, and dense crowds also lined the Embankment and Westminster Bridge. Maybe a quarter of a million people had come to see Elleano. Jack and I were on the North Bank at the starting point. Gerald Barry on the South Bank was ringing us up and telling us, 'Get that man on the wire.' The crowd started to slow hand-clap, and I asked Elleano if he had got his balancing pole. He had forgotten it. So Jack Triggs and I raced along the Embankment, past Charing Cross and over Waterloo Bridge to Elleano's caravan, seized a pole from the roof and ran back with it. I remember crowds scattering and bells ringing. Did trams then still run along the Embankment?

At 4 p.m. Elleano finally set out, but by this time tugs towing their strings of lighters were coming up on the flood. When a tug lowered its funnel to pass under Hungerford Bridge, Elleano was hidden in a cloud of smoke. As it cleared he was seen sitting on the wire. Twenty-five minutes after he set out he stepped on to the South Bank. The next day the Sunday papers were full of it and on the Monday there was yet another leader in *The Times*.

The last spectacle that Jack and I put on was the Closing Ceremony: Beating Tattoo by the Massed Band Drums and Pipes of the Brigade of Guards, Community Singing and Striking the Flags, when the Union Jack, flanked by the Festival flags, was slowly lowered. It was very simple, but to those who had worked for two years or more in the Festival Office, I think it was rather moving.

What did it all add up to? The South Bank was the centrepiece of the Festival, but one must remember that there were six other exhibition sites, plus a land and a sea travelling exhibition, all organized from the Festival Office. In the official programme there were other exhibitions and the arts festivals. But even this proliferation was not really what it was all about. The key to the real meaning of the Festival is in a green-covered booklet of some 160 pages listing the 'Events and Activities arranged by Local Authorities and Local Festival Committees throughout the United Kingdom'. Here you will find lavish, but ephemeral historical pageants; and simpler but more lasting projects such as re-gilding the face of the church clock. Some are strictly utilitarian – 'New Sewage Scheme'; some are just fun – 'Bonfire and Fireworks'. Then there are those jobs which until then nobody had got round to doing, for example 'Tidy up bomb site' (as if the mess was due to the children leaving their toys lying about). Re-reading the list I was pleasantly surprised at the number of places which celebrated 1951 by planting trees.

That is what the Festival was really about. It gave the people a goal and a deadline. For too long we had been saying 'Britain can take it'. That had been proved. Now we had to bestir ourselves and hold our heads high.

I believe that the spirit which united the country in 1951 is still with us, lying dormant. One day, someone will give it a shake and once again we shall throw back our heads – when there is something to crow about.

Festival Structures

RALPH FREEMAN

Partner, Freeman, Fox & Partners, engineers for the Dome of Discovery and consulting engineers, in association with R. T. James & Partners, for the South Bank

THE FIRST I REMEMBER of the Festival was being asked to go to a house in Lennox Gardens in, I think, October 1948. There I met a group of young architects, headed by Hugh Casson, and some others including Bernard Sendall. It seemed they were looking for an engineer to help them design stick and string buildings – their own description! – for an exhibition planned to be held somewhere in London. The buildings, they said, would not be ordinary or conventional, but light, exciting, with lots of wire, canvas and glass. I believe this original introduction was due to Basil Spence, whom I had got to know in the Army towards the end of the war.

The next move came early in 1949. My firm – Freeman, Fox & Partners – was approached by the Festival people, this time with a very clear and direct brief: to undertake with the appointed architect, Ralph Tubbs, the design of the Dome of Discovery, which was to be the centrepiece of the South Bank Exhibition, as it was now being called, and get it built. The job was urgent. There wasn't a moment to lose. A huge, 365-foot diameter, pancake-shaped dome had to be conceived and designed from scratch, put out to tender for construction and built, complete with foundations, supporting structure and numerous platforms and staircases, floors, walls, and all the ordinary paraphernalia of an exhibition hall, by mid-1950 *at latest*.

Fortunately we were in a position to take this work on. My father, a past master at knowing how to tackle things quickly and efficiently, directed the work himself and soon established the closest rapport with Tubbs. Result – the main dome structure was designed, detailed and out to tender in two months, and the contract for it let, to Horseley Bridge and Thomas Piggott of Tipton, Staffs, a month after that. The geodetic triangular rib structure and smooth metal cover was to be made of aluminium alloy, a material we'd never designed in on this scale before, and the ribs were to thrust on to an all-welded steel box ring girder, itself held aloft 40 ft above ground by a series of slender lattice steel masts leaning inwards and forming a complete triangulated support system all round the ring. This system, which was elegantly simple, was my father's concept and greatly welcomed by Tubbs who I think had been in some difficulty in his search for the best solution.

Soon after we'd taken on the Dome we were asked to meet the Festival directorate again, this

The Dome of Discovery under construction, 10 July 1951, showing aluminium alloy arches to support aluminium roof; in the foreground, part of the Transport pavilion.

time to discuss the more general and pressing problem of how to get the South Bank Exhibition built in the time required. The obstacles were formidable – so much so, we gathered later, that two other organizations already approached had said, in so many words, it couldn't be done. The exhibition was to open in the first week of May 1951. The buildings had to be ready for the interior designers six months before, and some earlier than that.

The site was literally being created at the time by the construction of a new river wall from County Hall to beyond Waterloo Bridge; and this work, with the reclamation and filling of the area behind it all moving steadily downstream, was not scheduled to be completed till early 1951. Meanwhile most of the accessible areas behind the wall and within the proposed exhibition site had already been allocated by the LCC as working space to their river wall contractor, Costain. Between the Charing Cross railway bridge and Waterloo Bridge nearly all the rest had been similarly allotted to the Festival Hall contractor, Holland & Hannen and Cubitts.

We said there was only one way – to invite these two 'sitting tenants' to undertake the whole of the construction work on terms to be negotiated with them, and to channel all the architects' drawings and instructions to them through a single supervisory and co-ordinating agency. This would mean a cost-plus type of contract with only the contractors' overhead and profit percentages negotiable. With the LCC breathing down the Festival people's necks lest there should be the slightest interference with their river wall contractor's operations, and the opening date for the exhibition already firmly announced by the Government, there simply was no alternative.

They went away and considered our advice. Very soon they were back, this time with a much bigger and even more challenging brief than the Dome.

They accepted our advice about how to get the job done – and would we be prepared to take it on and, if so, on what terms? Taking it on, it transpired, meant not only the control and supervision of construction and negotiation and settlement of all payments; they also wanted us to provide structural engineering service to those of the architects who hadn't already made their own arrangements with other consulting engineers, *and* to undertake responsibility for the structural soundness and stability of *all* the buildings, whether structurally designed by us or not – which meant we would have to check and satisfy ourselves about the designs of the various engineering consultants engaged by some of the architects.

All in all, this was a big demand. We felt we could only take it on if we could share the load. So we approached our old and trusty friend R. T. James, senior partner of R. T. James & Partners. They were much better known than we among the architectural fraternity, and 'Jimmy' James had trained in our firm under my father before setting up in practice on his own twenty years before. We immediately agreed on an arrangement between us whereby they would deal with all the buildings and site problems in the area downstream of the railway bridge, leaving us to cope with the upstream area, where the Dome of Discovery was to be, and with the overall administration and dealings with the authority.

Before presenting our proposals we cleared the other uncertainty by making preliminary approaches to both the sitting contractors, to confirm our expectation that they would be willing to co-operate on reasonable terms to get the exhibition built under the supervisory system we were proposing. I well remember our first meeting with Costain's representative, John Whiter, their Managing Director. No one could have been more helpful and co-operative, and he and his wife have remained firm friends of ours ever since.

This done, we put our terms to the Festival people along with our assurance, based on our conversations first with Jimmy James and then with Costain and HHC, that in that way the job could be done in the time. It hadn't taken us long to reach this point, nor was the authority slow in accepting our proposals. From that moment – about mid-1949 – it was 'all systems go' with a vengeance. It was just as well that we and James had a few talented young engineers not already fully committed on existing work, and were able to recruit some more, because we were immediately descended upon by all the architects who did not have their own consulting engineers with pressing demands to work out and solve their structural problems. At the same time we had to establish our own overall structural soundness and safety standards (the buildings were exempt from LCC building bylaws, but were expected to comply generally), make our number and maintain contact with the Festival's Director of Architecture (Hugh Casson) and the upstream and downstream area Co-ordinating Architects (Misha Black and, again, Hugh Casson). This meant attendance at regular weekly or fortnightly meetings as Savoy Place, all of which proved to be of absorbing interest.

Very soon the contractors had their offices set up on the site with their agents and staff; and we had our resident engineers and their staff. The architects' and engineers' working drawings began to flow. Before long the entire site was transformed into a veritable hive of activity. Miraculously, almost all those areas that had been labelled as reserved for the river wall contractor and the Festival Hall contractor suddenly seemed no longer to be needed for those purposes. Earth and all manner of debris – old street paving stones, concrete and brickwork – had to be carted away and ready-mixed concrete brought in. The first foundation work was for the Dome, a circle of insignificant-looking flat concrete blocks let into the ground. We had early decided that on this uncharted site, full of old cellars and footings, there would be no time for normal sub-surface investigations. We (and therefore our client) would have to rely wholly on engineering judgment. We decided that all foundations for the buildings would be sized to exert a pressure on the ground of not more than half a ton per square foot. Whether this was extravagant will never be known; but no building collapsed or even settled noticeably, so it was presumably sound.

The authority said from the outset that it wanted to adopt normal competitive tendering for any sections of the work where this might be feasible. In the end, only one building inside the main exhibition site – 'SB 20', a restaurant to be built on a curve to embrace the abutment of Waterloo Bridge – was singled out for this treatment. The architects were Maxwell Fry and Jane Drew; after proper competitive tendering the contract went to Kirk & Kirk.

Some of the architects were perhaps a little short of practical experience of getting things built, but whatever they might have lacked in this respect was more than compensated for by their energy and enthusiasm to provide the detailed information needed as soon as the need was identified.

My recollection of those days is of innumerable meetings and design problems: progress meetings at Savoy Place, progress meetings with the contractors, meeting after meeting with individual architects and with the engineers of those architects who had from the outset of design retained their own engineers. We were steadily building up our own staff to tackle all this work.

And then, on Saturday 11 March 1950, my father died. He'd been at the office as usual the day before.

I was making my customary Saturday morning round of the site when word from my mother was relayed to me. This sudden removal of the leader of our exhibition team was a serious blow. My reaction, however inadequate, was immediate. Someone had to take over, and that someone had to be me. Fortunately, supervision of the Dome contract was already in the capable hands of my partner Gilbert Roberts, and my two other partners could cope with most of the firm's other work. I was relatively free to concentrate on the exhibition – 'relatively' because in April 1949 I had been offered and accepted the Royal Household appointment of Consulting Engineer, Sandringham. This, though only a part-time job, was demanding a certain amount of personal attention. That 'everything comes at once' was never more true than of the second quarter of 1950.

Working drawings were pouring in, to be registered, checked and issued to the contractors with the necessary written instructions, often quite complicated. Planning and designing of water mains, drains, electricity network, fountain displays, pavings, tree positions, public lavatories and all the 'infrastructure' (the word hadn't been invented then or, if it had, it wasn't used) that was to fill the spaces between the buildings. There was also endless correspondence, with the authority, contractors, architects, the LCC, public utilities and many others. I could never have managed this without the tireless and incredibly accurate work of my then secretary Ann Brunsdon.

About mid-1950, when some buildings were well advanced but others were lagging somewhat, despite everyone's best efforts, our client – understandably I suppose – became concerned about progress. I sensed, though of course they never voiced this in my hearing, that with my father's death they'd begun to doubt our ability to see the job through on time – as if it depended only on us! For myself, I knew it would be a struggle; but, by this time, little that we could do or omit to do would seriously interfere with progress, which depended mainly on the production of the remaining working drawings by the architects for some of the buildings and the builders' ability to build fast enough to catch up any time lost. In all events the authority, for better or worse, decided to set up a 'Controllerate of Architecture', with Howard Lobb as Controller. His duties were not very clearly defined.

It was vital that he and I should work harmoniously together, and we did. Short of removing my firm altogether Howard could not be placed in an executive position vis-à-vis the construction contracts, and it is to the credit of the authority that it decided not to take this step. Lobb, and his assistant John Ratcliff, performed a valuable roving supervisory commission. They reported progress to the authority, attended all progress meetings and reported to us with great regularity any defects they spotted in the contractors' workmanship. They were also a valuable intermediary between us and the architects.

Most of the buildings were sufficiently finished to be handed over to the display designers and their contractors by late 1950, but there was little let-up in our work. 'Site works' were still in full swing. The smallness of the site made it very difficult to get paved areas finished while still allowing essential vehicle access to all the buildings. Besides innumerable pipes, cables, electric and telephone cables and other underground services to be laid, forty or fifty quite large trees had to be brought in and planted – a major engineering planning operation in itself. A full-size 120-ton, 5½-foot gauge steam locomotive and tender, built in England for the Indian Government Railways, was road-transported to the site, off-loaded on to a platform and then rolled sideways into place outside the Transport pavilion. A 90-inch optical telescope destined for Australia was erected in the Dome of Discovery.

And there was the Skylon. An architectural design competition for a 'vertical feature' had been mounted. It produced, I recollect, nearly two hundred entries and I was privileged to be the engineer member of the judging panel. There were a dozen or so quite outstanding designs. It fell to me to advise my colleagues that the one they preferred of the first two short-listed entries could not by any stretch of the imagination be built in the time available. The choice thus went to that ingeniously mounted cigar-shaped object, designed by Powell and Moya and engineered by the late Felix Samuely, which acquired the name 'Skylon'.

The last few weeks before the opening day were a nightmare for everyone and certainly for me. Endless last-minute demands of architects, designers, the exhibition management and countless others had to be received, processed and passed on. Right up to the last moment the two main contractors, Costain and HHC, were the willing maids-of-all-work. Exasperated they must often have been, and with good reason; yet they never failed to do what was required of them fast. My last inspection was at midnight on the night before the opening, when I was dismayed to see how much clearing up had still to be done, including the removal of a display contractor's hut still in a prominent position in the Dome. The amount of clearing up that must have gone on in those last nine hours was beyond comprehension.

Between us all, we had done it. HM King George VI put the final seal on the work of all the thousands who had been involved when he declared the exhibition open on 4 May 1951, accompanied by Queen Elizabeth and their Royal Highnesses Princess Elizabeth and Princess Margaret.

The South Bank perimeter: top, *part of the 'abacus' screen by Edward Mills;* above, *'look-outs' over the river, Seaside section;* right, *view of the South Bank, upstream section, from the North Bank:* Ruari McLean *wrote, 'Personally, on that first morning when I first saw the Festival looking across the river from Charing Cross Station, it was so utterly beautiful and exciting that I wept.'*

The Lion and Unicorn Pavilion

R. D. RUSSELL, ROBERT GOODDEN

Designers of the Lion and Unicorn pavilion, South Bank

IN THE LATE 1940s Dick Russell and Robert Goodden were sharing offices in Buckingham Street, Strand. Though not strictly in partnership they worked in collaboration whenever their clients' brief offered opportunities to both of them. The winter of 1948/49 was an exciting time. They had both been appointed very recently to Robin Darwin's staff at the Royal College of Art and had taken up their duties that autumn term. Like so many other architects and designers who were making a new start to their career after the interruption of the war, their imagination was set alight by Gerald Barry's vision of a great national festival to mark the centenary of the Great Exhibition of 1851. They had both contributed to the 'Britain can make it' Exhibition of 1946, and Goodden had designed a section of Basil Spence's Enterprise Scotland 1947, so there was reason to hope. It was impossible not to hope.

The opportunity came in the course of that winter with an invitation from Hugh Casson to call at the Festival Office to discuss the designing of one of the South Bank Exhibition buildings. Might the two of them design it in collaboration, they asked? Certainly, but in that case would they like to take on the interior display as well as the building itself, because he had intended to commission a building from one of them and one of the interior displays from the other. Of course they jumped at the offer and could hardly believe their good fortune. Apart from Wells Coates's cinema, it would be the only instance in the South Bank Exhibition of a building and its contents being designed by one team. The site would be in the downstream section, immediately to the south of the Royal Festival Hall (which was already under construction), with its west side hard against Hungerford Bridge railway viaduct. Its purpose was easily understood though never, in the three years life of the project, exactly described. It would house an exposition of what came most often to be referred to as the British character, with overtones of national traditions and achievements, though warlike achievements were strictly excluded. They would be given a brief to work to and the building would come late in the planned sequence of construction, so they had time to think.

If the designers had been given a free choice of the themes which the South Bank Exhibition was to celebrate, this was the one that they would have chosen to house and to display. As the project would clearly need a lot of their time the first step was to ask permission of the Royal College of Art to undertake it. 'Of course you must do it', Darwin said, 'and you must do it well enough for the college to gain in reputation from it.' A number of RCA students later helped on individual details of the display. The college's involvement was increased when the scale and nature of the display proved to demand a wider range of invention than Russell and Goodden could lay claim to, and they persuaded Richard Guyatt to join them. Perhaps Darwin felt later that the promise he exacted had been honoured, for he came to believe that the commission to design the pavilion had been given to the Royal College of Art and not to the individual designers.

During the early months of the commission the designers settled in their minds the general character of the building, which they saw as a spacious, airy and serene setting for a story which would excite many changes of mood and would need a simple frame to hold it together and to complement its diversity. It seemed wise to go no further than that until the brief was known. But the brief proved singularly elusive and the first script writer acknowledged defeat and made way for a second. Meanwhile the months went by until some point in the summer of 1949 when Hugh Casson agreed with the designers that the design of the building could wait no longer. So it took the form of a simple rectangular space with the proportions of a triple 40-foot cube placed lengthwise along the side of the viaduct. It had solid walls on the north (Royal Festival Hall) and west (viaduct) sides and large areas of glass filling the whole of the south and most of the east sides. The whole was covered with a 'lamella' roof of English oak the curved surface of which swept up again at the eaves to form a wide overhang on each long side which also acted as lateral wind-bracing. J. M. Richards, writing at the opening of the exhibition, described the building as a barn; and so it was, a dutch barn made weatherproof, whose unarticulated interior would accept with good grace whatever it might be decided to put into it.

That, at least, was the intention. It was modified at a late stage when the Festival Office notified an overlooked requirement for two small service rooms which were placed in a two-storey block against the wall on the viaduct side. But these two storeys rose to only half the height of the hall so that the roof, and the great flight of doves which winged their way beneath it, could be seen from end to end from most points of the building. This excrescence, while projecting from the hitherto blank west wall, needed daylight and ventilation, and so a diaper of small eye-shaped windows was pierced into the wall. Two lighted and ventilated the service rooms while the rest let in shafts of afternoon sunlight but were too small and separated to give a view of the trains from Charing Cross. As happens so often the unwanted intrusion was welcome in the end. The projecting block gave the visitor a moment in which to adjust his mind between the contemplation of two very disparate themes: a light-hearted presentation of Eccentricity as an essential element in our character and, in the very centre of the hall, a solemn acknowledgment of the influence on the national development of Christianity, the Law and the Constitution; and a front of limestone masonry on the solemn side of the block made a place for a majestic inscription carved by Barry Hart. In order to increase the space available for display without destroying the spaciousness of the interior a light gallery was introduced with a flight of stairs at either end. The whole construction stood quite freely on the floor like an enormous piece of furniture, unconnected to the structure of the building. Its width was about one-third of that of the building and it ran for almost the whole of its length.

With the arrival on the scene of Hubert Philips the brief at last took shape. In frequent and always enjoyable meetings between the Festival Office team* and the design team the sequence of characteristics was gradually hammered out. There would be an introductory statement of the purpose of the building and its display, and that would be the more important for the difficulty which everyone found in expressing in a few plain words what the pavilion was there to show. The thing had no name until half-way through the process of devising and designing it. It was in point of fact the designers who, true to their trade, suggested that, since a descriptive name was so elusive, perhaps we should have recourse to a symbolical one – for instance, the Lion and the Unicorn. The Lion would stand for the more dependable traits in the national character, the Unicorn for the more volatile.

Thus the first division of space within the building, the concourse between the entrance doors and the gallery stair, held only two things to localize attention away from a first appraisal of the general effect of the whole interior design; and they were linked into one. High on the west wall of this space pranced gigantic figures of the Lion and Unicorn made of straw in corn dolly technique by Fred Mizen of Great Bardfield; and under them the summary legend: 'We are the Lion and the Unicorn, twin symbols of the Briton's character. As a Lion I give him solidity and strength. With the Unicorn he lets himself go.' The Lion was speaking because the Unicorn was otherwise engaged. He was up to his tricks straight away. He had a rope in one front paw which lifted the latch of a colossal rattan birdcage hanging from the roof and released the great flight of doves to soar to freedom up the length of the hall.

*Hubert Philips wrote the brief, Peter Stucley identified the concrete things which converted the brief into a visible scene, and Laurie Lee titled the whole sequence in poetry and prose.

The Lion and Unicorn pavilion, South Bank, architects and designers R. D. Russell and Robert Goodden.

These were sculptural expressions to last for only a few months, and so were executed in deliberately perishable materials. The placing of the doves in flight needed careful forethought. Each bird was suspended at three points so that it could be given an individual tilt both lengthwise and across the wings, and so three screw eyes to each bird had to be fixed in the lamella roof before its scaffolding (whose forest of stanchions filled the space where the doves' path of flight would lie) was struck. In consequence the position in space of every bird had to be fixed in advance and plotted on plan and section. But the exercise was rewarding. By adjusting the angle of flight of each bird so that there were as many different positions as birds in a group, an effect of fluttering wings was given to the flight as a whole although each bird was motionless and all the birds identical.

The gallery was given to the English language, with principal sections on the translation of the Bible into English; the works of Shakespeare; and idiomatic usage of the present day, the latter with examples in recorded speech devised by Stephen Potter. The section on the Bible was introduced by a copy of the Oxford Lectern Bible laid open on a fifteenth-century brass eagle lectern lent from Cavendish Church, Suffolk.

Laurie Lee, chief caption writer, with egg roundabout and smoke-grinding machine in the Eccentrics' Corner.

Robin and Christopher Ironside designed and made to scale five sets for Shakespeare plays which were shown in miniature theatres grouped in front of a screen in the form of an open book. Opposite this was a showcase filled with volumes of translations of the poet's works in forty foreign languages, together with a number of English editions including Mr Foyle's first and second folios. These, like the four masterpieces of painting which concluded the whole display and many other borrowed treasures, were exposed (within touching distance) for half a year to all the hazards of public viewing with only a sheet of quarter-inch glass for protection – a risk which nowadays would be unthinkable – and yet came to no harm.

When these books were being set out in their case on the night before the opening of the exhibition, one volume brought the team to a standstill because there was no scholar of the Chinese language at hand to say which way up it should be placed in the case or whether the title page would be the first page or the last. A number of visitors were touring the South Bank that evening under some kind of dress rehearsal viewing plan, among whom providentially was a young Englishman who read and spoke Chinese. The book was thrust into his hand in the certainty that he would replace it in the case in legible position. He read a page or two from the Chinese and declaimed the lines in English, to the admiration of all present, handed the book back closed – and vanished.

At the far end of the gallery the visitor was faced by a very large mural painting by Edward Bawden occupying the full height and width of the end wall, which here, to give rigidity to a very light structure, was crinkled into angled vertical facets, like the leaves of a partly opened fan but each about six feet in width. His theme was Country Life in Britain. The space at floor level in front of this wall was given, as has been said, to the British Eccentrics, presided over by a life-size figure in white plaster of Lewis Carroll's White Knight whose spirits were lifted by the only other use of recorded sound in the building – his own voice uttering a continuous stream of quiet self-congratulation and encouragement.

The way now led back towards the entrance, past the projecting block with its masonry wall and carved inscription and into the central space. On the right-hand side stood the solemn monument to Christianity, a life-size cast of a Celtic cross; the Law, a composition of a High Court judge's robe and wig of heroic size surrounded by the great tomes of enacted law and of legal precedent; and the Constitution, symbolized by the Union flag and its contributory crosses of St George, St Andrew and St Patrick. Behind these three tall groups and against the lower part of the west wall with its eye-shaped lunettes, a long mural painting by Kenneth Rowntree extended the length of the

Display shelves in the Lion and Unicorn pavilion, redesigned after a disaster (see opposite page).

central space, its subject a running sequence of scenes from British history. On the left-hand side, with the glazed east wall beyond, was placed a collection of examples of British craftsmanship of all kinds and materials, and mainly of the last century and a half, including work of that day.

Just as the designers had made of the gallery a thing that had settled lightly upon the scene, so now their aim was that the artefacts should claim all the visitor's attention and that the means of supporting them at a convenient height to see should make as little interruption as possible to the open and airy character of their setting. They were placed therefore on a long table-top of half-inch thick plate glass in very large sheets, the manufactured size uncut, supported by the lightest possible construction of brass rods drilled into brass balls at their points of meeting to form a triangulated structure which was held taut by stranded wires in tension. The strength of this undercarriage depended on a perfectly tight fit of the rods into the balls and on the tension of the wire. When it was delivered an ominous amount of play was found in the joints.

Any exhibition interesting enough to be worth a visit opens to the public only because of the wholly unreasonable optimism of those who have prepared it. The date of opening was too near for it to be possible to consider having the joints re-made, so the tension in the wires, which was adjustable, was increased until the framework was nearly rigid, and when the heavy glass tops were lowered on to it the whole thing appeared stable. When everyone in the building (which included the designers) was absorbed in the task of setting out the precious pieces of craftsmanship, a noise like a pistol shot rang out; a few moments later another, and then another. Under their own weight the slabs of glass were flexing beyond their elastic limit and every bang was a clean break right across. What could be saved was saved, but it only amounted to one-third of the display surface needed. When immediate enquiries were made it appeared that the Lion and the Unicorn had already been supplied with the country's entire stock of large pieces of plate glass of the thickness required. Eventually more was run to earth and was treated this time, as were the salvaged pieces, with sanity and caution. The glass was cut to much shorter lengths and hardwood bearers were introduced at intermediate points in the undercarriage. It must be admitted that the risk taken was unnecessary. When Natasha Kroll's arrangement of the Craftsmanship section was complete, the loss of effect from the slightly heavier character of the undercarriage was negligible.

Beyond this section and almost at the close of the whole sequence was a life-size tableau of Alice going through the Looking Glass. The lovely child from

The White Knight in the Lion and Unicorn pavilion: a model based on Sir John Tenniel's illustrations to Alice through the Looking-Glass, *symbolizing 'the fantastic genius in the English character'.*

Tenniel's drawing was modelled twice, one version being the exact mirror image of the other, and the two were placed one before and one behind an empty frame. To dispense with such an essential prop as the Looking Glass itself was not just a wilful piece of exhibitionism. The solid mirror image instead of the optical one enabled the story to be read from a much wider range of viewpoints than a mirror could provide, and in any case Alice herself had to be got to the other side. Alas, memory no longer finds an answer to the question: why was Alice there at all? But the verisimilitude of the device was proved in the early morning of the day following the opening when one of the cleaners went to give the non-existent glass a polish and, meeting no resistance, hurt herself in almost falling through the frame.

And so the visitor came to the pavilion's finale, a screen for the Landscape of the country on which were hung paintings by Gainsborough, Constable, Turner and Paul Nash; then out on to the terrace which was the pavilion's own and on which was placed, right on the ground like the bells of Constable's East Bergholt, the great bell of the Lion and the Unicorn, cast specially for the South Bank at the Whitechapel foundry and rung by remote control at noon, to the great surprise of any who happened to be too near. It is now the tenor bell of Kelvedon Church in Essex.

Left, *plan of the Lion and Unicorn pavilion from the guide to the South Bank*. Below, *straw Lion and Unicorn made by Fred Mizen, craftsman of Great Bardfield. Wallpaper designed by Richard Guyatt*. Opposite, *gallery looking towards the river with a mural by Edward Bawden on the end wall.*

In the beginning was the word,
and the word was with God,
and the word was God

A Jazz Mural

VICTOR PASMORE

THE COMMISSION to design the ceramic mural for the south wall of the Regatta Restaurant, which flanked the staircase entrance to the Festival from Hungerford Bridge, was a tremendous challenge at that time since it coincided with the creative explosion in the visual arts which spread throughout the world following the renewal of free expression after the war. It was essential, therefore, to carry out this commission in a form which would symbolize the full implications of this spirit. Fortunately the huge scale of the mural, together with its prominent position at the entrance to the Festival, provided the necessary scope to do just this.

The Regatta Restaurant was an elegant building designed in the best tradition of modern architecture by Design Research Unit and so provided an excellent ally to the purely abstract style in painting which I myself had come to adopt in response to the new situation. Moreover the commission provided a unique opportunity to demonstrate the validity of this style when brought to bear emotionally on the cubic and utilitarian functionalism of modern architecture.

Of the various ways of extending architecture by the addition of painting and sculpture two stand out: one is to reinforce it harmonically by repeating its forms; the other is to transform it optically by means of contrast. I decided on the latter course as the best way of demonstrating the new spirit in emotional terms. As it happened I had been working privately on a series of spiral motifs from a purely empirical point of view. I thought that the powerful flowing movement of these motifs would provide a complementary image sufficiently dynamic to change the architecture. So, with the idea of 'exploding' the Regatta Restaurant, I painted a full-size maquette on the floor of the gymnasium at the Central School of Art.

The architects gave me full support in this venture even to the extent of granting my request not to have the tiles 'pointed', a decision which greatly distressed the tile craftsmen. But I had to explain that we were not tiling a swimming pool, but constructing a jazz painting, so the more uneven the tile grid the more movement we would get in the painting. Nevertheless the process of having the design copied on to tiles for firing in ceramic also proved inhibiting as it had to be done only in small sections in a tiny workroom. As a result neither I nor my assistants could ever see what we were doing. When finally they did arrange the complete work on the ground I wanted to rearrange the painted tiles in new and independent positions; but this proved to be too costly an operation.

Ceramic mural by Victor Pasmore, Regatta Restaurant, South Bank.

Apart from the excitement of painting this mural the experience gave me an intimate insight into both the technical and aesthetic aspirations of modern architecture. Moreover my association with Design Research Unit in the construction of this restaurant at the Festival of Britain marked the beginning of a long, fruitful and practical association with architects which is still in operation today.

The Riverside Restaurant

JANE DREW

Architect, Riverside Restaurant, South Bank

THE RIVERSIDE RESTAURANT, one of the buildings in our area, was originally destined to face the old Shell Building on the north side of the Thames. It was a horrible view; but on visiting the site I perceived that one could steal a little more site (what was known as the Willment site) and go right on under Waterloo Bridge and look at St Paul's, which seemed to be the one decent view. I immediately went to Sir Gerald Barry and asked if we could have a little more land. He replied that if I could square things with the Port of London Authority he had no objection. This proved to be quite a job because they wanted the building designed so that it would collapse at once if hit by a ship. The greatest problem, however, was how to erect it, as it was going to be the last part of the site to be built on.

We had been having quite a lot to do with aircraft factories at that time because of the involvements we had had with prefabrication in kitchen design. It seemed to us that by constructing the roof of a double skin of aluminium with a cork sandwich we could make one that could quickly be assembled on site by aircraft rivet technique. This we did. The restaurant was meant to be up for six months but was still in sound condition and watertight some ten years after.

Building it was not uneventful. At that time the Kingsway Tunnel was used by trams which came out of the tunnel into the open along the north side of the Thames from Waterloo to Westminster and operated all night. One night I was supervising the lighting of the underside of Waterloo Bridge when I turned round to find myself confronted by two large British policemen. Apparently our lighting had blinded the tram drivers in the tunnel and a queue of trams had now formed on the other side of the bridge.

One of the things that we, in common with many an architect, were anxious to do was to use our sculptor and painter friends. In the Riverside Restaurant we used Barbara Hepworth, Ben Nicholson and Eduardo Paolozzi. I used to stay with Ben Nicholson down at St Ives during the period and visit Barbara (they had just separated and relations were strained). Ben Nicholson was to do a large mural at the entrance to the restaurant and some distance in front was to be a slowly moving mobile sculpture by Barbara. As the design evolved we were terribly short of cash – I remember we had exactly £400 for the mural. Then came the idea of making the mural curved. I went down to St Ives to see if Ben would like the idea. He did very much, but he also did all the arithmetic and proved it was now slightly longer and so he should be paid more!

Ben believed that the workmen would not realize how valuable the mural was, so when the time came for it to be erected he wrote to me to be sure that all the workmen wore white gloves and knew its cost. I duly went to Selfridges, bought lots of white cotton gloves and bearded the workmen with these. Getting them to put on the gloves was quite an affair. I don't think Ben really believed I would do it and he turned up on the site himself in his characteristic beret. He then complained that I had not got any curved glass in front of the mural and that the public would damage it. Curved glass was quite outside the budget. The

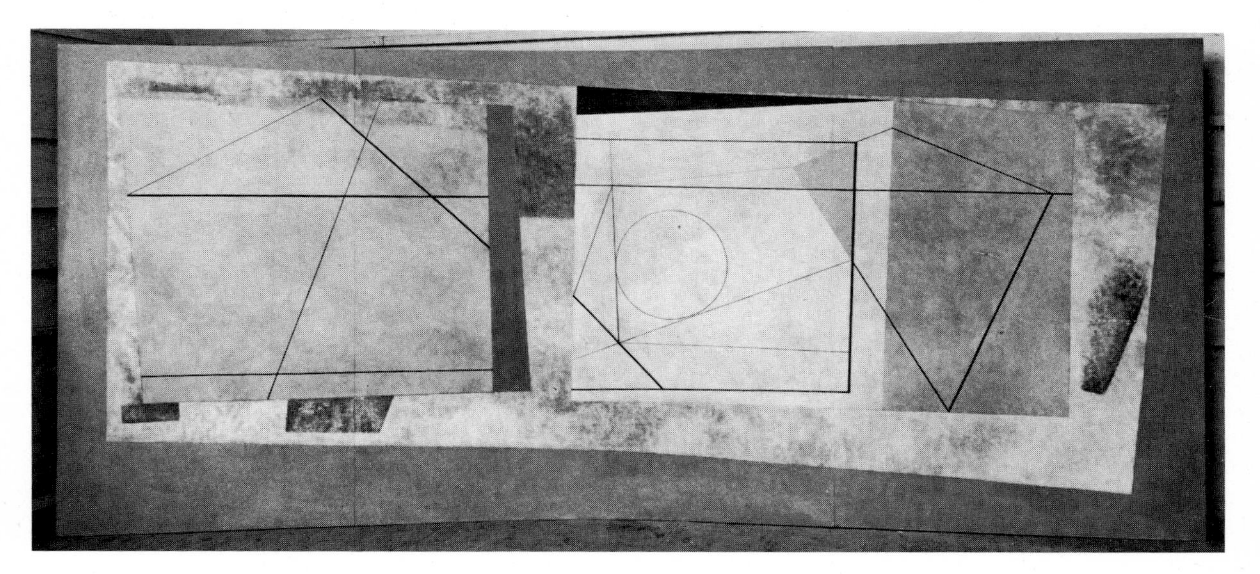

Mural by Ben Nicholson, at the entrance to the Riverside Restaurant, South Bank.

only thing I could think of was to make a sunk ha-ha in front of the mural and fill it with pebbles. I saw Ben off for his train to St Ives; later that day he rang up saying that the pebbles would simply give the public ammunition to throw at the mural. I pointed out that they were all cemented down and for the time being he was assuaged. The mural did not get damaged at all. Later Sir Frederick Gibberd bought it for the VIP lounge at Heathrow Airport where it is now.

Above left, *under the first arch of the Riverside Restaurant: left to right, Mr Turvey, foreman of Kirk & Kirk, contractors; Jane Drew; Maxwell Fry; and Mr Thompson of Kirk & Kirk.* Centre left, *model of the Riverside Restaurant under Waterloo Bridge.* Below left, *interior of the Riverside Restaurant.* Above, *Waterloo Bridge entrance from under the footbridge to the Royal Festival Hall. The engineers were Ove Arup and Partners.*

Opposite above, *drawing of the Waterloo Station entrance and the Rocket Restaurant, architect Gordon Tait.* Opposite below, *the '51 Bar. The competition was won by Leonard Manasseh.*

51
BAR

The Agricultural and Country Pavilion

F. H. K. HENRION

Designer, Country pavilion, South Bank

WHEN I WAS ASKED to design two pavilions, one on agriculture and the other showing British flora and fauna, under the title Country pavilion, I had no idea of the problems which had to be faced and overcome. Having to deal with people, animals and plants and their inter-relationship proved a most challenging job. Civil Service routine, which had to be followed at all times, demanded a requisition in quintuplicate for every exhibit, along with precise specifications, descriptions and serving requirements. This applied to every plant and every animal as well as to every display. The service requirement of some animals

The foot of the giant plaster oak tree in 'The Natural Scene', designer F. H. K. Henrion, landscaping Peter Youngman.

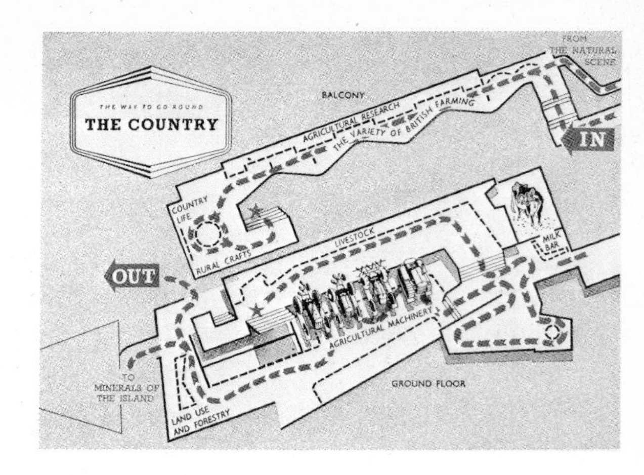

Plans from the guide to the South Bank.

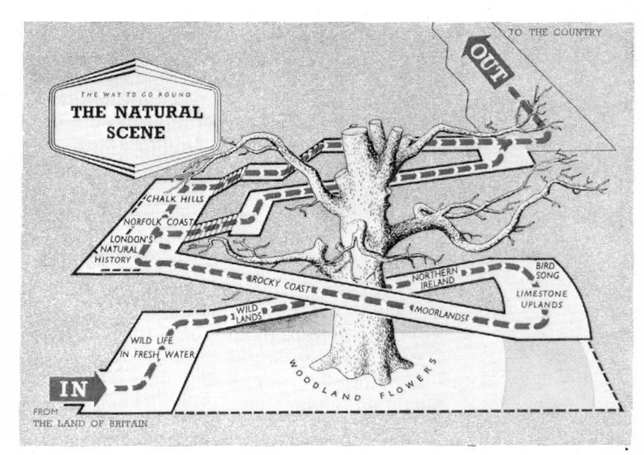

seemed particularly complex: the valuable horses which arrived without horseshoes and for which daily transport had to be provided to take them to Hyde Park for exercise; the daily delivery of plankton from the Lake District as a diet essential to all the live fish exhibits; or the breeding of 5,000 butterflies, a year in advance, so that a new batch could be supplied once a week for the 'Live Butterfly' window: this, in turn, made it necessary to organize Boy Scouts all over the country to dig up the appropriate wild flowers which alone would feed the particular butterfly species, delivered in that week. To make a reasonable showing at the Festival opening in May, it meant that special grasses had to be grown in Aberystwyth the previous summer and then transported to a special greenhouse built at the Cambridge Natural History faculty. Various universities and plant research stations grew fruit trees, grain, berries and hops as exhibits in a specially designed air-conditioned greenhouse. As these were conditions never experienced before, no one could anticipate the rate of growth of any one plant. I had to design special plant furniture with aluminium containers, each adjustable in height, in case its vegetable content grew faster or slower than the experts had guessed.

Scenes from the cycle of the country year in the Country pavilion; in the left background, a mural designed by Constance Howard *(see p. 45).*

Over five months, five thousand prize animals – bulls, cows, horses, sheep, goats, chickens and ducks – had to be exhibited as they were so valuable that none of them could be shown for longer than a few weeks. Planning their arrival and departure, as well as their exercise before the exhibition opened, was part of the designer's job; likewise, to settle the dispute between the Union of Road Sweepers and the cowmen as to whose job it was to remove the cow pads every day before the opening of the exhibition.

As some of the wild life exhibits were shown in acryllic plastic – at the time a very new process – we needed five adders in mid-winter. The only way to obtain them was for the British Embassy in Paris to prevail upon the mayor of Nice to organize an adder hunt. In due course, an ominous box marked 'Poisonous snakes' arrived at London Airport. From there I had to take them to the laboratory where they had to be killed, prior to setting them in plastic. Thus Gallic adders posed as their British cousins. But they took their revenge. In the heat of mid-July, their bodies swelled in such a way that they broke through the plastic and the whole display, of which they formed a part, was dripping with blood. People fainted left and right, the whole area had to be roped off and, as always when something went wrong, the designer was called in. I put the whole gory mess in the back of my car and tried to get rid of it through the local refuse collection. This, however, meant hacking both perspex and adders into small pieces to make them fit into a dustbin. Rarely can a designer have been required to do such a Herculean labour. No sooner had I recovered from the shock when I was informed that one of the large fish tanks, with all the fish and plankton, had burst, causing a short-circuit as the water went into the electrical controls. However, the fish were recovered and survived until the end of the Festival, after a new tank, this time reinforced, had been installed.

It was a challenging but very worthwhile job and I should not have liked to miss the frustrations and excitement for anything.

The Sea and Ships Pavilion

Right, *plan from the guide to the South Bank*. Below, *exhibit in the Sea and Ships pavilion*. Opposite above, *part of the shipbuilding display, with a fountain by Richard Huws to the right*. Opposite below, *to the left, giant bas-relief*, The Islanders, *sculptor Siegfried Charoux; to the right, ship relief by Ernst Pollak.*

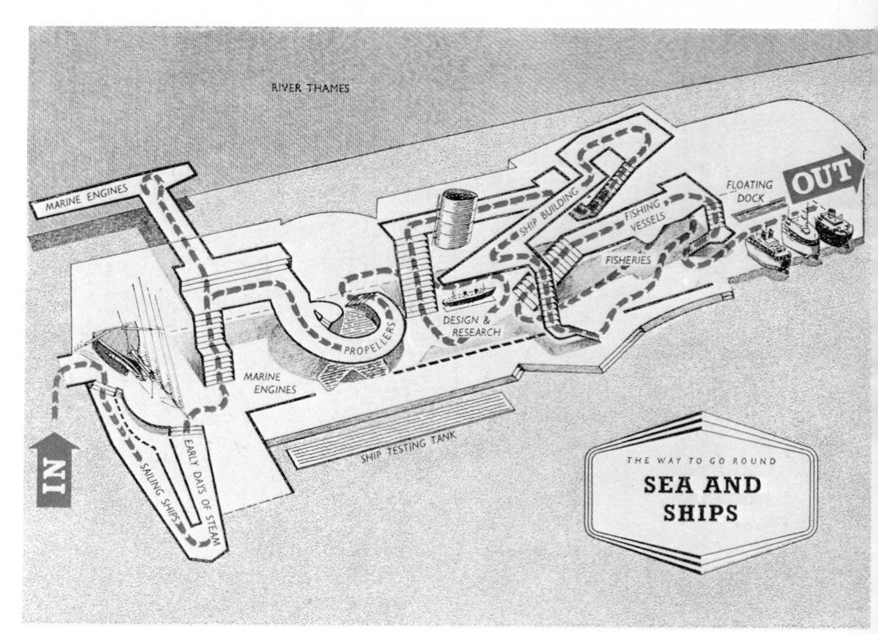

SHIPBUILDING
SHIPBUILDING

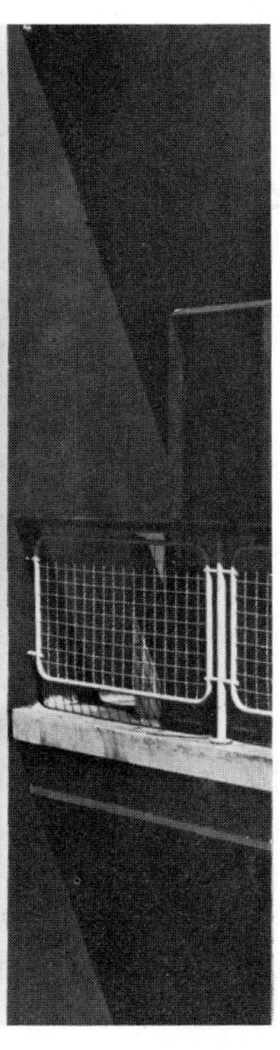

Architects and the Festival of Britain

JOHN RATCLIFF

Deputy Director, Architecture; Deputy Controller, Construction, South Bank

WHATEVER THE APTNESS of the title *A Tonic to the Nation*, it was certainly a tonic for architects when they were appointed by the Festival of Britain Office to take part in the South Bank Exhibition. In 1948, architecture too was still in the throes of post-war austerity: rationing of timber and steel, scarcity of labour and other similar problems. For those who had qualified before the war, and who had been concerned with hutted camps, airfield construction or similar wartime building operations, the opportunity to indulge at last their pent-up design capacity was heaven-sent. And it is remarkable, in my view, that in spite of such a lack of opportunity to flex their design muscles, such a concensus of design approach emerged that it later became known as 'Festival of Britain Style'.

For the Festival's South Bank Exhibition area, instead of a single master-minded architecture, it was the policy to appoint separate architects for each pavilion. Recommendations for such appointments were made by the Architecture Council, Festival of Britain, and the emphasis was on those younger men who had yet to make their reputations. However, room was left for two non-nominated appointments through the competitions for the Skylon and '51 Bar, won respectively by Powell and Moya, and Leonard Manasseh. Each architect was given his brief and a budget and left to produce his design.

For all the sympathetic outlook of the Festival of Britain Office, encouraged, of course, by the Director General, Gerald Barry, it had, nevertheless, to conform to the Civil Service pattern of appointments, contract action and, of course, financial control. I often found myself, therefore, as a catalyst between the unworldly section architect on the one hand and the sophisticated 'dyed in the wool' civil servants on the other. With exhibition work, of course, financial control was all the more tricky, especially as there were two major financial reviews, and we were constantly prodding the Director of Finance to see what hidden contingencies he had up his sleeve, hopefully to improve standards or to launch a new project.

I think one success story of the South Bank Exhibition could be said to have been the integration of the many individual architects into one team. Architects are not notorious for design collaboration, especially when it comes to aesthetics. There were, therefore, three co-ordination architects – Hugh Casson, Misha Black and Ralph Tubbs, in charge of the downstream, upstream and Dome of Discovery sections respectively. It was their task to weld the individuality of each section architect into one coherent visual whole: not forgetting the spaces between the buildings, which is where the landscape architects – Frank Clark, Peter Shepheard, Peter Youngman and Maria Shephard – came in. I coined, for administrative convenience, the terms 'hard' and 'soft' landscape, which seem to have become a vernacular expression. All designs, including buildings, display, lighting, signs, were considered by the Design Group and endorsed by the Presentation Panel. In the wings were the Architecture Council, Science Council, Council of Industrial Design and Arts Council, to see that there were no gaps in theme or presentation, and a proper balance between the parts.

At the start, the idea was to use 'temporary' materials for the pavilions, as would seemingly befit the design philosophy of a temporary exhibition. Experimental samples of different coloured canvas were set up to weather at the Surrey Docks – the dirtiest atmosphere in London at the time – and the idea of an enormous 'Big Top' tent preceded the Dome of Discovery. In the event, so that the displays could be installed protected from the weather, in order to survive the English winter of 1950/51, it transpired that nothing less than 'permanent' construction would do. Canvas was, in fact, only used to any degree in the introduction to the Homes and Gardens pavilion and the Seaside.

Although the whole of the South Bank Exhibition was exempt, by statute, from the London Building Acts and Bylaws, the section architects, far from having a freedom spree, found themselves subjected to a degree of control, in respect of structures and safety, far in excess of normal requirements. For the Festival Office took the question of safety very seriously. It must be remembered that experience of design for crowd conditions on that scale was very limited in the immediate post-war years (witness the failure of football stand barriers subsequently) and many standards had to be worked out *de novo*. For the architects, one of the most irksome details was the requirement to design all handrails to resist a minimum horizontal force of 50 lb per foot run, which made a nonsense of many elegant design submissions.

It may have seemed disappointing that, with such an open brief, so little advantage was taken to use advanced structures. Exceptions were the Dome of Discovery and the use of stressed skin steelwork roofs (Transport pavilion) but, in general, the South Bank Exhibition will hardly be remembered for structural innovation. Not only were the pressures of the time factor, availability of materials and skilled labour responsible, but some architects (Homes and Gardens pavilion) deliberately opted for a simple and economic structure in order to be able to spend more of their budget on other features. Timber was still scarce and had to be avoided in the buildings, although a *sine qua non* in display work because of its adaptability, but there were, even so, some interesting examples of the use of timber in laminated arches (Station Gate) and a lamella roof (Lion and Unicorn). Amongst other novelties was the manufacture, transportation and erection, by a newly developed vacuum 'sucker', of the 'largest sheet of glass in the world', to serve as a viewing window in the Power and Production pavilion. In general, however, the extensive use of glass only became an example of a lesson in exhibition design to be learnt the hard way. For one of the basic tenets of modern architecture at that time was the opening-up of buildings by large amounts of glazing. In many cases, however, this was exactly contrary to the requirements of the interior display designer who needed, quite simply, a dark box into which he could introduce controlled artificial lighting to illustrate his theme. It was, in fact, the opposite of the Crystal Palace approach. There were exceptions, of course: for instance, the great sliding screens to the Transport pavilion which could be opened in fine weather to reveal the aircraft suspended from the roof; or the Sea and Ships pavilion, designed as a shipyard gantry with outdoor displays.

Introductory building, designer Denis Clark-Hall, to the Homes and Gardens pavilion.

Behind the teeming activity of section architects, display designers, co-ordinated by their co-ordinators, must be mentioned more mundane matters. First, there were the permanent public works improvements that were specifically authorized as part of the Festival of Britain and which were intended to facilitate the entry approaches to the exhibition site: traffic roundabouts on the approach roads, thirty-five special car parks, the Bailey Bridge linking the north and south river banks, the new escalators from Waterloo Station Underground, and the construction of a new river wall downstream from the Hungerford railway bridge. Then there was the winkling-out of reluctant tenants, notably in the railway bridge arches, which was the responsibility of the LCC valuer. One of these, Carlsberg Breweries, who occupied arches at the centre of the exhibition site up to January 1951, caused many palpitations as the search for acceptable alternative premises took such a long time. Imagine the possible to-ing and fro-ing of brewers drays in an otherwise pedestrian precinct! The LCC chief engineer was also responsible for what would nowadays be called the infra-structure of the site – drains, water supply, electrics, low voltage services – all of which had to be planned and often executed long before the detailed pavilion designs were available.

There were over twenty architects, three main contractors and seventeen display contractors, with target completion periods of sixteen months for the buildings and six months for display. What information they lacked on drawings had to be made up at site meetings, and I often found myself in the position of a supposedly benevolent dictator trying to placate harassed but deferential contractors and irate architects. The whole was, as might be expected, leavened by trade demarcation disputes and strikes. On one occasion, the electricians, making the best use of the element of surprise, plunged the whole site into darkness; but the next time they were forestalled by the loyals who had taken good care to seize the keys of the switchrooms first. Progress was bedevilled by design revisions, due to the laudable but sometimes exasperating desire to improve, and the wettest February in 1951 for eighty-one years. Morale was boosted by visits from VIPs, not the least their Majesties the King and Queen. As the magic day of 4 May 1951 drew near, and completion on time seemed more and more impossible, a big gamble was taken. In spite of the amount of overtime worked by all concerned, it was decided to stop work on the last Sunday before opening day, and allow all workmen to bring their wives, families and sweethearts to satisfy their curiosity. The effect was magical, for there is nothing like the prodding of a nagging wife and family, and the whole job was completed on time.

There was another project with which I was much concerned, outside the South Bank; this was the Live Architecture Exhibition at Lansbury, in London's East End (see pp. 138–43). Why 'Live Architecture'? It was to be a demonstration in the flesh of those

Left, *exterior view of the Telecinema, architect Wells Coates.* Below left, *suspended offices, Chicheley Street entrance, architects Architects' Co-operative Partnership.* Below right, *the '51 Bar, architect Leonard Manasseh. The tall water tower, capable of holding 5,000 gallons, supplied its contents to the adjacent Power and Production pavilion.*

intangibles – town planning, building science and architecture – and it took the form of a collaboration with the LCC, who were redeveloping their first 'neighbourhood' at Poplar, which had high priority under the Abercrombie-Forshaw County of London Plan. In addition to the permanent housing, shops, schools and churches, each designed by different architects appointed by the LCC, there was a small temporary exhibition site.

The subjects of town planning and building research are not exactly thrilling to a lay public, even when leavened by a 'Rosie Lee' cafeteria and signposted on the East India Dock Road by a tower crane suitably decorated. I was responsible for the theme in each subject and, in addition, with the goodwill of the Design Group, for the design of the Building Research pavilion. The problem was how to make these indigestible subjects palatable. In the event, the kernel of the Town Planning pavilion – constructed with canvas as a large tent – was the end piece entitled 'Heart of the Town', which was a model, optimistic in retrospect, of what a town centre should be. Building Research was even more intractable, the answer being introduced by a scaled-down version of an inter-war jerry-built 'semi-det' – dubbed Gremlin Grange – illustrating all the faults which building research could cure. The Building Research pavilion was constructed as a series of boxes each expressing and displaying its subject matter: stability, rain penetration (with real water flowing over patent glazing!), heating, lighting, noise and maintenance.

Below, *garden by Maria Shephard next to the* Regatta Restaurant*; in the background, a sculpture by Lynn Chadwick.*

Right, *the southern front of the Sea and Ships pavilion with the Skylon and the Dome of Discovery.* Below, *Barbara Hepworth sculpture, entrance to the Riverside Restaurant.* Below right, *Henry Moore sculpture in front of the Country pavilion, architect Brian O'Rourke, designer F. H. K. Henrion.*

The Festival Lettering

Preface to the booklet *A Specimen of Display Letters Designed for the Festival of Britain* 1951

CHARLES HASLER

Designer; chairman, Typographic Panel

ABCDE
MNOPQ
THE ITALIC

Above, *part of an alphabet from the Specimen booklet.* Below, *examples of the special Festival types in use on the South Bank. The view of the Sea and Ships pavilion includes the figure of Neptune by Keith Godwin.*

THE TYPOGRAPHY PANEL has given much consideration to the subject of suitable letter-forms for external use in the various Festival projects, with particular reference to the titling of buildings.

In such a large-scale exhibition as that on the South Bank, it is obviously necessary to avoid a monotonous use of lettering. At the same time, a general affinity of character must be preserved. This is best achieved by the use of a 'family' of alphabets, i.e. one with variations of weight and width, which is also amenable to varying treatments by architects and designers.

The problem here was to produce a display letter which is British in feeling, of good 'typographic colour' and one capable of being used architecturally – possibly in large sizes, flat or three-dimensionally – without loss of character.

In considering this problem, it was thought that an Egyptian letter would best fulfil all these requirements, though it was also felt that the modern Egyptians lacked sufficient 'colour' and character; even the necessary architectural appropriateness.

Nothing could be more British in feeling than the display types created by the early nineteenth-century typefounders, and our researches have led us to re-examine the Egyptian types cut by Figgins, Thorne and Austin between 1815 and 1825. It is very largely on these that the basic Roman and Italic in the present series are modelled.

The range illustrated in this specimen consists of a basic Roman and Italic with light, extended and condensed versions, each complete with numerals and punctuation marks. Lower case letters are at present provided with the basic Roman only, but these (with the exception of the extended) could also be provided for the other alphabets if required.

We do not wish architects and designers to feel that they are confined to sign-written or cut-out versions of these letters; on the contrary we would like to see individual ingenuity exercised within these forms, the three-dimensional in particular. The only limiting factor will be the adherence to the basic shape and proportions of the letters chosen. But we do feel that this variety of related alphabets will provide plenty of scope for inventiveness.

Right, *Henry Moore sculpture and the windmill on the Country pavilion in silhouette*. Below, *the Royal Festival Hall, architects* Robert Matthew *(then Chief Architect LCC) with* J. L. Martin, *Edwin Williams and Peter Moro*.

Night on the South Bank: left, *coloured canvas screen facing the Fairway, designed by Architects' Co-operative Partnership;* below, *view from Waterloo Bridge: in the background, the Sports pavilion, architects Gordon and Ursula Bowyer; centre, the Centenary pavilion; right foreground, base of the Shot Tower;* opposite, *Skylon showing interior lighting; landscaping includes plant pots specially designed by Maria Shephard.*

PLEASURE GARDENS BATTERSEA PARK

Battersea Pleasures

INTERVIEW WITH

JAMES GARDNER

Co-ordinating designer, Battersea Pleasure Gardens; member of the Design Panel

BEVIS HILLIER How did you come to be involved in the Festival? Was it a direct invitation from Hugh Casson? Did you know Gerald Barry?

JAMES GARDNER No, in fact Barry had appointed the rest of the team and they were all cracking before I came in. Gordon Russell then head of the CoID said he wanted me in because I was the only designer he knew who could display goods – or something as awful as that! So I came in some months after the others.

BH And you had in fact been the prime spirit in the 'Britain can make it' Exhibition.

JG That's it. Well, I guess that was a big job, and it came off.

BH What was your background before that, were you connected with the Ministry of Information during the war?

JG No, I was in the Army – camouflage and deception. The *deception* side was really something. Before the war I was drawing for advertising, then Jack Beddington asked me to do an exhibition for Shell. Jack Beddington and Pick of the Underground were the two educated patrons in those days. I wish we had people like that now – he got me to do an exhibition, with Barnett Freedman advising on colour, called 'Aircraft, how they fly'. And that was very successful. After the war, Beddington got me straight out of uniform for 'Britain can make it'. That, of course, put me in the exhibition racket. Quite frankly, one doesn't decide on a line; a job comes up and if you make a success of it you find you're doing that thing forever or until the phone rings and something unexpected knocks you into another groove.

BH Did you just plunge into the Festival and begin designing straight away or did you have lots of discussions?

JG We five, the co-ordinating team, were all running our own businesses, except Casson who was fully involved, so we would meet at Savoy Court in the Strand at seven o'clock in the evening and go on to goodness knows what hour. We would plan themes and layouts, and select designers for the different sections. Of course we had to answer to expert advisers, the theme conveners. It was a National Show, so there had to be some sort of authority. But the South Bank side grew rather a big pyramid of theorists and administrators and each designer became rather separately orientated to the conveners for his own section. For instance, while I was co-ordinating the downstream section with Casson, I was also designing the 'Origins of the British People' in detail. Meanwhile what went on between Henrion, who was designing the agricultural section, and his theme convener was his affair. There were big policy meetings. I remember at one of them Barry decided that people must all have a day away from interruptions to 'think', and hired a quiet hotel out on the Hog's Back. There was only one old lady resident and the hotel sent an attendant to follow her when she went for a walk – to be sure she didn't run away.

The whole show was to commemorate the 1851 exhibition, yet with all this think-tank business it was only towards the end I realized we hadn't any exhibits on the old Crystal Palace. So I prepared a little drawing of a mini glasshouse, velvet curtains and palms, Victorian castings for the detail, and tabled it next meeting. Barry loved it so we went ahead. No one cared that it wasn't in the official budget. As it turned out this bit of nostalgia was the last bit of the South Bank show to remain standing; you may remember seeing it perched on a raised platform to one side of the Festival Hall.

BH But weren't you particularly involved in the Festival Gardens?

JG Oh completely, that's when my hair turned white. Barry, the inspiration behind it all, was finding the South Bank rather too clinical for his tastes. Architects and the scientists seemed to be running away with it. He wanted a place where people could relax and have fun – elegant fun. Remembering the old pleasure gardens at Vauxhall he decided we'd have a Festival Gardens. Battersea Park, then given over to allotments and a cricket pitch, was to be the site.

Opposite, *fireworks in the Main Vista, designers John Piper and Osbert Lancaster.*

The Showboat, *designer James Gardner.*

BH In Battersea, were you given more or less *carte blanche*? You were the person that decided everything?

JG That wasn't the intention, it's how it turned out. Casson and I were put on to it as we were the lightweight pair, a bit more imaginative, maybe. Then Casson got so involved in South Bank affairs he handed over to me, then I got so involved I arranged for a chap named Jefferies to represent me on South Bank, and moved up river. Barry, who appreciated that bureaucracy and fun mix like oil and water, decided to streamline; just four of us would handle the whole project: the man who had run the Shakespeare Theatre, Leonard Crainford, was the administrator; Cecil Cooke of the Central Office was to see we didn't get out of line; and the man from the Treasury, George Campbell, was to watch how the money was spent – very much a Scot with fierce eyebrows and aggressive nose – we called him old moneybags, not entirely a friendly epithet.

We would sit round the table feeling like conspirators. Everyone was against the idea, one would think 'pleasure' was a rude word. The *Standard* would carry a leader – 'Spend the money on St Thomas's Hospital' – it had recently been bombed – and so on. I suspect politics and that Herbert Morrison, who was backing the idea, was in direct line of fire for these attacks. As for the Chelsea and Lambeth Councils, I remember the Mayor of Lambeth crying at a meeting at County Hall, 'Oh my poor trees,' he sobbed. All this opposition, plus the destruction of a beautifully rolled cricket pitch, was too much. The idea was shelved.

BH That's news to us. So how and when did the idea start up again?

JG One evening, about ten months later, old moneybags stopped me on the stairway at Savoy Court. He jabbed a finger and said, 'Remember Festival Gardens, G? Suppose I said we had' – then he mentioned a figure about half of what I had estimated – 'could we do it?' I hesitated. 'Oh, all right but I must have the answer by ten tomorrow morning.' He grinned, knowing the answer would be yes. Of course, I said yes.

BH Do you mean to say you risked a commitment with only half of the budget?

JG Well, I reckoned we would get the major features sponsored – anyway, I believed in it. Rather a do or die situation.

BH So it was *on* at last. How did you start?

JG First, I spent a miserable morning wandering round the site in the rain, wondering that very thing. How to start. Then I asked how many people the area would have to hold at one time at a peak Bank Holiday? Then I reckoned each person would need two square yards to move in, if they were walking, then I multiplied up and designated that area as hard paving – at least that would keep people off the flowerbeds. Next came circulation. If people followed their noses they would all end up at the boundary, so I made a continuous route round the edge of the site, with a number of way-throughs that led people from the edge back to the inside. This kept the public circulating fairly evenly over the whole area. It worked. Next I had to think up things that would keep the public happy as they circulated – something new.

I invited a number of bright guys for dinner at the Café Royal and we talked crazy ideas until the early hours – what the Americans call a brainstorming session, I guess. The only notion that actually came out of it was the treewalk. You remember it? One climbed a spiral staircase and walked among the foliage past a giant cat on a swing, a tree-town on a branch with a little underground train hanging underneath, a Chinese dragon and so on. I hadn't realized that trees don't stand still but are on the move all the time, so building the catwalks wasn't that simple. When it came to planting, I had to bring in an expert and was very lucky to get hold of Russell Page. He was a great individualist, cool and autocratic but deeply versed in the tradition of planting great gardens – he taught me a lot.

The grounds were in a terrible state after the flooding and we had to have a spectacular show of flowers the next spring. Undefeatable, Page put down a layer of cinders, over this eighteen inches of mushroom-bed compost, and in went the bulbs. Sometimes the beds were planted around the buildings before they were erected so we had to protect them with picket fences. There were hundreds of marvellous shrubs, particularly rhododendrons from the Rothschild estate, and new trees – interesting trees.

We found it necessary to cut down a number of the old trees, really large ones, and to prevent a public outcry we would do this late at night, having all the machinery there to cut the trees into logs and remove them by morning. I would disguise the stump by placing pots of geraniums on the top and putting a hexagonal seat round it. No one noticed, but early one morning the minister responsible for Parks happened to be walking a dog in Battersea Park and heard the crash as another great tree went down. That, of course, gave another headline for the *Standard*. In fact the trees we removed were all on their last legs but people get emotional over trees, quite naturally so, and this argument would not have helped us at all. One of Russell Page's notions was for the row of little striped kiosks with bamboo posts which you will have probably seen along the riverfront. It's amazing that these were only built of hardboard and erected in the damp – it rained, of course – and yet they have stood for twenty-five years!

The Grand Vista was the top event – a firework platform at the far end – a lacy screen like the Crystal Palace, with a great bank of trees behind it, then a lake with fountains, some of which were designed by Osbert Lancaster, and shallow steps leading down in the Venetian manner, flanked by two high colonnades designed by John Piper. This was the area where people watched the firework displays reflected in the lake. We had really terrific shows. Then Guy Sheppard designed a beautiful little theatre in plaster pastiche but very elegant; the fact that it was built round a scaffolding frame was not apparent at all. Inside, very cosy, plum velvet silk fringes, and there would be Leonard Sachs compering a Music Hall Show. We had a grotto where you could actually smell spices in the South Wind and the saltiness of the North Wind and so on – then down to an underwater world in ultra-violet light to eventually come out in another part of the grounds. This was one of my mistakes, as a family would leave Granny to wait at the entrance until they came out.

We had three pubs, five restaurants, a permanent open-air theatre which, by the way, had to be built in red brick because that's what London Parks required – I think it's still standing – and, of course, an Emett railway. Up to then Emett was only known for his spidery drawings of crazy locomotives, so I got him to actually build real ones. We had a station, a tunnel and I'll always remember the first run of the engine *Daffodil*. Believe it or not, it only went at five miles an hour, nevertheless it managed to knock down an old lady.

Battersea was problems within problems. For example, we built a scaffolding pier out on to the

The Dance pavilion, designer James Gardner. It was 'the biggest single pole tent ever erected in the world' and is shown here half up – a pause to give it an airing.

river for a pavilion that the sponsors decided not to build. So I was stuck with a scaffolding pier. What to do with it? Eventually I built a Mississippi Showboat on the end of it. Rather comical, paddle wheel whirling around in mid-air, smoke puffing from the tall chimneys and a Belgian street-organ playing like mad. Having built the showboat, what was one to put in it? So I had to think up a show. One of the best features was Oscar the Octopus. He slithered around in a big tank. Made of rubber, of course, but very realistic. Some time after the opening the RSPCA forwarded me a letter they had received from three old dears. It called their attention to the fact that we had an octopus in captivity and that the legend stated that it was fed on *spinach* – just one of my jokes – and would the RSPCA please deal with it.

Of course the real point about the Festival Gardens was designing for crowds of people. One had to imagine what English people *do* to enjoy themselves. After a visit to a Scandinavian Pleasure Gardens, I designed a large circular dance hall which turned out to be the biggest single pole tent ever erected in the world, and which John Edgington, the top tentmaker, said just wasn't practical – true in a way, as I had made the canvas top cantaloupe like a melon. So I went to their competitor, Benjamin Edgington, who made it work. I will never forget the moment when the great tent top went up. A whistle was blown, then four giant tractors started off pulling steel ropes away from the centre, so that the great mass of canvas weighing tons slowly crept upwards. This tent was near the fireworks platform so I provided a 'rain' fountain at the top, so the tent could be wetted before the fireworks started. Except, of course, the people running the show would forget to turn the valve. I remember seeing fireworks bouncing

Drum majorette and orange girls.

down that canvas roof – but it never caught fire. It turned out that the English are too shy to dance in public so we had to engage tame dancers to start the ball rolling. Then it worked.

Apart from all these designed features there would be performers of all sorts. Acrobats, a Punch and Judy theatre, cockatoos on perches, mechanical elephants and a pneumatic giant. There were orange girls dressed up as Nell Gwyn, and of course a Festival Band, with a sleek-thighed but tough majorette.

Towards the end of the preparatory work, the administrators put a 'Fixer' in on each site, that is, at the South Bank and at Battersea, to see we opened on time. Frankly, Battersea just couldn't open on time – Royalty or not. Firstly, we had started eighteen months late owing to the trouble over funds and the cricket pitch. Then we had an inexperienced contractor accustomed to building wartime airstrips. And we had a lot of labour troubles. The only time all the men were really motivated was when they had a strike meeting. There were a lot of strike meetings. To cap it all the river flooded and turned the whole area into mud soup. Sad to see foundation blocks sliding over and tanker trucks pumping up mud to dump it down river. We couldn't drain the site as there was nowhere to drain it to – we literally had to carry the mud away, and that took time. The result was that when the Fixer arrived we were already well behind schedule and I was fighting for a three-week postponement. The committee just sat round the table and said it must open on time for the King. The final crisis occurred when I had left the site for four days to deal with problems at the South Bank end. The Fixer decided to do his stuff while I was away. When I returned, the site looked for all the world as though some great monster had walked around vomiting tarmac. The contractors had been instructed to lay the stuff over all areas marked as pathways and standings with the result that the main vista, instead of having a Venetian pavement and shallow steps leading down to the lake, was an undulating landscape of tarmac. What to do? I sat on the running board of my car, an old Beardmore taxi, and thought it out. Eventually I decided to try the president of the RIBA. When I arrived he was in conference, so I sat in the entrance hall on a little red seat for a miserable hour and a half, waiting. Eventually when I saw him and put my case – that a client cannot interfere in this way with a designer's approved scheme – he agreed wholeheartedly, but he couldn't take action. Firstly, I was not an architect or member of the RIBA. Secondly, it was a government project and no one but a fool would sue a ministry. My heart sank, but I pointed out that though the committee I was concerned with had little respect for designers, at least as powermen, the Establishment had great respect for the RIBA. Would he come down to tomorrow's meeting and back me. Well, he did, and I had the joy of seeing Costain's men bulldoze up all the tarmac.

So we opened in good order, but three weeks late. Most people seem to be impressed by openings. To me an opening is a depressing experience. A gaggle of people flossing around in Moss Bros suits and fancy hats take over, and, as far as I am concerned, this means the end. On the appointed day Festival Gardens just opened its gates to the public. I was in disgrace. But who cares, the public absolutely loved it.

BH Looking back, don't you feel all that work was worthwhile, rewarding?

JG Well, I just work. But I must say it is rather nice to meet latter-day friends who found it exciting as children, maybe even got engaged there. It did put a moment of dreamworld into a lot of people's lives. Unfortunately, it didn't have a happy ending. After three good years the LCC, finding it was troublesome to maintain, let London down by handing it over to Fortes and a man who had run a pleasure beach at Porthcawl. You see it now – no comment.

A Painter's Funfair

INTERVIEW WITH

JOHN PIPER

Artist; designer, with Osbert Lancaster, of the Grand Vista, Battersea Pleasure Gardens

BEVIS HILLIER In 1951 you were an established artist.

JOHN PIPER Well yes, I suppose one was established, but I must say, I didn't feel at all secure, not in the least. At that particular time I was rather wondering in what sort of direction I was going because I had been a totally abstract artist between 1934 and 1939 and then I was a 'war artist'.

BH Is that what forced you to become representational?

JP Not really. I wanted to be representational, it was a good excuse. It wasn't that I wasn't really happy, in fact I was very happy being an abstract artist, but I didn't ever regard it as a final end in itself. I thought it was an awfully good way to learn how to paint, by putting a simple area of blue against a simple area of red and seeing the reaction, different kinds of texture, etc. Inevitably one got to know a lot of abstract artists and one got carried along on the tide. By the time war broke out I was just longing to get on to what I regarded as real work.

During the war I was attached to the Ministry of Information. But, before that, very early in the war, I had done a lot of record drawings – that thing called 'Recording Britain'. We were allotted counties. I had Bucks and then Berkshire. I did that for a long time and then I did those pretty nearly record drawings of Windsor for the Queen Mother, which was really doodling, while the War Artists' Advisory Committee got going. I had actually volunteered for the RAF and was due to report in at Medmenham on the Monday. And then I was told that I was reserved and the WAAC had been founded; and then quite soon after that Coventry Cathedral was bombed and I was telephoned to go there.

BH How did you hear about the Festival and how did you first come into it?

JP I think I might have first heard of it from Hugh Casson.

BH Were you old friends?

JP Not very, but we did become so later.

BH What did he suggest to you that your involvement might be? Did he suggest murals or models or what?

In John Piper's studio at Fawley Bottom Farm: left to right, Joy Mills, John Piper and Osbert Lancaster working on a model for part of the Main Vista.

JP I think the first idea was for a mural at the South Bank. I think he wanted a sort of architectural congerie, I think that's what it was and that's in fact what I did. Battersea was a later idea.

BH That was your only involvement on the South Bank?

JP Yes, it was, just this mural, which was quite a size. It was painted on board. I think they had, not a ply, but a hardboard surface. It was laminated board which was supplied by a contractor here to Fawley Bottom. I remember it being put up, it was quite a game.

BH Were you given *carte blanche* as to subject, or was it suggested by the people?

JP I think it was probably suggested by Hugh, this collection of buildings.

MARY BANHAM So you weren't one of the people commissioned directly from the Arts Council?

JP No. James Gardner was my employer at Battersea. It was dotty, really, working for Gardner. We never met each other at all, or hardly ever. He was always busy with a lot of other things and we just went our own sweet way; and there was some other overlord over both of us. I've forgotten the names but the whole thing was wonderfully and adorably vague, you know! I didn't believe that we were going to get whatever large-seeming sum it was, but I think Osbert Lancaster and I did get paid that in the end. He and I, with a bit of help, decided how we were going to divide the design work. It worked very well – Osbert was either living here or around the area, commuting here a lot, anyway. And so bits of his ideas got incorporated into my design and vice versa. It was a really joint effort. And his wife, Karen, made the most beautiful models herself. Osbert would draw things, sort of doodle in the evenings after he'd done his proper cartoons and Karen would make them into a model, bring them along and we'd put them up. It was all great fun and exciting. I had very strong feelings that this thing would never get built.

MB But it did, didn't it?

JP Oh yes, and of course I had to be 'interpreted', I don't know whether Osbert had to be. There was an intermediary architect, as you probably know, a firm; the chief partner in it was a man called Dex Harrison, D-E-X, which I thought was a most marvellous name. He was quite a sympathetic man but frightfully offhand – he had a sweet brother who was quite a different type, he wasn't an on-the-spot business man like Dex, who was rather efficient. He was a sensitive chap who tried to interpret my rather dotty drawings so that they would stand up.

BH You were involved mainly with Battersea. Did you have any overall vision of what you were trying to do? Were you appealing to, for want of a better word, vulgar, fish and chip Brighton front taste, or were you doing something more sophisticated?

JP What I was doing was quite clear. I thought that among the most popular features of the English landscape with trippers, good old-fashioned 'fish and chip' trippers, were follies, always have been – castles and follies – and I thought that if the authorities would run to the cost of building a gigantic folly at the Festival Gardens, it would be super. And that's just how it started, and we never looked back, really. It was very much influenced by Desiderio Monsu – seventeenth century, I think. He was dotty, half Genoese, half Venetian. I was originally introduced to his work by Osbert Sitwell, because you know what a kind of researcher in curios of that sort of folly kind Osbert was. And there was a book at Renishaw when I was doing illustrations for Osbert's book, which had Desiderios in it. They were very much up my street, as I say they were just like giant follies. They were like Italian Chambords, you know the roof at Chambord, that sort of thing.

BH When the work was finished, how did you feel your vision had been realized, well or otherwise? And how did you feel the people at whom it was aimed were reacting to it?

JP I thought it was realized astonishingly well, I thought it was fantastically good. Exactly what one hoped it would look like. And the people were very pleasing because they looked very much at home and they weren't taking the slightest notice of it, the way people don't.

BH They were just enjoying it.

JP Well, I hope they were. I don't think they thought it was funny or interesting or anything – just thought it was natural.

MB Do you think it looked familiar to them, somehow?

JP I think it did, I really think it did.

MB They knew how to behave in this environment?

JP Yes, I think so. You could climb up the spiral staircase and go to the top and see what things looked like.

BH Now Misha Black has said to us that although nowadays you may think of it as a load of fun with everyone giggling at Savoy Court, in fact it was a grimly serious business. Was it very hard work for you, was it hair-raising in the sense that you thought it would never be completed; or was it, in fact, very great fun to work on?

JP Great fun to work on. I didn't care whether it got completed or not, really. That sounds rather grand but it isn't; I am a painter and doing that wasn't my life, as it were, but it was something I thought interesting and exciting to do. But I never really thought it would come off. If I remember correctly, it had a frightfully bad press – or none at all. Not only did the public not notice it, nobody noticed it, except one American who thought it was absolutely wonderful and said so in print somewhere – rather small print! People loved the funfair and that got all the publicity.

MB It probably didn't get much publicity because it didn't have a lot of opposition from the Beaverbrook press, like the South Bank.

JP I think that's possibly right.

MB Gardner said that he had the man who ran the Tivoli Gardens over and he was thrilled to bits with it and wanted to know why we were so self-effacing in Britain, because this was a marvellous garden, better than anything they had in Denmark, anyway, and that we ought to keep it. But, of course, they didn't.

JP No, it would have been rather fun if they had. There was nothing against it because it was quite well built.

BH What was your favourite feature of the whole ensemble? What do you think came off best?

JP Those towers, the tallest thing.

MB In the Festival Catalogue, you are credited with: the Grand Vista including Entrance Towers, Arcades, Rotundas, Tea Houses, Lakes and Fern House.

JP Yes the Fern House is the thing the LCC wouldn't let us have; but at least we had the cane Crystal Palace structure in front, but they took the ferns away.

MB What were they made of, they weren't real ferns?

JP I think they were made of woven cane and painted. I saw our contribution to the Festival Pleasure Gardens as a background, like Brighton pier. But not only that; I was very moral about it, I seem to remember. I was very pro modern architecture. Brought up on the old 'Archie Review': Jim Richards, Wells Coates and Justin Blanco-White who is still to this day building houses for the Edinburgh Corporation. And I thought that the Festival Gardens in this Desiderio-ish folly kind of design was an enrichment which might even – in one's rather pretentious way – affect the development of modern architecture.

MB Do you think it has done?

JP *No*, not in the slightest, I don't think so. In fact, as I was telling you, it was very cold-shouldered by all the critics. I don't think it was even noticed in the *Architectural Review*. If you go through the pages of the *AR* you won't get a smell of it.

The Emett family with Neptune.

The Far Tottering and Oyster Creek Railway

ROWLAND EMETT
Designer, Emett railway, Battersea Pleasure Gardens

In 1950, drawing exclusively for *Punch*, I had, every now and again, featured the goings-on of the Far Twittering and Oyster Creek Railway. A courageous though desperate system, its locomotives became more and more snuffling and long-funnelled, and its bemused personnel were, as someone so rightly said, too late for the past and too early for the future.

We had heard something of the exciting things that were going to take place at Battersea and the South Bank, if and when the Festival of Britain came to pass, and one day, in London, we received a letter from James Gardner. Perhaps, it went, you might care to consider the possibility. Could one not envisage something like your *Punch* railway, passenger carrying, taking people about an exhibition, say at Battersea?

This was very nice, of course, but it seemed wildly improbable, and I don't think we took it very seriously. Some weeks later, however, Mr Gardner's secretary telephoned my wife. She sounded a little perturbed, and slightly ominous. 'Oh, Mrs Emett,' she said, 'the meeting about the Railway is tomorrow, and *Mr Emett's drawings are not in!*' 'They are being delivered by hand first thing in the morning!' said Mary, without turning a hair. Bit by bit the ideas took shape. It was settled that the railway should run all along the south boundary of the Battersea Pleasure Gardens, with a station at either end, a tunnel, a serpentine cutting (which became Twittering Woods) and a bridge over the line. There were to be three engines, and about three or four coaches for each train.

I was now put in touch with a Mr Harry Barlow, of Southport, who was to build and run the railway. He built and operated miniature passenger railways for various resorts in the north of England. He wilted visibly when confronted by my tentative locomotive drawings, but bit by bit he recovered, and began to shine with enthusiasm – an enthusiasm which he sustained throughout. He was to provide his speciality, magnificent diesel-electric powered frames, upon which were to be erected the hand-beaten engines I was to design.

Gradually the first engine *Nellie* began to take shape. I seized every opportunity (and invented lots, myself!) to dash up to Southport to see the progress. I shall never forget the wonder of seeing this mad engine, which up until then had only existed in spidery ink squiggles, gradually filling out and burgeoning forth into three glorious beaten-copper, polished-mahogany dimensions! I think Mr Barlow was as overcome as I was on the day he ceremoniously unlocked the workshop-door and, to the cheers of the assembled workmen, *Nellie*, delicately poised on her 15-inch track, steamed into the light of day.

Meanwhile, it was decided that the railway should be known as The Far Twittering and Oyster Creek Branch Railway and when, in a preliminary announcement, this was made known we had a communication from that well-known philosopher and radio comedian Gillie Potter, the self-styled Bard of Hogsnorton. He told of a village in *his* neck of the woods called Little Twittering, from which, it appears, he frequently pontificated, and *what* was I going to do about it? This was quite a blow, as, to me, Mr Gillie Potter's power seemed only slightly less than that of Attlee. I explained that our name came from 'West Wittering', and in any case, because of the birds . . . However, we agreed to modify the name, and as all the F. T. & O. brass plates were cast by then, we settled for Tottering. Not *quite* so evocative of bird-song at even, but the Bard declared himself happy (though, I felt, *still* a bit Hogsnortonish).

By now, work was getting well under way at Battersea, dogged by the most outrageous weather. I recall endless days when the track workings were a sea of mud, days of frustration in Twittering Woods, endeavouring to hoist glass cases of waterlogged owls into position, and wringing out stuffed woodpeckers whose colours were running all down the tree-trunks. But the weather *did* improve, things really *did* begin to take shape, and the two stations finally came to life.

Now these station buildings were intended by Harrison and Seel, the architects, to be pre-fabricated in cast plaster panels, following the old-brick, pebble and elderly clap-board effect suggested in my drawings. I wasn't at all happy with this arrangement, as I felt it would mean a lot of detail repetition (though, of course, quick and comparatively easy to erect). It was finally agreed that they should actually be built on the site, of real weathered brick, flints and old weather-worn planking.

The main station, at the western end of the line, was Far Tottering. There was a small separate booking office, much given over to elaborate fretted-out overhanging barge-boards, and, inexplicably, a lady's bicycle caught up in the topmost finial. (Perhaps some early Edwardian Ladies' Lib?)

The long platform accepted the trains on either side (so that there could be one Coming and one Going), and was flanked by the pride of the system, the station buffet. This was a long, lowish building in faded clap-board, meandering quietly along the platform and which, in a sudden burst of enthusiasm, soared upwards at one end into a steep Loire-château roof, ending in a fitful clock-tower, with a stopped clock and permanently deranged cuckoo. The building, mainly supported by old London gas-lamp posts, had a graceful lean away from the prevailing wind.

There were many nice railway touches about this station: a luggage-crane, based on a wooden-roller mangle, from which hung a wealth of Gladstone bags, leather silk-hat boxes and the like. A wicker bird-cage, containing a depressed sea-gull, was consigned to Oyster Creek. This crane carried a stern warning: 'It is forbidden to wind other people's luggage up and down.' And there was a water-tower, comprising an elderly hip-bath poised aloft in the branches of an unexplained tree, growing out of a striped lamp post. *This* carried the legend: 'Engine Water. Bathing Prohibited.' Indeed, the railway teemed with forbidding notices – 'Do NOT tease the Engines' . . . 'Do NOT feed the Bats' (this at the tunnel entrance) . . . 'Passengers must NOT cross HERE, so *there*!' And, of course, the one that stated quite simply: 'IT IS FORBIDDEN'. All these strictures carried the normal railway penalty of forty shillings.

Oyster Creek was the station at the other end of the line and was frankly fishy. The booking office was in the style of an old Cornish net-loft, hung with ancient pilchard nets and a wealth of green glass net floats. The platform canopy and the roof-ridge were edged with giant scallop-shells. By the booking office door was an incredible Weather-predicting Machine, glass cased. Varnished skipping-rope handles advanced and retreated along their string, turning the weather-dial and controlled, I think, by the expansion of a measure of R. White's gingerbeer, tightly sealed in its glass-marbled bottle. The whole was called, simply, To-day's Weather.

Further along the platform a large baleful lobster hung moodily from a signal-arm. 'WARNING', stated the forbidding notice-board. 'When Red Lobster is hoisted, Tide is OUT', and added, spitefully, 'By order'. Nearby stood a small steam hand-barrow fire engine, flanked by a red-painted glass-fronted case, with a large chained hammer hanging from it. This case contained a nice wad of crumpled newspaper, two sticks of fire-wood, three lumps of coal and a box of matches. The accompanying notice summed up, I think, the timeless flavour of the whole railway: 'IN CASE OF FIRE', it said, chattily, 'Break Glass, remove Contents and Light Fire in Fire Engine'.

There was a general feeling that high tides had now and again lapped over the station, and the booking office, notice-boards and so on were encrusted with limpet-shells. These I had sent up from Cornwall by the basketful, and having drilled a centre hole in each, I proceeded to nail them up in carefully considered patterns and limpet-like groups. This resulted in the Great Limpet Strike. A deputation of gentlemen with shovels waited upon me, and pointed out that wielding a hammer was not fit work for me, and that *they* would arrange for this to be done. I was assigned a team of three, and so we proceeded. *I* was allowed to select a limpet-shell from the basket (in charge of the first member), and pencil-mark its position on the woodwork. The second member held the shell in this position. The third (and key) member inserted the nail and applied the hammer.

The Emett locomotive Nellie*: 'long-funnelled, brass-knobbed and dedicated utterly to never giving one puff if two will do'.*

When the line of the track was being finalized, it was found that a shallow cutting would go right through John Piper's magnificent Vista, and he became a trifle concerned about disembodied 8-foot high funnels drifting up and down in front of the intricate end set-piece. I offered to 'Piperize' my funnels by making them, say, Doric columns, in rich William Blake blues, scratched away in meaningful textures. We finally compromised, and ran the trains through a tunnel at that point!

The weather improved, the construction began to catch up, and the Festival Gardens finally opened.

We shall never forget the opening day: the railway was literally beseiged, and the trains (both the Coming and the Going *and* the Spare, which was somehow pressed into the schedule) never had a moment to themselves. And this was to go on practically the entire time the gardens were operating.

One day the BBC descended upon Oyster Creek to do a special television feature, and I, in one scene, had to arrive at Far Tottering station (carrying a stuffed owl in a bird-cage) to greet the interviewer. There were quite a number of takes, and I had to keep returning to Oyster Creek to entrain again (with stuffed owl) to make another 'entrance'. An interested and ever-increasing crowd gathered at Oyster Creek to see these unexplained departures.

On my last arrival at Oyster Creek a grubby urchin detached himself from the crowd, and thrust forward an autograph book and a stub of pencil. FAME, I thought. I will sign, and they will *all* press forward, clamouring for signatures. I signed, with a flourish, and graciously returned the book. The boy took it, glanced at it, and then, with a look of ineffable scorn on his face, tore the page out, crumpled it up and threw it under the engine. 'Oo's this, then?' he demanded. 'Thought yer was Danny Kaye!' (There *was* quite a resemblance at the time, I suppose. The *New York Times* once referred to me as an under-nourished Danny Kaye.)

From start to finish, it was all the most wonderful and exhilarating experience, yes, even the dark days of continual rain and Flanders mud. The railway generated world-wide interest, and we had newspaper and magazine features and pictures from fifty-eight countries: second only, we were told, to the 'Skylon'. Mr Harry Barlow, the concessionaire, was delighted, and stated that he recovered the entire cost of the railway in three weeks.

I received a fee of £1,500, which in those days was what I believe is called handsome. It was, I might say, simply for supplying visual ideas, on paper: the Flying-Dutchman life between Cornwall, Battersea, Southport, Sussex; the weeks in the drawing-offices; the sudden safaris into deepest Peckham and even beyond for rare and curly brass-work. Well, they just couldn't keep me out of it; and I wouldn't have missed an hour of it!

The Tree-Walk Dragon at night.

The Tree Walk and the Paper Sculptures

BRUCE ANGRAVE

Designer, Tree Walk, Battersea Pleasure Gardens; designer, Outdoor Games section paper-sculpture figures, Indoor Sports and Games, and Outdoor Sports sections; designer, Crazy Car, Land Traveller Exhibition

I CAN'T RECALL the circumstances in which James Gardner commissioned me to design the decorations for the Tree Walk in the Festival Gardens. But I do remember floundering about in the mud in Battersea Park, many months before the Festival took shape. I think I was armed with a tape measure, and feel sure that I was actually selecting the trees from which the Tree Walk was to depend.

I remember the decorations for the Tree Walk in more detail. There were, as I recall, two towers, each carrying a spiral staircase, situated at either end of the Tree Walk. The entrance tower carried at the top my conical 'Whether House' with its four open porches and ogival roof. The Whether House stood about 8 ft tall above the tower, which was I suppose about 30 or 35 ft high. Endlessly in and out of the porches moved my 3-foot carved wood figures – of a Farmer, a Stout Lady, a Slim Lady and a Business Man. All were looking suspiciously at the sky and wondering what the weather was to be. That is why it was called a Whether House – because no one in England ever knows whether the weather will be wet or dry.

Further along the Tree Walk one encountered 'Branchville', a row of houses, shops and offices built out on a suitable limb. One of the houses drooped over and hung down like a limp and expiring plant or Salvador Dali's *The Persistence of Memory*, in which soft watches hung floppily over twigs like badly tossed pancakes. Underneath the branch of Branchville ran, logically, an Underbranch Railway, connecting one end of the town with the other. Nearby was an immense furry cat on a swing, persistently pushed by a small mouse. The cat was designed to strike the mouse on its backward swing so that the mouse, which was mounted on a spring, recoiled and appeared to give the cat another shove.

Past the mouse and through the fork of a large tree one emerged on to a long span of Tree Walk, alongside which hovered my *pièce de resistance*, the 40-foot fiery dragon. This was based on the best Chinese models, with bared teeth framed in curling tusks, barbed horns and a lizard-like serpentine body with huge bat-wings and outspread talons. It was built of steel framing covered with spray-on plastic of the kind fashionable at the time for cocooning battleships. There were no concessions to humour in the dragon. It hung there sinister and ominous. Its malevolence extended even to me when one day, staring up at it in mesmerized admiration, I fell over a low wire fence and badly skinned my shins. The exit tower of the Tree Walk was surmounted by my Bird Cage, filled with fluttering metal birds, some of which were pouring out of the open door and soaring into the sky.

My other contributions to the design of the Festival of Britain were all concerned with the Land Traveller, an immense portable version intended to bring the delights of Britain's New Dawn to the larger northern cities. I was commissioned by the co-ordinating designer Richard Levin to create a set of eighteen paper-sculpture figures for the Outdoor Games section. These were set in pairs in nine circular display frames and symbolized early and present forms of golf, cricket, football, etc. I remember driving with my father up to Manchester in his now vintage Humber 'Vogue' saloon. The back of the car was crammed with paper sculptures in large dress boxes. It rained all the way there, as it always does when I carry paper sculptures, causing much anxiety over the stretching effect of the humid atmosphere.

I also designed a section called Indoor Sports and Games, the central feature of which was a 'pyramid' of life-size highly decorative and colourfully painted 'acrobats'. Each acrobat, besides balancing upon the shoulders of the one below him, was engaged in some activity such as darts, table tennis, squash or archery. Two more acrobats, one on either side, were juggling with the impedimenta of more indoor sports and games.

Another section of mine was Outdoor Sports, consisting mainly of rolling hills dotted with hikers, cows, cats and birds, and a foreground of decorative trees festooned with sports equipment. A shiny new bicycle leaned against one tree. It was while working on the installation of these that I met Peter Judge, a very ingenious diorama designer and animator, who had created, in his kitchen in Belgravia, an entirely automatic Pollock's Theatre scaled up to about six times normal size. As I passed the remarkable proscenium arch of this device, a head looked out at me and said politely, 'I say, would you mind watching part of the machinery for me while I switch on the power at the other end? Something is binding.' Minutes later, after I had witnessed a piece of metal catapult, with a loud crack, from within a dense array of gears and wheels, he thanked me courteously and so began a friendship that lasted twenty years.

My other contribution was a Crazy Car: an electrically driven 1923-ish tourer with eccentric wheels and dubious springing, which bounced and crashed its cartoon occupants without mishap through the six months of the exhibition. And what do I remember most clearly about that? Well, the entire sum allocated for the design and construction of the Crazy Car was absorbed by the construction contractor, leaving nothing for me.

Popular Arts

BARBARA JONES

Designer, the Coastline of Britain, Seaside section; Outside Broadcasting mural, Television pavilion; figures of lion and unicorn for the Lion and Unicorn pavilion; Battersea Funfair; organizer and designer, Exhibition of British Popular and Traditional Art

I HAVE NEVER worked harder in my life, and most of the time it was marvellous. The Festival started very slowly and methodically. I was to design the Coastline of Britain part of the Seaside section, the Outside Broadcasting mural in the Television pavilion and later a big carved lion and unicorn decorated like roundabout horses for the Lion and Unicorn pavilion. Everything was planned well ahead to go without a hitch as no exhibition ever had: every building was to be absolutely finished in 1950 and everything else was to be got absolutely ready and sent 'into store at King's Langley'. These ritual words of the early days meant that everything would be *there*, labelled and documented in triplicate, ready to be popped into place at a swift signal from the Festival Office. I never met anyone who sent anything there; we reckoned that if *we* couldn't master the sheaf of thin sheets (six or seven each of salmon, canary and eau-de-nil, covered with 2-millimetre-square boxes for

Airedale tiled fireplace exhibited in 'Black Eyes and Lemonade', Whitechapel Art Gallery, 1951 (see p. 131).

ticks, one sheaf per item), then neither would the people sent to find the exhibits in the future.

But I did set up one of those large charts of times and jobs that are now called critical path analyses. Below the South Bank jobs came various capers at Battersea Gardens, an exhibition at Whitechapel Art Gallery called 'Black Eyes and Lemonade', its poster and catalogue and an illustrated book on the same theme, to be published at the same time. Shorter jobs were written on strips of coloured paper and pinned on the chart for timing: posters for provincial festivals; paintings for the Festival's regional guides to Britain; paintings for the Arts Council of the South Bank site before demolition began (one of them was of the interior of the shop of George Burchett the tattooist); Festival catalogues and window displays for shops; Festival essays for magazines here and abroad and drawings for them, Festival, Festival, F.o.B.

The Coastline of Britain was started first; red sandstone, chalk, sand dunes, seaside towns, all had to be visited, painted and photographed, and a way found to show each different aspect of our complicated geology, from 400-foot cliffs to estuarial mud. We decided for instance that sand should have a sand-picture; the Victorians bought them the size of a postcard as souvenirs. We made one 6 ft long, painting each area with thin glue and throwing on the appropriate sand. The surplus fell off when the glue was dry and we did another bit; it was like painting the Mona Lisa by numbers. We collected some of the coloured sands ourselves in jam pots, but the whitest sand in Britain had to be sent down from Scotland. It looked grey. So we coated it with Vim to pep it up.

The cliffs were represented to scale by tall thin white cones, each with a little flag on top to tell its name and height. These were among the first things settled and ordered; the flags were almost the last things delivered to us. Sea anemones, fish and seaweed were painted on receding sheets of glass like a transformation scene; sea birds were a mobile inside a big scarlet wicker cage woven like a lobster pot. It stood on a beach of pebbles, and somewhere else there was raffia grass from Covent Garden market – all hopelessly old-fashioned now. On the last day but one I suddenly saw an unpainted bit up under one of the yard-square domed sky-lights. While I was on the ladder, the next dome fell, grazed my shoulder and shattered on the pebble beach below.

There were spare domes, and another one went up, but there was no spare pier. This had been painted and laminated into plastic, and I had fitted in the 'Coastline' title and its description and my name as designer, all as agreed through the committees except the ordained type sizes, which were tiny. These never filtered through to me, and my lettering was in scale with the pier; the description was easy to read, I thought, and 'Coastline' was in the sort of lettering that goes above whelk stalls; 'Jones', though much smaller to match, was shamefully bigger than anyone else's name, set under plastic, beyond remedy. I think it was patched over with more plastic later and re-done properly meek, almost invisible. But I forgot about my crime in a more serious crisis. When the lights of the whole Seaside section were tried out together, my Coastline, that had been lit up successfully on its own for weeks, was seen suddenly to be no longer linked to the rest; it remained a dark mystery for the opening day.

The television mural also had problems with electricity (there is always something). First there was a still unheated pavilion to work in – with snow on the ground outside. That was cured when Wells Coates produced electric fires where none were known to exist. My scaffold glowed, but then the electricians had meetings about strikes and all possible power went off for the duration. My own union, however, was not having meetings, and I could be left with safety lights in the dark pavilion and sometimes, by a kind accident, with the fires as well.

In the Television pavilion I was an artist, working with my hands like all the other Festival artists, and as the South Bank site was a closed shop we were all members of the Sign and Display Trades Union. On the Seacoast I was still an artist, but also a designer, supervising only: no hands, no union. It was so complicated that as a designer I could order a wheelbarrow load of concrete and then, as an artist's assistant, fetch it and lay it.

At Battersea I designed the setting for a traditional fair, with a helter-skelter and a roundabout in an enclosure of side-shows. Some were to be real, like coconut shies and shooting galleries, others were to be fantasies on such old freak-shows as the Fat Lady and the Skeleton Man that exhibited alive would now be in bad taste. Unfortunately the fair was cut for economy to a simple square of booths and shops. When these were finished there was still a big blind wall to be jollied up and we used one of the rejected fantasy side-shows. We painted the blind wall with a red and white striped tent under a fascia board with the portrait of a gigantic tabby cat and the announcement: 'MOGGO. The Largest Cat Alive. Entrance 6d'. For several years afterwards visitors seeing my own fine tabby would tell me of their disappointment at Battersea, trying to find an entrance to see Moggo. The economy loss of the fair was sad, and so was the economy loss of the water-roundabout, a carousel of baroque shells turning under strings of lights and manned by cat-gondoliers. The pay-booth got built, though, and was used for selling ice-cream.

At some stage during one of the summers there was an odd day on the river. It had been decided to have a pair of narrow boats moored at the South

Bank; they were newly and beautifully painted with their roses and castles. A small committee of those interested in preserving the canals and this traditional decoration went to Brentford to fetch them in by water – it would only take a couple of hours. But there was a strong east wind blowing, the tide was against us, and it took the whole lovely day. We had bread and butter and salami and gin and vermouth with us in case, and when they were all finished we threw the bottles in the Thames with decorated messages offering prizes if they were returned to the Festival; but they never came back.

Right at the beginning it was obvious that something large and strong would be needed for transport, so we bought a second-hand Austin taxi for £30. A passenger seat and a near-side door were put in and the whole of the back was left clear for cartage. The dynamo had to be rewound in Port Sunlight, and pre-war taxis were heavy to drive and heavy on petrol, but it was a perfect Festival car, conspicuous outside London and in private hands surprising anywhere. It was therefore very disarming as a collecting cart for the exhibition at Whitechapel, a bonus added to its size and reliability. No one suspected that anything borrowed for the glorious Festival and taken away in such a car would not be safely returned, and they were right.

The Whitechapel Art Gallery's Exhibition of British Popular and Traditional Art was arranged in association with the Society for Education in the Arts and the Arts Council. I think the society originally had in its mind more tradition and smocking and Staffordshire dogs than were in mine. We brought the whole popular art scene right up to date and so far as I know this was the first time it had ever been done: things currently on sale in the shops and posters on the hoardings, plaster and plastic ornaments and a fine 1951 fireplace in the shape of an airedale dog were all displayed as works of art. People began to realize that indeed they were. Visitors were eased into the idea by a row of ships' figure-heads and cases of other acceptable art-objects, and were brought gradually to accept comic postcards and beer labels. All through the exhibition the new and commonplace were seen near the old and safe, and by the end most people felt able to accept a talking lemon extolling Idris lemon squash and Bassetts Liquorice Allsorts isolated under a spot light. A few adjustments had to be made; we had borrowed two waxworks from Madame Tussauds – Queen Anne for general appeal and the beloved late Chief Rabbi for Whitechapel. The first local visitors were delighted to see him, but later the Synagogue felt that he was too near the talking lemon for dignity. So we swapped the waxworks round, though the visual balance was destroyed, and Queen Anne stood nearer to the lemon.

Also near the lemon was a group of pictures by

Talking lemon extolling Idris lemon squash, exhibited in 'Black Eyes and Lemonade', Whitechapel Art Gallery, 1951.

Miss M. Willis, a primitive painter who was working on huge canvases in a small flat over the tattooist's shop when I was recording the South Bank site. Her work was remarkable, and there were a lot of photographs in the papers, especially of the painting of *Lord Kitchener in his Coffin*. We invited the directors of a number of London galleries down to see the paintings, sure that one of them would take her up. One director explained why they could not: 'They aren't like *other* primitive paintings, you see, not bright and pretty.'

One person who was impressed by the paintings was Miss Picton Jones from the Manchester *Guardian*. We talked for a long time and she told me about other festivities. Surely we were going to the fireworks at Liverpool? One of the greatest displays ever held, to be staged on the river – we must go. We went, unthinking: it was a dazzling evening and there were millions of people, packed thick for miles. Only a little corral beside the press stand was not yet filled, and I remembered Miss Picton Jones's card, still in my bag – surely she would like us to use it? We were put alone in the little corral, in the front row. The Mersey still glittered as the sky faded. No fireworks. No sign of activity. The crowds began to stir, and suddenly far down the river a single rocket went up and the fantastic display came slowly up the great river on barges, moving fountains of light far into the darkness.

One of the yardsticks we used in choosing the old exhibits for Whitechapel was memory – when you think of the posters you can remember seeing as a child, what comes up first? That question evoked for a surprising number of people the Start-Rite Shoes poster of a little girl and boy, back view, setting out down a long road lined with poplar trees, so we had that. Posters led to tin plates on barns and railway stations. The first choice was usually the Stephen's Ink blot, but then people would say, 'there was a yellow plate with a pig – Thorleys. I've never forgotten that.' So I telephoned Thorleys, who said 'yes of course, but you'll have to come and look for it – all our old advertising stuff is in a shed. Anything left over has been shoved in there for years – do come in old clothes!' We needed boiler suits, rubber gloves and Wellington boots, but it was all there, crammed into a warehouse on the Regent's Canal. The latest discards were near the door, clean and new, but beyond them far to the back were rolls and bundles thickly black with London grime. We peeled off the top layers to find more than a century's advertising: posters, tin plates, glass plates, leaflets that unfolded to show chicks bursting from the egg, and portraits in oils of prize animals fed on Thorleys. The collection filled a whole room of the gallery.

And there, back at the beginning of that sentence, is the sad difference between 1951 and now – 'I telephoned Thorleys, who said "yes of course"'. Messrs Thorley might well say it again, I hope so, but I am now writing another book, this time on the popular arts only of today, and dozens of enquiries have taken three letters to get an answer, and dozens of letters have never been answered at all; I can count the instant cheerful responses on the fingers of both hands. Twenty-five years ago thousands of people all over the country worked like wartime with the Festival for D-Day. The word itself was magic; one phone call would awake the dead – 'I am working for the Festival of Britain and we need a photographer's cow for an exhibition. . . .' 'Would you mind a brown one? She's a bit ropey, but we'll soon smarten her up. When d'you want her?' And the old stuffed cow would be returned to her full glory of hollow back, splay feet and big tits, and delivered on the nail. Today it might take six months to get the answer no.

I think that the Festival had a real and lasting effect on private life in Britain. Clothes, streets, houses and thousands of things in daily use have slowly got brighter and lighter ever since, and this change can be traced directly back. But paralleled to it has grown another change, a mental sluggish gloom, a love of crises and despondency. Doing a successful thing again usually goes flop, so another Festival of Britain, centred on London, would be to invite failure; but we do need a new celebration to wake us up again – perhaps a Carnival for Devolution?

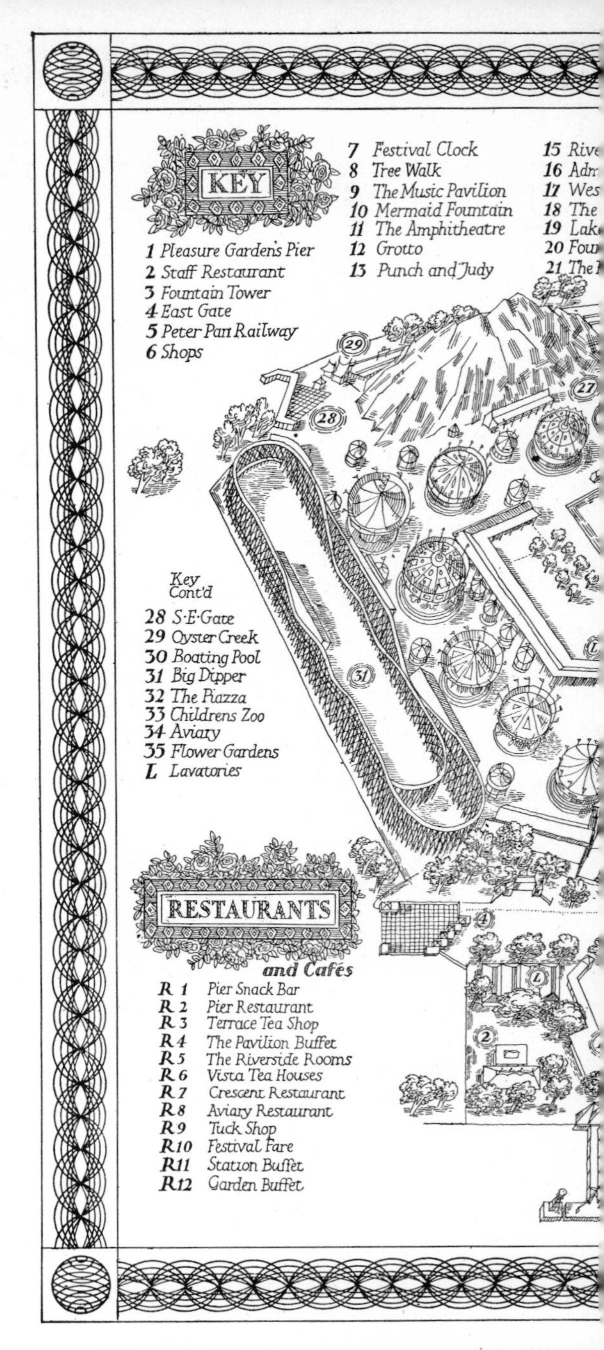

Above, *Battersea Pleasure Gardens: plan and key drawn by E. W. Fenton.* Left, *Crescent Restaurant, architect Patrick Gwynne.* Far left, *the Guinness Clock, designers Lewitt-Him; on the hour, its eccentric automata whirred into motion.*

Left, *one of the towers flanking the Main Vista.* Above, *the Fountain Lake illuminated. The lighting consultants were A. H. Barker and Partners.* Right, *chandeliers illuminate the Main Vista.*

Above, *three typical details at Battersea*. Above right, *entrance to the funfair, detail by Hans Tisdall*. Centre right, *cockerel mural, Hans Tisdall*. Below right, *the Children's Zoo, designer Fred Millet*.

Below, *the Pneumatic Giant, half inflated and fully inflated to 40 ft.*

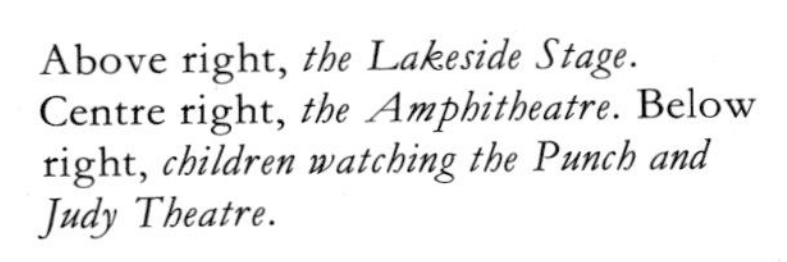

Above right, *the Lakeside Stage.* Centre right, *the Amphitheatre.* Below right, *children watching the Punch and Judy Theatre.*

WHAT ARCHITECTURE, HOUSING AND PLANNING CAN DO FOR US: LANSBURY

Lansbury: The Live Architecture Exhibition

FREDERICK GIBBERD
Architect, market area, Lansbury

To MANY PEOPLE it may be hard now to remember what London was like in 1951, so short is the memory for the visual scene. No super stores, no shopping precincts, no prestige office buildings, no parking garages, no urban motorways. Above all, no towers and slab blocks to destroy the silhouette. London was still a horizontal city with an even skyline broken only by the towers, domes and spires of public buildings and wooded hills like Hampstead and Highgate.

But it was a tired environment: tired, depressed. Perhaps drab is the most evocative word. It was not just the great voids created by bombs and fire; willow herb and even trees had obliterated from those ruins all reminders of death. They had their own picturesque beauty ('fearful' is what they would have been called in the eighteenth century). It was the patching up of damage, the makeshift materials, the absence of new building other than squalid huts ('semi-permanent accommodation') and the general neglect. The English scenery is subtle and muted; lacking the brilliant sun and black shadows that can make even an Italian slum look romantic, much depends on the surface quality of building materials, which, if allowed to deteriorate, can reduce the finest urban scene to one of dejection.

The scene was depressing, but the spirit of the time was enormously envigorating and no more so than in the construction industry. So much had to be done, a huge backlog of building, to say nothing of the bomb-damaged city centres. There was a willingness and sense of urgency. Reconstruction not conservation was the fashion. Everyone had their reconstruction programmes. Town planning was still regarded as an art and both it and architecture had not yet become so absorbed into huge government and local authority organizations that private practice was restricted. Sir Patrick Abercrombie was rushing round the country explaining his proposals for rebuilding city centres like Hull and Portsmouth, and even younger architects like myself were given opportunities denied to our counterparts today. I was involved in the design of Nuneaton's bombed town centre, a slum clearance scheme in Hackney, Harlow New Town, London Airport and a steelworks: three of which were to receive Festival of Britain awards. The housing and schools programmes were under way and a start had been made on four new towns; the Government had staged an exhibition of prefabricated-house types in Northolt, which was a revelation to those steeped in traditional building methods. All kinds of new ideas were floating about: neighbourhood planning, pedestrian shopping centres and industrialized building.

An exhibition on the arts and sciences of rebuilding could be of exceptional interest and value to those faced with the problem of rebuilding. Of value, too, to the layman who had only the vaguest ideas of what the 'New Britain' would actually be like. But an exhibition of such technical subjects as planning and building sciences might not be appropriate to the South Bank. There was also the problem of space. A committee was set up with the task of advising on how the exhibition should be staged. Very soon, those who thought they were in the know were buzzing with rumours of their findings, perhaps the most picturesque being to roof over Exhibition Road.

I had been sounded out about being the controlling architect for the South Bank but it was not my forté. Town design and architecture were, and I had very definite ideas about how such an exhibition should be staged. I wrote a piece and sent it to the Exhibition Committee. The idea was to take a bomb-damaged area and rebuild it as the exhibition. The scheme as a whole would be an example of town planning and the buildings themselves would form an exhibition of architecture. Construction and building science could be demonstrated by using different systems for the construction of the buildings, some of which would be left in an unfinished state. After the exhibition was over the scheme would be completed and handed over to the people. The cost of the exhibition structures would be saved and there would be a social

Opposite, *Shopping Centre and Market Place, Lansbury, Poplar, architect Frederick Gibberd, showing the clock tower with its viewing gallery.*

PEEP
SUN BONNETS

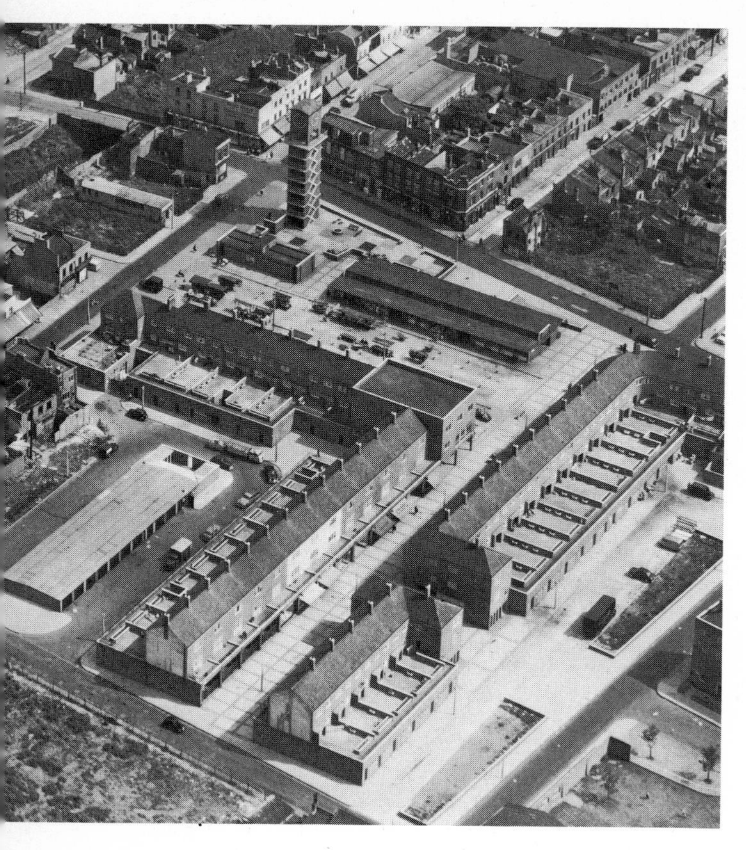

Aerial view of Chrisp Street Market.

gain. Being much impressed with the Harlow Development Corporation, I proposed that a similar body should be responsible for realizing the scheme.

What impression this report made on the committee I do not know, but the Festival organizers came to the decision that the bomb-damaged area of Poplar should be rebuilt as a 'Live Architecture Exhibition' intended to show the British achievement in architecture, town planning and building research. The buildings were to be completed, exhibition material being shown in temporary structures. In 1948 a site of about 30 acres was chosen on the East India Dock Road. It was part of one of the new neighbourhoods proposed in the plan for that heavily damaged area and was to be called Lansbury after the veteran politician.

The London County Council, as the planning authority, were responsible for the scheme. Under the direction of Arthur Ling, the senior planning officer, the overall design was prepared, which can best be described by the press handout at that time:

The buildings, of varying heights, will be grouped round closes and spaces of different sizes, each with its individual character. In some cases there will be children's playgrounds in the centre of blocks, completely protected from traffic. The layout is in fact a series of neighbourly groups linked together by open spaces. While this type of layout is new to the East End of London and the contrast between new and old forms of development is likely to prove striking, the architectural treatment of most of the buildings will include the use of London stock bricks and purple grey slates which are traditional building materials for this part of Poplar.

Four architects were commissioned to design areas of housing, F. R. S. Yorke was given a primary school and I the shopping centre and market square. Architects were privately commissioned to design two churches and a Roman Catholic school, and the London County Council themselves were to do some housing.

The scheme was intended to show a cross section of the different kinds of development planned for Lansbury as a whole. Town planning, architecture and building science were to be explained in temporary exhibition buildings. An innovation was what the London County Council called 'accelerated landscape', what we now call instant trees, and there was of course a vertical feature – a tower crane, not at that time familiar in the London scene.

That is how it was all carried out. Housing in terraces and low flat blocks form pleasant spaces on a human scale. The shopping centre and market square is a three-storey development of masonettes over shops, there are two pubs and a single-storey covered market for the sale of perishable goods. The buildings are grouped to form a narrow shopping street, which extends into a rectangular market square, the whole being exclusively pedestrian: the first shopping precinct to be built in London.

The London County Council was a cumbersome machine (no less than ten committees were involved in Lansbury) and it was riddled with internal strife. It was hardly likely to make the kind of adventurous decisions that one would expect from a single body such as the one I had proposed. The overall design within which we were all required to work tended to be conventional and a bit tame. Certainly there were no architectural innovations, except perhaps in the reinforced concrete framed church by Cecil Handisyde and the clock tower in the market place. The clock tower was commissioned by the Borough of Poplar, who wanted that Victorian symbol of civic pride. It was much to be welcomed as it could form a contrast and focus in an otherwise horizontal development.

One of the joys of towers is what is revealed when you climb them. I suggested we should not stop at a clock but also make it an 'Outlook Tower' from which to survey the surrounding panorama of dockland. And so it was that I designed a tower with two intersecting staircases (one for going up and the other for coming down), which start together but do not meet until the viewing platform – the prototype is the famous double staircase at the Château de Chambord. The building was given architectural expression by exposing the concrete framework of the landings and staircases, which cross each other like scissors, the diamond shapes formed by their intersections being left open for the view. It was a practical folly that gave pleasure, but only for a short time. The fear was suicides; the base was surrounded with spiked railings and the viewing platform enclosed in wire mesh. So it has remained, and the small paved garden at the foot of the tower, designed as a retreat from the bustle of the market, is now a barren waste.

Compared with the exhibition on the South Bank Lansbury was a pretty tame affair. Town planning and architecture, let alone building science, are not subjects of wild interest to the public and the site was very much out on a limb. In terms of architecture, it was all too modest and lacking in exciting 'architectural statements' like the Dome of Discovery to attract the younger generation of architects. But it was immensely important, and I suppose everyone who was in any way involved in the rebuilding of Britain was influenced by it.

As an environment it was at that time a revelation. Bright, cheerful and human in scale, it formed an exciting contrast with its drab and derelict setting. In planning terms it showed the advantages of comprehensive development, how different kinds of buildings can be arranged to form pleasant urban spaces; how the motor car can be controlled and what pedestrianized shopping was like. The exhibitions in the pavilions explained the new theories and ideas about town planning and building research.

There was, too, a very great advantage in that it was permanent. It did not go to the breakers; even the vertical feature, the tower crane, went on to move many thousands of tons of building materials. It accelerated development enabling a start to be made on rebuilding the devastated East End. As soon as the exhibition was over it became a living organism and continues to be so; the houses are still homes and the market square still thrives as a social focus. The rest of the neighbourhood has since been rebuilt and the 'Live Architecture' is buried in a vast wilderness of tower blocks and slabs of every conceivable shape and size. Alas, the exhibition did not prove to be the pattern for Lansbury as a whole. Even though it has been cruelly neglected, the development still has an air of quiet distinction and, though it may be dated architecturally, it is a place with its own character: an intimate, friendly and human character, which planners and architects are now seeking to revive elsewhere.

Background to Lansbury

Extract from the guide-catalogue for the Architecture Exhibition, Lansbury

WITHIN AND TO the north of the sudden loop in the Thames which almost encircles the Isle of Dogs, close to the heart of London's busy dockland, lies Poplar – part of the East End home of the traditional Londoner, the cockney. Its name is derived quite simply from the many poplar trees that once grew there.

For more than fifty years, Poplar has been one of the metropolitan boroughs which, with the Cities of London and Westminster, comprise the Administrative County of London. At one time, it was part of the Manor of Stepney, later becoming a parish in its own right. But long before it became a borough, Poplar was a firmly established community, rich in historical associations and with its own local loyalties, traditions and customs, which have endured to the present day.

The history of Poplar during the last three hundred years is part of the history of London as a port, and of Britain as a maritime nation. Indeed, the growth of Poplar was entirely due to its position on 'London River', its historic Blackwall Stairs being a well-known point of embarkation for sea-going ships as early as the sixteenth century. Martin Frobisher sailed from there in 1577 on his second voyage to attempt the North West Passage as did Captain John Smith, on his expedition to found the first permanent English Colony in America.

The East India Company. In 1614, the East India Company began the construction of a dock there for the building, repair and victualling of their famous 'East Indiamen'. The dockyard attracted workers, local trade expanded, secondary industries grew up, and this process continued throughout the eighteenth and nineteenth centuries, as the Port of London grew in importance and more docks were added. Contemporary prints show these reaches of the Thames dominated by the forest of bare masts and yards of the countless ships that carried trade to all parts of the world.

The development of iron-built ships and the passing of the sailing ships, however, caused a gradual decline in shipbuilding on the Thames, and finally, this industry almost died out. But the docks still remained, for their importance as a terminal and distribution point was as great as ever, and the population of Poplar today is still largely dependent on the fortunes of the shipping industry.

George Lansbury. Like many parts of London which became urbanised in the early nineteenth century, and particularly in Dockland, where the

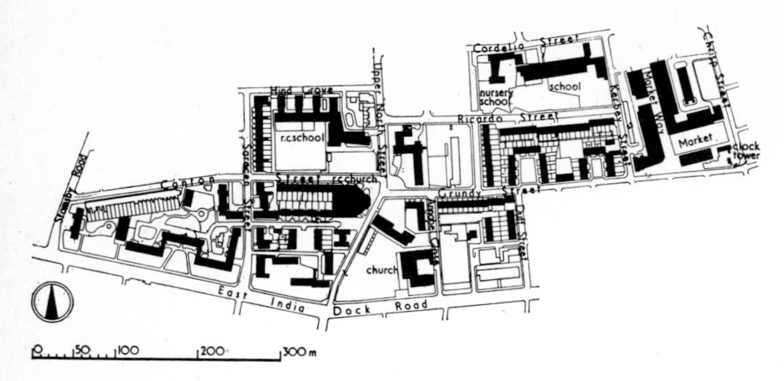

Plan of Lansbury.

inhabitants were mainly poor, the standard of living and housing conditions were of a low standard. Parts indeed became very dilapidated, and although improvements were made, the task of rebuilding such a vast area, quite apart from the cost, was almost too enormous to contemplate.

The names of many well-known men and women are linked with schemes for improvement, and some of them came from Poplar itself. The best known, and one of the best loved of these was George Lansbury. For forty years he served Poplar as a member of the old Board of Guardians of the Poor, and of the Poplar Borough Council. He was its first Labour Mayor in 1919 and again held this office seventeen years later. From 1910–1912 and from 1922 till his death in 1940, at the age of 81, he was Labour Member of Parliament for one of the Poplar Divisions. He devoted his life to working for a better world and a new Poplar.

The County of London Plan

The urgency of rebuilding increased greatly as a result of the war, for the areas round London's docks suffered much damage from bombing in 1940, and Poplar was one of the chief casualties. But with this urgency came opportunity. In the same years, while the capital was still under air attack, the London County Council appointed Sir Patrick Abercrombie, Professor of Town Planning in the University of London, and Mr J. H. Forshaw, then Architect to the Council, to examine the whole problem of London's future development. The result was the publication, in 1943, of the County of London Plan.

This was a most comprehensive study of the major defects of our Capital, followed by proposals for long-term development, divided into stages. Apart from emphasising the general lack of coherent architectural standards throughout London, the Plan presented four main physical problems for solution:

(1) Traffic congestion
(2) Great areas of depressed housing
(3) Inadequate and badly distributed open spaces
(4) Intermingling of industry with housing.

London has grown in a sprawling fashion, gradually swallowing up the surrounding villages and open fields, and replacing them by drab suburbs with ill-defined boundaries. In spite of this, recognisable communities still survive with strong local loyalties.

A sense of community, of neighbourly responsibility, satisfies an essential human need. The underlying purpose of the Plan was to encourage this sense and stimulate or revive these communities and loyalties. The Plan proposed that each community in an area to be redeveloped should be composed of several smaller units of convenient size to be known as 'neighbourhoods'.

The Three Square Miles. One of the most urgent problems was the reconstruction of Stepney and Poplar, an area of over three square miles.

It was proposed that the whole of this enormous area should be redesigned and rebuilt. The overcrowded, insanitary and obsolete buildings, with their drab, monotonous and cramped surroundings were to be swept away, and in their place, eleven new neighbourhoods were planned. These neighbourhoods were to house between five and eleven thousand people, each as it were a small town within a town, with its own houses and flats, schools, churches, parks and public buildings, grouped to maintain or recreate the three old communities of Stepney, Bow and Poplar. Each community was to have amenities and public buildings appropriate to its larger size and complementary to those of the neighbourhoods.

The Festival of Britain

In 1948, the Council for Architecture, Town Planning and Building Research of the Festival of Britain suggested that one of these neighbourhoods would be an ideal site for the Exhibition, which was to be one of the Festival's most important features. What could be more effective than to demonstrate the possibilities inherent in good town planning, architecture and building, by putting on show part of a replanned, living community in the process of going about its daily life?

Lansbury. After careful investigation by the Festival of Britain authorities in co-operation with the London County Council, the choice fell on one of the three neighbourhoods making up the Poplar community, plans for which were already well advanced.

This neighbourhood, since named as a memorial to the late George Lansbury, is a triangular-shaped area of one hundred and twenty-four acres between the East India Dock Road on the south, the Limehouse Cut – a canal – on the north and a railway on the east, and was designed to house some nine thousand five hundred people. A complete neighbourhood would, of course, have been too large for a manageable exhibition. A carefully devised cross-section of a neighbourhood would, on the other hand, be more

Drawing of the Exhibition of Town Planning and Building Research, Lansbury.

suitable in size and still demonstrate satisfactorily how the proper planning of open space and buildings would ultimately transform the East End and, later, other parts of London. The development of a thirty acre site, one quarter of the area of the future neighbourhood, was therefore accelerated.

To complete the picture a special temporary Exhibition has been organised for the Festival of Britain as an introduction to the whole Exhibition of Architecture. There is a Town Planning Pavilion and a Building Research Pavilion in which are explained in diagrams and models, the principles to be followed in providing for the needs of a new community. It is part of the object of this Exhibition that construction should go on through the summer, thus putting on show current building methods and materials.

'Gremlin Grange' was intended as an object lesson in how not to build *(see p. 112)*.

EXHIBITION OF SCIENCE SOUTH KENSINGTON

The Story the Exhibition Tells

Introduction to the guide-catalogue for the Science Exhibition at the Science Museum, South Kensington

J. BRONOWSKI

Science historian; caption writer for the Science Exhibition

THE WORD SCIENCE means Knowledge. This is an exhibition of things which we know. It shows what we know about nature and how we have come to know it, step by step, in the sturdy progress of discovery. People are often tempted to draw a more romantic picture of science: to see it as something remote or frightening, a magic and a mystery. Science is none of these things. Science is knowledge.

Nor is science a strange and special kind of knowledge. Its underlying ideas are not difficult and not at all extraordinary. They can be understood and enjoyed by everyone. This is an exhibition for everyone, in which the ideas of science are shown as common knowledge.

Nothing in this exhibition, therefore, is meant to puzzle or to astonish. There are no trick miracles here, and no mechanical marvels. Instead, here is the modern world itself, standing straight and handsome on its base of science. The wonders of this exhibition are not larger than life; they are the fabric of modern life; and they have grown of themselves from science.

This is an exhibition which looks inside nature. It shows the processes, living and dead, by which nature works. Here is the world for all to see, built transparently from the clear ideas of science. This exhibition is meant to make you feel at home with the knowledge of science, and to make you take pride in it, because it shows science as it is – fascinating, yes, but real and downright.

THE WAY IN

You come into the exhibition through five rooms which take you, step by step, into the heart of matter. Going through these rooms you seem to shrink like Alice in Wonderland, and the things round you seem to grow larger and larger. There are pencil and paper in the first room. Now you find yourself apparently shrinking, first to the size of the pencil, and then to the thickness of the paper; you see that the pencil lead slides off in layers as it writes. Another step, another thousand times smaller, and you see the structure of the graphite crystals which make up the pencil lead. And then a last step, you are ten thousand million times smaller than you began, and now you see into the atoms themselves. Each atom has a heavy centre like a small sun, and the electrons move round it in clouds. You can see what it looks like in the artist's impression on the opposite page.

You have plunged headlong through these five rooms into the structure of matter, and are now ready to see, in a more leisurely way, how we come to know about it.

A FIRST LOOK ROUND

The exhibition's story at its simplest is told on either side of the main central gangway. Opening off this gangway are bays where particular aspects of the story are presented in more detail. These are distinguished in this Guide by being printed in smaller type.

The story is in three parts. The first part displays the PHYSICAL AND CHEMICAL NATURE OF MATTER. Matter is made of atoms, and there are over 90 kinds of atoms, because there are over 90 elements, each made of atoms of one kind. From the centre gangway we see how these elements make up the earth's crust, and we have a glimpse of the inner structure of the atoms themselves. There are side displays which look more closely at rocks and crystals, and at the finer structure of atoms, particularly of radio-active atoms.

The exhibition continues by showing the chemical behaviour of elements and their combinations. This chemical behaviour itself depends on the structure of the atoms, and this is shown in alloys and in some compounds of carbon. The carbon compounds, which are found in all living matter, then lead us to the chemistry of living processes.

The second part of the exhibition – THE STRUCTURE OF LIVING THINGS – deals with plants and animals. It shows how they are built up from cells which live and multiply and die. The factors of heredity lie

Opposite, *entrance, Science Museum Exhibition, South Kensington, nearing completion.*

BIOLOGY
CHEMISTRY

Model of a living cell.

curled up within these cells, and when a male and a female sex cell unite, these factors show themselves in the descendants. So the plant or the animal grows and fulfils itself, shaped jointly by its heredity and its environment.

The third section is aptly described by its name, STOP PRESS. Here are shown some of the latest topics of research in science, and how they have grown naturally from the underlying ideas which we have met on our way round. These new advances concern such matters as the penetrating rays which reach us from outer space, what goes on in space and in the stars, and a range of subjects from the electronic brain to the processes and structures on which life is based.

The Science Exhibition

BRIAN PEAKE

Architect and co-ordinating designer, Science Exhibition

THE APPROACH into the building at the rear of the Science Museum, which was erected in time for us to insert this Science Exhibition, is somewhat long and, after the entrance courtyard, circulation had to be through another long courtyard in which not very much could be done, as approach had to be given for fire engines, access, turning and egress. From this inner courtyard a ramp went up to the first floor of the new building on to a viewing platform where it was possible to see the whole of the exhibition spread out below, with the exhibits laid out under a hexagonal grid. This hexagonal grid was a common unit of pattern in the exhibition, as it represented the pattern of the atoms of carbon. The lighting feature was also intended to illustrate further this atomic structure of matter.

After passing through the five rooms illustrating the composition of the atoms of carbon (these rooms were mostly in the dark and could not be easily photographed), one descended by ramp into the main hall where a display of chemistry and physics, detail design by Ronald Dickens, was set out. In the centre of the building, in the basement, was a little cinema. The little foyer to the cinema had specially designed fabrics based on crystal structure diagrams.

The last section in the exhibition was on living structures. Also included in this section were the Walter Mechanical Tortoises, which wandered about by themselves until their batteries were exhausted, when they automatically returned to their charging 'womb'. As a counter to these, we also had some live tortoises, which until the exhibition opened were looked after by one of my assistants. My most vivid memory of the whole exhibition was the appearance in my office on certain mornings of this assistant with a glum look, reporting further 'mortalities' among the tortoises!

Left *and* opposite above, *periodic table of the Elements, display designer Ronald Dickens.* Opposite below, *the exhibition as seen from the viewing platform. The hexagonal grid represented the atoms of carbon and the lighting pattern was related to the atomic structure of matter.*

In the Periodic Table elements in the
same group have the same number of
electrons in their outermost shell.

PERIODIC TABLE OF THE ELEMENTS

LAND TRAVELLING EXHIBITION

The following is part of a description written at the time of the Festival of Britain

RICHARD LEVIN

Chief designer, Land Travelling Exhibition

DESIGNING THE WORLD'S biggest-ever travelling exhibition will not go down in the books as 'my favourite assignment'.

The Exhibition is to visit Manchester, Leeds, Birmingham and Nottingham. In Manchester and Birmingham it fits into existing halls; in Leeds and Nottingham into an enormous tented structure specially built for it. So the first complication was that three different sets of layouts had to be prepared for all the Exhibition units.

The theme of the Land Traveller is similar to that of the South Bank Exhibition, but because it is visiting the industrial towns of the Midlands, the emphasis has been placed more on industrial design.

The exhibition foyer is simple in form but contains a dramatic sculpture symbolising the skill of the people. The first section of the exhibition proper is called the Corridor of Time, and here the story of the development of Britain's skill and resources is displayed in a series of power-driven pendulums, the effect of infinity being achieved by the use of large facing mirrors. The public actually walk underneath the swinging pendulums.

The second section deals with Design and Discovery, and here is shown the development of design through the ages and the inventions and discoveries which have affected it.

In the four main sections will be displayed some of the best examples of modern industrial design which Britain is producing today, as well as a full-size theatre, a prototype observation carriage and a galaxy of gas turbines.

The Exhibition, which covers some 40,000 square feet, is to travel by road. We are also taking with us a 120′ by 50′ Exhibition Facade constructed in steel and translucent plastics. This contains a number of searchlights which are directed through a red translucent roof. The beams are interrupted by a rotating vane which alternately deflects the searchlight beams through the front of the Facade and the roof. It is expected that the 10,000,000 candle-power light will be visible over an area of 1,500 square miles.

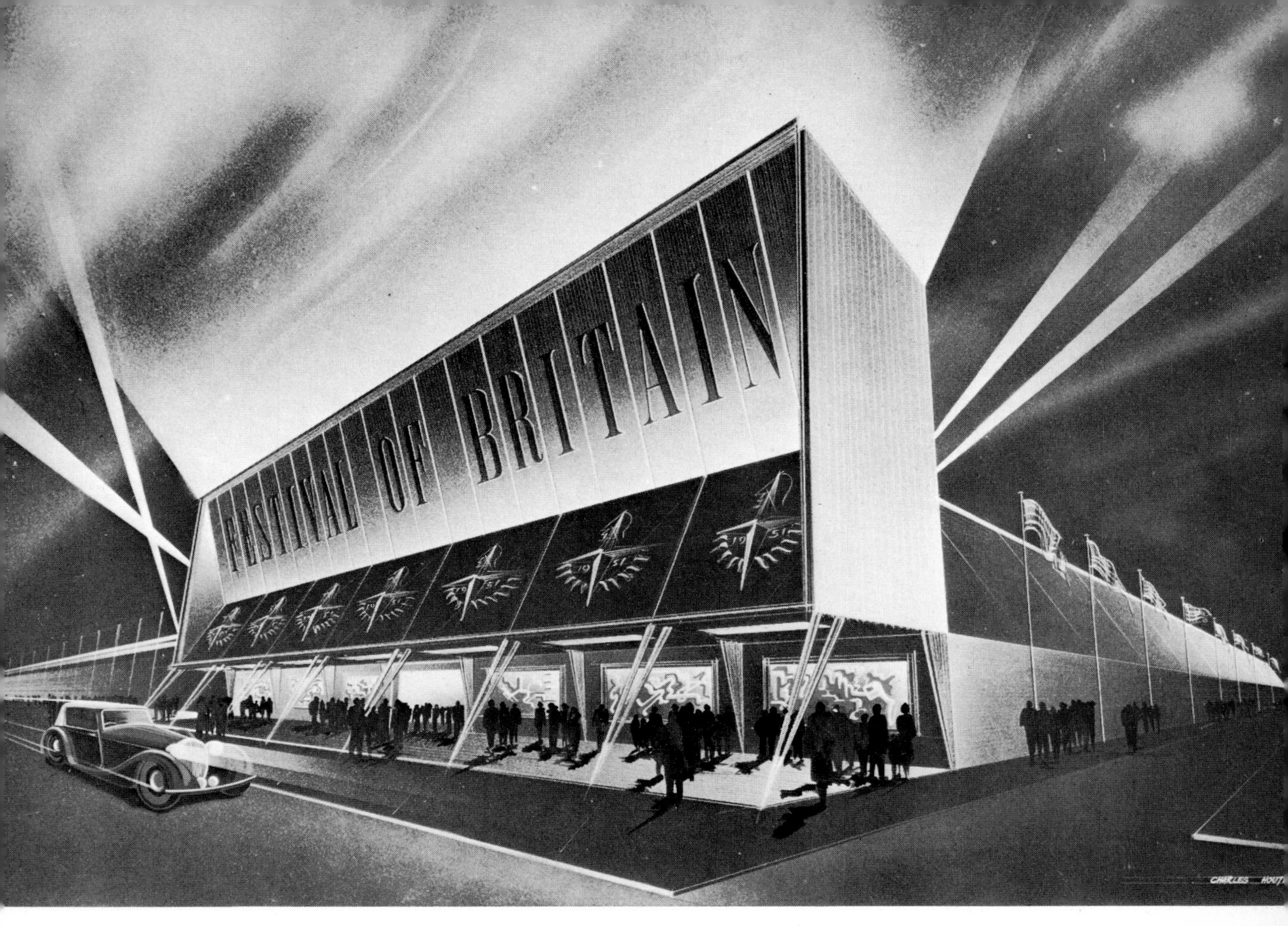

Opposite above, *the Corridor of Time*. Opposite below, *Hall of Fashion, display by Natasha Kroll, stage setting by Clavé*. Above, *drawing of the entrance to the travelling exhibition at night, by Charles Houthuesen, 1950*. Right, *the Arena; designer of the roof mosaic Eleanor Esmonde White*.

FESTIVAL SHIP 'CAMPANIA'

Britain in Festive Guise

JAMES HOLLAND

In charge of display in the upstream section of the South Bank; member of the Design Panel; resident designer at the Festival Office

ALTHOUGH THE Festival of Britain owed something to 'Britain can make it', held at the V & A in 1946, it derived as much, and probably much more, from the experiences and techniques developed during the war and immediate post-war years at the Ministry of Information, and later at the Central Office of Information, where a band of designers had acquired considerable skill in making bricks without straw. For the Festival was conceived not so much as another shop window for marketable products as a boost for national morale, pride and achievement, tangible or intangible. Improvization characterized all Festival planning. Any use of conventional structural materials gave opportunities for critics of the Festival project – and there were many – to accuse the organizers, and the Government, of diverting these from housing and rebuilding in general.

My own involvement followed a long apprenticeship in the Ministry of Information and subsequent experience as Chief Designer, Exhibitions and Display, at the COI. At the Ministry my colleagues had included Milner Gray, Misha Black, Ronald Dickens, Beverly Pick, Peter Ray, Cecil Cooke and Richard Levin, all of whom, in varying capacities, were later very directly involved in the Festival. A design panel, consisting of Misha Black – by then in private practice – Hugh Casson, Ralph Tubbs, James Gardner and myself was brought together to plan, supervise and co-ordinate all design activities in connection with the Festival. We worked as a team, and although we allocated particular responsibilities among ourselves, there was no supremo, and all aspects of all projects were subjected to the critical scrutiny of the panel as a whole.

Perhaps the key moment was when we knew that the Government had agreed to us having the South Bank site. Up to then a great many schemes of varying possibilities were being pursued, including plans for tented structures and re-usable units to be installed on the 1851 exhibition site in Hyde Park; an experimental rigid-framed tent was slowly disintegrating under test in the docks during 1949 and 1950. The Office of Works advised us, and the Government, that to mount a structured exhibition on the site in the time available was out of the question. But with the South Bank now available anything was possible. Bombing had partially cleared the site, a new embankment could reclaim many acres of foreshore mud, and some existing fragments might be saved, among these the Shot Tower and some of the complex of railway arches.

It would be impossible now to give a very coherent account of the early planning days and nights at Savoy Court. New projects and possibilities flowed in continuously: Pleasure Gardens at Battersea to out-Tivoli Copenhagen's famous gardens; a competition for a vertical feature on the South Bank; a live re-housing and community development on a blitzed site in the East End of London; a land travelling exhibition; a floating exhibition; a project known as the Newton-Einstein House, gravity defying, a grounded sputnik before its time, and only reluctantly abandoned much later because of unforeseen health hazards. But high points do stand out. The day we were told the South Bank was ours Hugh Casson and I were set to produce, for press release that same evening, bird's-eye impressions of how an exhibition might fit into this site. Curiously, although weeks and months were then spent on producing a master plan, in essence the final layout differed very little from the cockshy sketches produced in a few hours and published in the next day's *Times*. But there is probably a degree of inevitability about the treatment of any circumscribed site at any particular period. The South Bank, a quadrant held between radiating bridge approaches, bisected by a multiple track railhead, and lying between the curve of the river and another railhead, certainly did impose its own limitations.

An important aspect of my involvement in the Festival came when, with Bernard Sendall, Gerald Barry's Deputy Director, I was summoned to the office of the Secretary of the Navy. There we were told that the Admiralty had given permission for the escort carrier *Campania*, 16,000 tons, to be loaned and converted to a Sea Travelling Exhibition. Thus ended the search for a suitable ship that had so far only brought us lunch with Greek ship-owners in the City – at that time anything that floated was still in demand for bringing basic cargoes to Europe.

The Campania, *drawing by James Holland.*

I hurried to Gareloch, where *Campania* lay in deep water among the moth-balled reserve fleet, an uncompromising lump of grey and rusty steel, but with a large hangar deck well suited for our purposes.

By this time the Festival Office had been set up as a temporary government department, and as the resident designer I had working with me on general assignments a group of young architects and designers. These included several Polish architects, serious and dedicated young men, who sometimes found it difficult to reconcile their precise and detailed approach with the traditional and rather slap-happy, rule-of-thumb interpretations of the northern shipyard that handled the conversion and installations. Indeed what the shipyard would make of perhaps over-ambitious plans was unpredictable, and we were relieved when eventually several hundred workers came down the gangplanks for the last time, albeit they seemed to have rather many of our door handles and other small fittings inadvertently packed into their tool boxes.

Campania provided more than its share of problems. A warship is normally handled by a crew of many hundreds, packed into cramped mess decks, and does not convert very readily into a showboat. Nor did service on the Festival ship compare with current rewards of the Merchant Navy. When *Campania* finally sailed there were some tense moments between an understandably irascible captain and a rather assorted crew and catering staff. I soon discovered that the behaviour of an aircraft in flight is far more predictable than that of a ship at sea, subjected to the infinitely variable stresses of wind and waves. The hangar of the *Campania* had all the stability of a biscuit tin, and the architects developing the internal structures found that their usual margins and tolerances had to be multiplied many times. Large as the hull appeared, the flight deck could carry little weight additional to the necessary lifeboats. But white paint, skeleton masts and plentiful bunting transformed a rather graceless hulk into the semblance of a floating fairground that certainly must have astonished those foreign skippers who encountered the *Campania* on her way up channel in the course of her Festival tour.

Perhaps the most demanding and often tedious part of a co-ordinator's task was to reconcile the many theme and subject specialists and the designers commissioned to handle their particular sections. Nor were the experts always in the wrong – some designers could be obdurate about abandoning a concept that, striking or elegant as it might be, presented a misleading picture. Hindsight inclines me to think that often we were trying to tell too involved or too technical a story. The mixture of instruction and amusement was not always easy to maintain.

EXHIBITION OF INDUSTRIAL POWER, GLASGOW

In common with the other Festival exhibitions, the Exhibition of Industrial Power at Kelvin Hall, Glasgow, had been planned to tell a story – the story of Britain's contribution to heavy engineering. It was concerned not only with machines, but with the men who made them and the people who used them. It set out to show British inventiveness and the effect it had had on the world. Against this background were shown the outstanding products of British heavy engineering at the time of the exhibition.

The Exhibition of Industrial Power was organized by the Scottish Committee of the Festival Council under the Rt Hon. Thomas Johnston, as chairman, and by the Council for Science and Technology under the chairmanship of Sir Alan Barlow. Alastair Borthwick was in charge of organization and theme, and the Chief Architect was Basil (later Sir Basil) Spence.

The general theme of the exhibition was a simple one. This is how it was described in the guide-catalogue: 'There are two main sources of power used by heavy engineering today. They are coal and water.' To demonstrate this general theme, the first part of the exhibition was the Hall of Power, designed by Basil Spence, who as co-ordinating architect was responsible for the layout of the entire exhibition. This was followed by the Hall of Coal, designed by Hulme Chadwick; the Hall of Steel, Power for Industry and the Hall of Electricity, all three designed by Albert Smith; the Hall of Hydro-Electricity, designed by Arthur C. Braven; the Hall of Civil Engineering, designed by Douglas C. Stephen; the Hall of Shipbuilding and Railways, designed by Jack Coia and the Design Group, Edinburgh; and, finally, the Hall of the Future, dealing with atomic

Above, *mural by Fred Millet on the lower Steel Gallery*. Opposite above, *the entrance to the Coal section; the symbolic sun was created by a stroboscopic flash contained in a perspex sphere; relief sculpture by Thomas Whalen*. Opposite below, *general view of Irrigation, in the Civil Engineering section, designed by Douglas Stephen*.

Above, *Coal section*. Below, *drawing by* R. T. Cowern, *1950: proposed treatment of the final display.*

energy, 'the power of the future', designed by Basil Spence.

This is how the guide-catalogue described, in part, the Hall of the Future:

On entering, the visitor walks in the present, looks down on the past, and looks up to the future. In a series of pits below floor level the great pioneers of the past are seen at work. Above is a shining cone rising from the floor, its tip pulsating and throwing off great crackling flashes of lightning to a night sky which curves above it in a twinkling hemisphere – the limitless future. On the floor level, suspended as it were between yesterday and tomorrow, is a display on present-day atomic research. . . . What atomic energy will mean to us is still largely a matter for conjecture but Rutherford made the first significant discoveries nearly thirty years ago. The use which has been made of these discoveries and the work which is being based on them today will determine whether we are entering an age of undreamed-of plenty and comfort, or whether we are working out our complete extinction.

The scientists have placed a great new source of power in the hands of the engineers, the basic power of the sun. If it is used for peaceful ends, anything is possible. This is the theme which William Crosby has taken for the final spectacle of the exhibition, the gigantic luminous mural which screens the exit from the Hall of the Future.

ULSTER FARM AND FACTORY EXHIBITION, BELFAST

An interior view in the Factory showing the rope display, designers W. M. de Majo and L. Bramberg.

THIS EXHIBITION was organized under the chairmanship of Sir Roland Nugent who headed the Festival of Britain Committee for Northern Ireland. His foreword to the guide-catalogue for the exhibition pointed out that this was the first exhibition of its kind to be held in Northern Ireland. It set out to demonstrate the craftsmanship and productive skills of Northern Ireland's factories and farms as aspects of the pattern of British industry and agriculture. The co-ordinating and chief designer was W. M. de Majo.

The main exhibition building was a new factory on an industrial estate. The exhibition was in two main sections: inside the factory building were the narrative displays of industry and agriculture; in the grounds were the old and new farm features. In addition to the factory, the exhibition area included the following features: the reconstruction of a typical 1851 farmstead, a model farm of the future and various public facilities areas. The indoor exhibition in the main building included displays concerned with industry – textiles, general industries and new industries – and with agriculture – development, eggs and poultry, oats, potatoes, milk, fruit, food processing and livestock.

The Professional v. The Amateurs

INTERVIEW WITH

WILLY DE MAJO

Co-ordinating and chief designer, Ulster Farm and Factory Exhibition, Belfast

WILLY DE MAJO I was selected to be a co-ordinating designer in the Festival of Britain when the Northern Ireland Government asked the Festival Office in London for advice. They'd never done a large exhibition before and they wanted to be on the safe side and also to follow as near as possible the London procedure. My name was given by the CoID and the Festival Office with five others, and they came and interviewed us and in the end they selected me.

From that moment it was literally a question of the blind leading the blind. In a way that was the most extraordinary thing about the whole Festival, that there were so many amateurs acting as professionals or professionals who were in fact amateurs when it came to doing an exhibition of such size. There were no precedents at all; we had to think it all out from the word 'go'.

MARY BANHAM Do you think it could have happened in another country, because that seems an extraordinarily English way of carrying on?

WM It could have happened in America perhaps, I think that's the only other country – and with a bit more money! I was anxious to get the job, as it provided a once in a lifetime opportunity.

MB You wanted to get established after the war?

WM I was already established but more in the field of packaging and display. I really did my first exhibition stand in 1948 during the British Industries Fair and so I felt very proud that by 1951 I should have been considered for the role of one of the co-ordinating architects and designers. But once I was offered the job I considered turning it down. It was my wife, then, who said, 'For God's sake, there's a challenge. You do it, you'll do it well.' Once I got appointed there were questions raised in the Ulster Parliament. Somebody said: 'If we have to get a designer from across the water, why not an English Englishman instead of a Yugoslav Englishman?'

The main contacts were Mr Arnold Arnold MA, who was the Secretary in charge of the Festival, and Mr H. Jones, who was the Assistant Secretary of State. They were the first two to come and interview me. Then I had to go across to Belfast and be interviewed there before a bigger committee and eventually they offered me a contract. What was typical was the tremendous lack of time and money. My contract was signed two weeks after the date on which I was supposed to take over! Half the things the Ministry was supposed to supply they couldn't supply, like copy-writers and reference material. So many things were delayed I had to use my own initiative and sometimes my own sources and resources.

Then there was the problem of distance.

MB You were in London?

WM Yes, most of it had to be done by correspondence. They wanted it to go by ordinary mail – I was supposed to phone as little as possible – so we had to find all sorts of excuses to make calls.

There was also the problem of building up from an office of three people to a staff of twelve to fourteen which I felt was the minimum we needed to get the right results. There was also the question of space. I had a big squash court in my house in Chelsea which I turned into a studio; eventually the day nursery had to become the architectural drawing office, while my private study and library had to become an extra office for secretaries – so we were eaten out of house and home in a way.

MB You really had to *live* it.

WM That's it – for fourteen solid months. The initial briefing was done by two people, one from each of the Ministries, Agriculture and Commerce. Commerce was really running the show on behalf of the Ministry of Agriculture as far as finance, contracts and all those things were concerned, but on contents and on basic details we always liaised with both ministries.

They appointed H. Lynch-Robinson as architect for the Farm buildings and he also acted as adviser to the Festival Committee. Problems arose because I got stuck with an existing factory building with terribly low ceilings. The solution I arrived at was to stretch an airy-looking false cloth ceiling across the whole 35,000 square feet which gave an impression of height and was quite a technical feat.

We prepared some basic drawings and eventually made a model for approval by the Liaison Committee. And in fact from that moment, once we'd had the basic drawings OK'd, there was absolutely no problem on major policy matters. I had a fairly free hand and the Minister was very co-operative. However, we had some arguments, partly because they didn't move fast enough and I kept pushing them.

There was a big problem about a vertical feature. I insisted that we should have one because obviously it was good as a landmark and the factory itself was a bit out of town; it was in one of those modern soulless factory estates.

MB You weren't required to produce a vertical feature? Most of the other Festival exhibitions had one.

WM No, it was my idea. I felt we needed it so that people could see it from far away. The Ministry architect who had put up the building insisted that it wasn't strong enough and that my proposed design was likely to blow over. After considerable argument I won the day. Fortunately for me it did not fall down, not even after we had a 60 mile per hour gale one day.

There were also some rather protracted arguments about landscaping. I insisted, for instance, that we kept an old tree there which we saw on our first visit and they wanted to raze it to the ground and bulldoze the area. I felt that it should be kept as it would add an interesting dimension. Eventually I got my way and just a week before the opening, lo and behold, that broken-down tree began to grow little leaves! It was really almost like the chosen tree!

Then there was another problem about adding some more kind of human-nature element to it. There was a very old dried-up culvert there, it wasn't really a river, I don't know quite what you'd call it. It was about 2 ft wide and they were going to fill that in and I pleaded for its retention. Originally I intended to use it as an open-air barrier on that side of the factory ground and to widen it so that people couldn't jump it easily. Well, they wouldn't accept it. For security reasons I had to put a fence up, they were afraid of people falling into the culvert. But they allowed me to widen it and use it as a 'natural' feature, and that ended up in a little pond at the main entrance with a mobile rotating in the wind. That was quite a good feature; we didn't have anyone fall in, anyway it was too shallow to drown in!

Oh yes, the bandstand and the open-air restaurant. I insisted on having those two features as Belfast didn't have anything like, in London, the Battersea Funfair. I wanted something which people could enjoy. Not only be educated, but also have fun, and I wanted people to come mainly to relax, which was the great thing I found at the London Festival. Even after a heavy day of hard work I would go to the South Bank and just sit and look out from the Regatta Restaurant at this marvellous vista with its floodlighting and one could feel so relaxed and suddenly realize how wonderful London was. The officials said, 'You're crazy, Northern Ireland has more rain than any other part, apart from Scotland, and you're going to be flooded and no one will come and it won't do.' I ventured, 'I have a special relationship with God and I guarantee there will be sunshine!' Well, again I won my battle and, believe it or not, except for just before the opening, we had no rain.

Entrance to the Factory section, showing vertical feature.

The Farmyard in the Farm section, architect H. Lynch-Robinson.

MB I see you had beautiful sun for the opening, which is more than they did in London. You must have had a better summer in Northern Ireland.

WM Well, we opened a month later to start with, but we were very lucky and people came and *really* enjoyed it. I organized a special caterer, I insisted on that kind of detail right round. If I had to be in charge I wanted to choose the cutlery, I wanted to select the dresses of the waitresses and all that, and, in fact, the menus too. But it was great fun, because people really came, as I'd hoped, to enjoy, to eat and to have a day out.

Flooding – yes. Despite my good relations with God, the floods came three weeks before we opened, and all the new grass we'd sown was just washed away. Two weeks before the opening we just didn't know what to do, there were miles of mud and slosh. Fortunately the Ministry of Agriculture were one of the main exhibitors, so we got together with them and they said the only thing to do was to turf it. And through the resources of the Ministry – it cost another few thousand pounds – we turfed it. Some days before it opened it rained and at the opening it was lush and green. Nobody knew!

Probably one of the most unusual things pre the opening day was that there was nowhere to have an office. So I decided to buy a caravan, a huge one; it was, I think, about 30 ft long. It was marvellous, very nice-looking. I painted it blue and pale grey and put a big sign on it 'Co-ordinating Designer's Office'; on one side was my office and on the other a little buffet. I brought over from London a selection of frankfurters, continental sausages and cheeses, rye bread and so on. I also had 'muzak' piped in; in those days it was unusual for workers to be allowed to have that. And if anyone said, 'I'm tired and I want to go home,' I'd say, 'Come on, have something to eat, have a glass of beer, and off you go.' And I think that's why, unlike other Festival building sites, I had no strikes. That is probably why it was the only Festival exhibition which was ready to the last letter. And I was very proud of that, because after what I'd seen in London I was determined that our show should be finished when the Queen opened it. The King was already too ill by then. Originally he was supposed to open it.

Mobile by Veronica de Majo at the entrance to the Factory section *(see p. 157)*.

We'd been two nights and two days on our feet. At 5 o'clock on the morning of the opening, I did the last round and everything looked just perfect. Against many odds we had succeeded. The sun came up and it was absolutely marvellous to see the sun rising, it was almost orange. I felt really happy. I went home and I washed and dressed and went back. For some reason I didn't carry my co-ordinator's pass with me and by the time we came back to the exhibition it was about 9.15. The opening was at 10 o'clock and there were crowds already forming; they were all ready for the Royal Party and the police would not let anyone through. They didn't know who I was and they said, 'I don't care who you are – you can't come through unless you have a special ticket.' I said, 'I have a ticket, but . . .' So we argued and I tried several other routes and got the same answer, always. Eventually, I think it was about eighteen minutes to go before the opening when I noticed in the distance one of our local coppers, who knew me; he'd been on site. So I said to the sergeant, ask one of your mates, he knows me, and that got me through.

I was delegated to Princess Margaret's party to take her round, with the Minister of Commerce and Dr Rebbeck. The Minister knew very little about the exhibition and as you know the procedure is that you don't address Royalty unless they speak to you, so I was walking behind and kept feeding the Minister and telling him what was what. Princess Margaret soon realized that the man who knew the answers was walking behind, so then she started talking to me and from that moment on we really had a marvellous time. We spent quite some time, for instance, under the big ship tank in the shipbuilding section where she got very intrigued by how those models kept moving round the harbour without anyone seeing anything. She said, 'Have you got a little man in there?', so we got down on our knees, which was rather fun, and looked underneath the tank and I explained how the magnets worked. We had a marvellous luncheon party at the end in the open-air restaurant with all our friends and families and all the staff and everyone. But I was so tired after a session of two days and two nights, prior to the opening, that I fell asleep over lunch. I must have been the only designer to have missed the Royal Garden party which followed the opening ceremony.

8 RECOLLECTIONS

Visitors examine a plan of the South Bank.

The editors of this book felt it would be a good idea to invite recollections of the Festival and of life in 1951 from the important and unimportant, participants and deliberate abstainers, cooks, managers of temples of mystery and casual visitors, many of whom may have been only schoolchildren at the time.

Through newspaper articles, radio broadcasts and advertisements in the press, such contributions were requested. Some arrived as elegantly typed articles of several thousand words; others were written in longhand in the form of a personal letter to the editors.

We have divided the contributions finally selected for inclusion in this book – many of which have had to be edited for reasons of space – into two groups: 'Participants' and 'Visitors and Abstainers'. The former group includes anyone who can fairly claim to have taken a direct part, even if a minor one, in the Festival enterprise. The editors hope that the resulting symposium in both groups gives an overall impression of the effect the Festival had on those for whom it was intended, as well as something of the pleasures and pains of organizing the Festival in a short time.

Some of the most unassuming recollections by people to whom a day's family outing to the Festival was a gala day, in the still austerity-ridden Britain of 1951, give as valuable an insight into what the Festival meant to the public at large as some of the most olympian commentaries of the leading organizers.

Joining the team

JACK GODFREY-GILBERT

Architect; Senior Executive Officer in the Festival Office

Jack Godfrey-Gilbert explains Lansbury to the Duke of Edinburgh; in the centre, Hugh Casson.

IN DECEMBER 1949 I received a letter from Mr Gerald Barry who explained that a special branch of the Civil Service had been set up directly under the control of Mr Herbert Morrison, the Lord President of the Council, and that a new Architects' Department was being created under Mr Hugh Casson in order to design the buildings for an exhibition which was to be held in 1951 in order to commemorate the Great Exhibition of 1851. My name was on a list of young architects obtained from the Royal Institute of British Architects and if I was interested in an appointment with the Festival of Britain Office, would I kindly complete the attached questionnaire.

By January 1950 I was appointed Senior Executive Officer, to work with John Ratcliff who was Hugh Casson's deputy. On my second day at work for the Festival John Ratcliff told me that we were to go to the South Bank as he had been instructed by Hugh Casson to show me round the site. We walked across Hungerford Bridge, collected two pairs of wellington boots from the nearest hut and made our way to the group of huts in the centre of the site. In the largest of these I was introduced to the Senior Clerk of Works, Colonel Adlard. We made our way stickily round the site which was ankle deep in mud. It was raining and had been raining incessantly for days. Colonel Adlard pointed out the profiles and levelling pegs of the Dome of Discovery and other buildings and introduced me to various general foremen in charge of the setting out of the individual structures, the foundations of which had been designed by various consulting engineers. I was amazed at the size of the South Bank site as from the office it had looked quite small. The Shot Tower stood as an elegant reminder of the eighteenth-century method of making various sizes of ammunition, while the remains of the factory which had produced Coade stone and was now being demolished made me feel sad that Mrs Coade had died without passing on the secret to anyone of how to produce the famous artificial stone.

On my third day, I see from my diary that a meeting of the South Bank Committee took place on the site. Hugh Casson was in the chair and it was attended by Misha Black, John Ratcliff, Richard Miles, Ralph Freeman, myself and my secretary. The meeting lasted most of the morning and then we returned to Savoy Court for lunch. After lunch a memo appeared on my desk which said: 'From the Director of Architecture to Mr Godfrey-Gilbert, subject Letts Wharf, Willment site, South Bank, Date Friday 17th February. You will please survey the above and let me have a report on present conditions and future possibility as location for the Riverside Restaurant with your recommendations. Report required Tuesday next 22nd February'. I picked up the memo together with my pad and walked over Waterloo Bridge with my miniature camera. The site was covered in mud. Open barges were being filled with refuse from the City ready to be taken down the river and dumped. I paced out the site in my wellington boots after drawing a sketch plan, shot off a roll of photographs and did some rough perspective sketches. Then I returned to my office and wrote an appreciation of the situation, setting it out as briefly as I could. It was soon typed, together with the cover page, and with my sketches and mounted photographs I sent it with an 'As requested' memo to Hugh Casson on Friday evening.

On Tuesday morning I received a further memo: 'From the Director of Architecture. Thank you for your excellent report.' The next day Jack Ratcliff said, 'I am taking you to Poplar neighbourhood no. 9.' We drove down to the East End, along Commercial Road to East India Dock Road and I was instructed to turn left into Upper North Street. Jack produced a plan of Poplar with neighbourhood no. 9 outlined in red. We walked all round the 30-acre site which consisted mainly of open derelict landscape, formerly occupied by terraced houses which had been completely devastated by the bombing and cleared away. There were the remains of a church on the corner of East India Dock Road and Upper North Street with some of the gothic arches still intact. There were derelict remains of houses here and there but the remainder of the site was completely flat except for one large square house occupied by a firm of chartered surveyors with the name William Clarkson written across the front. The whole area had an atmosphere of foreboding, gloom and despondency. It was the centre of the Blitz on the East End. Jack said, 'This is where we are going to have the Exhibition of Architecture, Town Planning and Building Research. I want you to be my deputy and you are to be responsible for the co-ordination of this scheme.'

Of course before we could start building we had to clear away the remains of the church and one complication was to have the ground deconsecrated. This was done by means of a memo to Hugh Casson; quick as a flash a bishop arrived to carry out the necessary ceremony. One very serious problem however

Trinity Church, Lansbury, architects Handisyde & Stark.

was how to get rid of the William Clarkson building. They were chartered surveyors. They knew the law. It would mean a compulsory purchase order which normally took a tremendous time to come through. I decided to go and see the senior partner and rang them up. I was referred to a Mr R. R. English FRICS at his City office in Billiter Street. I spoke to him on the telephone. He told me in no uncertain terms that he took a very serious view of the whole matter as his firm had had a branch office in East India Dock Road for over a hundred years. I said, 'This is a difficult matter to discuss on the telephone. Please could I come and see you?' He granted me an interview and so off I went. During lunch I told him about the exhibition, how I was a Glorified Progress Chaser, and after lunch, during coffee, he said, 'Well old chap how can I help you?' I then explained that I needed to pull down his building as it was right in the middle of a very important exhibition site. I told him that I would obtain a Building Licence from the Ministry of Works so that he would then be able to build a new office to his present-day requirements, that the cost would have to be submitted to us and I would do my best to get financial approval for his new scheme. We were able to co-operate extremely well and the whole exercise went without a hitch.

I visited Lansbury every day. I drove through Cable Street, which was a short cut to Commercial Road, and there was still evidence of beautiful Georgian terraced houses in this road of ill repute, surrounded as it was by complete devastation. Time passed in a flash and before I knew it 1951 had arrived. This was one of the most exciting years of my life. Everyone was working flat out in order to get the exhibition on the South Bank and at Lansbury ready in time for the opening on the 4 May.

After the opening by the King and Queen, thousands of people came swarming over both exhibitions in no time. Lansbury was linked to the South Bank by river bus to West India Dock Pier where special road buses ran to the exhibition site. Everything was somehow completed. It looked gay, exciting, colourful; all the pavilions on the South Bank and at Lansbury had an air of something brave, something new, something exciting about them and their contents. The Dome of Discovery and the Skylon epitomized the production of new thinking, new ideas, a new world, high standards of design in everything. A new architectural language was born.

Organizing the Festival

GEORGE BACKHOUSE

Chief Executive Officer, Personnel and Organization, Festival of Britain

In 1948 the Festival Office was formed to undertake the organization and management of the official projects. The Central Office of Information, whose Exhibition Unit had hitherto been responsible for planning and managing official exhibitions, contributed staff to work with other specialists devising and designing the various projects. The speed with which preparations got under way resulted in very many plans and revisions until the overriding question of cost put a stop to further schemes. Estimates of the sum required could not be made until a list of projects had been agreed in principle, but finally a figure of £12,000,000 was fixed, less about £2,000,000 expected revenue. Shortly after this, in 1949, when all appeared to be going smoothly, there was a financial crisis; £1,000,000 was lopped off the budget and more replanning was needed.

At the same time as these estimates were being prepared, some staffing of the Festival Office was going on and this went ahead rapidly once the financial position was clear. The build-up of the organization fell into four main periods: research and planning; main preparation; Festival period; and dismantling, disposal and financial settlement. The administrative branches of the Office – finance, accounts, contracts, organization and staffing – were manned at the senior levels by established civil servants loaned from other government departments. The remaining staff of the Office was recruited through the then Ministry of Labour. The difficulties of recruitment were immense and not only because of the wide range of skills required. In a period of full employment, often with a five-day week and luncheon vouchers and good prospects, the Festival's need for a six-day week (and much unpaid overtime) with only a limited period of employment and no future was hardly attractive. It did, however, have the effect of bringing in many who were more interested in the purpose of the Festival than the conditions, and others who welcomed the opportunity of working, even if only for a short time, with the country's leading designers.

Interviews and selection boards seemed endless and a lot of time was spent in seeing candidates who turned out to be unsuitable. On the other hand there were welcome surprises, such as the girl applicant for an interpreter's post who came from the remote north of Scotland and had seven fluent languages. The qualifications for some posts were occasionally unusual but none more so than the requirement for the officer in charge of the South Bank Press Room to be an experienced drinker. Applicants for this post were plentiful but the other necessary qualifications narrowed the field considerably.

The head office of the Festival was at Savoy Court in the Strand. Additional offices were set up in Kensington, Victoria Street and Regent Street, as well as on the South Bank site, at the Science Museum and at the Architectural Exhibition at Poplar. Eventually an Advance Booking Office was opened in Northumberland Avenue and a Press Club in Old Scotland

Yard. The Booking Office became overwhelmed with applications, particularly from organizations, schools, churches and large parties from works and offices. This greatly relieved pressure on the exhibition turnstiles and particularly on the South Bank where on one day alone nearly 160,000 were admitted. A special Festival Office was set up in Glasgow to supervise the building and managing of the Exhibition of Industrial Power at the Kelvin Hall. This very attractive exhibition, thought by many to be the best, was not so well supported although there was no apparent reason for this. It was said in some quarters that as it was only a small part of the Festival of 'Britain' it did not do justice to Scotland. There was no hard evidence to support this but it may be significant that the handsome stainless steel and enamel Festival of Britain sign was removed from outside the Glasgow office by (it was reported) early Scottish Nationalists.

Long before some of the exhibitions were ready for resident staff, and indeed as soon as any construction started, it became necessary to provide a disciplined security force. An ex-superintendent from Scotland Yard was recruited to get together, over the months, security police and firemen. A total of a hundred and fifty was required for South Bank alone. The recruits were all experienced in police, fire or Forces security work. This force was kept busy as much during the preparation period as when the exhibitions were open. The classic story is of the loss of six wheelbarrows, each wheeled from the South Bank site with a load of rubbish by an employee who each time returned empty-handed to collect another. During the opening of the exhibitions there were the expected pickpockets and bag-snatchers together with unexpected frauds by some of the ticket staff at the entrances. This involved the surreptitious passing-back to the cashiers for resale, tickets already sold and handed in at the turnstiles. Checks and controls swiftly brought these offences to an end. Few exhibits were lost although a valuable cigarette box lent by Sir Winston Churchill was a particularly embarrassing loss as it had been borrowed after considerable persuasion, with the firmest assurances of safety and against a firm conviction by Sir Winston that he would not see it again. On the last night of the South Bank Exhibition there were the expected souvenir hunters of items of relatively little value and these were good-humouredly dealt with at the exits and obliged to go home empty-handed.

The operational staff, those employed as attendants, cashiers, publication sellers and cleaners, could not be recruited until a few days before the opening date because of the cost of the large numbers (1,200 on the South Bank alone). Apart from the supervisors, who were interviewed at the head office, the selections were made at the Elephant and Castle Labour Exchange by Festival staff in co-operation with the Ministry. As it was essential to confirm the engagement the day after the interview there was not time to take up the usual references. Instead, an arrangement was made with the Criminal Records Office at Scotland Yard to make a quick check on the same day as the interview. An interesting result of this was the finding by the police of a number of 'wanted' men including one for whom the Canadian police had been seeking for a serious crime.

Staff for the travelling exhibitions were recruited locally. In the case of the Land Traveller this meant at its four sites, at Manchester, Leeds, Birmingham and Nottingham. The sea exhibition aboard the ex-aircraft carrier *Campania* could not find staff at Southampton where it was fitted out but was able to do so at Liverpool where there was some unemployment.

Early in 1951 the South Bank site caught the attention of the trade unions and there was immediate competition between the National Association of Theatrical and Kinematograph Employees who had previously operated in government exhibitions and the Transport and General Workers' Union who already had some members on the site. They were both after the large body of attendants and other such staff. In the end, after some 'earthy' discussions and hard bargaining, a division was made with some in each union according to the duties. In the event this worked to the advantage of the Festival since the two unions could never agree on joint action. There were threats of stoppages and some exercises in brinkmanship up to the eleventh hour and even later, but these were all resolved without strife. There were a few strikes among the contractor's workers building the displays but these, although causing delays, were short and did not lead to disaster. In view of the vulnerability of the project the labour record was remarkably good. Generally there was an excellent response from the unions to the appeal by Herbert Morrison, as the Minister responsible for the Festival, for all help in making the Festival a success.

Although the conditions of the office staff may not always have been as good as for comparable work outside, the operational staff had to be paid the current going rate. Attendants were paid £6 a week, firemen and security police £8 15s, labourers £5 10s and interpreters £8 10s. Extra pay for over forty-four hours and for shift and Sunday duties helped to raise these rates slightly.

The Festival Office began to discharge staff as soon as the exhibitions opened, starting with those who had been engaged on research and design. The peak staff figure was 772, plus 29 industrials and 1,908 operational; this dropped rapidly as the Festival finished and during the fifteen months of clearing up, disposal and accounting. The office ceased to exist after 31 March 1953.

Those of us who worked in the Festival have our own personal recollections. The long (often fifteen-hour) days, the seven-day weeks, the irregular meals (if any) and many strange happenings are but one side of it. There was also the excitement of a new creation, a freedom to cut red tape, an opportunity for quick decisions and fresh and unusual ideas, and the uplifting effect of the high quality team work. The ultimate in the many desperate occasions must surely have been the night of 3 May on the South Bank when, as dawn broke, senior staff were dropping from exhaustion after hours of frantic arranging, cleaning and sweeping in preparation for the Royal visit prior to opening to the public. The high light of satisfaction, and of emotion too, was the closing ceremony on the night of Sunday 30 September.

That, despite all the setbacks, the Festival took place at all, and on time, was due to the tremendous enthusiasm of all who planned and created it. Its effect on the jaded nation was precisely what had been hoped for and the result was a new spirit throughout the country. Something special had been achieved and the world had seen it. If, twenty-five years later, we can revive some of that new spirit it will be no bad thing.

The achievements of 'Cockade'

T. W. HENDRICK
Production Manager, 'Cockade'

IN 1946 Sir Stephen Tallents KCMG, who had been in control of public relations for the Post Office, Empire Marketing Board and the Ministry of Town and Country Planning, had been deeply impressed with the visual value of three-dimensional models for promotional and instruction uses. He felt, however, that there was often a lack of artistic imagination in the presentation of models and displays and was certain that a consortium of designers, artists, craftsmen and craftswomen working together in harmony must inevitably raise the aesthetic standards to a considerable degree. This, in turn, would prove likely to induce discerning clients to make fuller use of such services in the field of exhibitions and displays.

With the enthusiastic co-operation of friends, Sir Stephen created an undertaking which he named 'Cockade'. The directors included R. H. Moll, Peter Barker-Mill and Richard Guyatt, Professor of Graphic Arts at the Royal College of Art. Notable among the design associates were Sir Hugh and Lady Casson, Christopher Ironside, Robert Wetmore, Frederick Dickinson, Elizabeth Corsellis, Donald Bell-Scott, Grace Bryan-Brown and Roger Hopkin. The control of workmanship in scale models and the construction of exhibitions and displays was in the very experienced hands of F. E. Ward and R. G. Basden.

In 1950 I had the honour of joining the enterprise as Production Manager, by which time it had gained an unrivalled reputation in the design world. Its clients included several government departments as well as the prominent undertakings in many branches of industry. At the design stage of the 1951 Festival of Britain Cockade held a unique position. Here, under one

Flight of plaster doves in the Lion and Unicorn pavilion.

roof, was gathered all the essential creative talent and skill necessary for the entire production of exhibits and displays. The organizers immediately called on Cockade's services for most of the pavilions on the South Bank; several projects were also commissioned by section designers at Sir Misha Black's Design Research Unit.

For the Sky section of the Dome of Discovery, Frederick Dickinson designed an extensive exhibit to illustrate the 'History of the Telescope'. Against a discreetly lit dioramic background, scale models of the telescopes of the great explorers of the heavens – from Galileo onwards – were presented in every detail, often with groups of figurines posed in admiring attitudes. As may be imagined, a considerable amount of research was entailed in this and the other displays described here. In the Sea section of the Dome, the whaling industry, past and present, was illustrated in a series of scenic dioramas by Grace Bryan-Brown. The artists and craftsmen in the studio and workshop also produced a large model of a blue whale, with little men clad in sweaters and sea-boots engaged in the gory task of 'flensing' the monster.

But one of the most amusing exhibits in the Dome was the 'Tempest Prognosticator' – a full-scale model designed by Roger Hopkin from reference to an ancient print. This elaborate and highly ornate apparatus was evolved by a certain Dr Merryweather (no epigram intended) who had observed that during the period before the onset of a severe storm, fresh water leeches tended to become particularly agitated. The learned Doctor decided to harness the physical energy of these surprisingly hysterical aquatic bloodsuckers to operate an early warning system. On the circular base of his apparatus he installed glass jars, in each of which a leech was imprisoned and attached to a fine chain that led up to a miniature belfry – from whence the tinkling tocsin would be sounded on the approach of a tempest.

In the Transport and Communications pavilion Cockade installed a very large scale model of the then projected BBC Television Centre at White City. This was built to a scale of $\frac{1}{16}$ in to the

Model of a whale for the Sea section in the Dome of Discovery.

Coat-of-arms designed by Richard Guyatt for the Lion and Unicorn pavilion.

foot, so that the little figures of men in the foreground averaged only $\frac{3}{8}$ in high – yet one of the craftsmen carved a figure which, seen under a magnifying glass, was undoubtedly Winston Churchill – complete with cigar! In the same pavilion we also erected a scale model of the TV mast at Sutton Coldfield. This was of metal lattice-work, 7 ft high and only an inch in diameter, yet a tiny lift was made to ascend and descend within the mast – and in the lift there was an electric light.

The Power and Production pavilion contained a series of dioramas designed by Roger Hopkin under the direction of the section designer, Robert Gutmann. These incorporated scale models of an ideal factory layout, as employed by Courtaulds; a typical assembly line for tractors at the David Brown plant; and the use of colour and lighting in the cloth-raising department of Hervey Rhodes factory. Cockade also made a large cut-out wall map of the British Isles to illustrate the location and concentration of industries.

Professor Richard Guyatt, a section designer for the Lion and Unicorn pavilion, designed a majestic coat of arms in brass, aluminium and steel; this was a most impressive feature, no less than 33 ft long and 11 ft high. He also designed the exquisite yellow flocked wallpaper that lined the walls of the pavilion. He was responsible for the Crown of Poetry and the English Language section of the exhibition, in co-operation with Lady Margaret Casson and Harold Bell-Scott.

For the Lion and Unicorn Professor Guyatt also designed a lofty display of great dignity to represent the British Law. This comprised a cabinet containing legal volumes, draped with a red velvet robe and surmounted by a full-bottomed wig. The sword and scales of Justice were also incorporated in this impressive feature as well as replicas of Magna Carta and the writ of Habeas Corpus. His Commonwealth feature comprised a tall mast of polished hardwood and brass, bearing a trophy of flags. In another part of the pavilion, Christopher Ironside and his brother Robin (well known as scenic designers for the Royal Ballet at Covent Garden) produced delightful model designs for scenes from five of Shakespeare's plays; these were exhibited in highly decorative metal showcases.

But the highlight of the efforts of Cockade's designers, artists and craftsmen was undoubtedly in the production of the Centenary pavilion. The section designer, James Gardner, entrusted this project to the unit and Christopher Ironside was assisted by Robert Wetmore in the overall design of the contents of the pavilion. This feature was a large-scale representation of the Crystal Palace and showed the opening of the Great Exhibition of 1851 by Her Majesty Queen Victoria. The structure of steel and glass was built on a grid platform supported on moulded pillars, adjacent to the Shot Tower. It was approached by a steel staircase and the public entered to view a large model of Victoria's court at the opening ceremony of the exhibition, held a hundred years previously.

There were no fewer than fifty figurines, each approximately 10 in high, representing the Queen, her family, her ministers, prelates, courtiers, gentlemen-at-arms and beefeaters. These were designed and exquisitely modelled in porcelain by Christopher Ironside; their robes and uniforms in authentic colour and resplendent with decorations were made by Marie Hill, Margot Burry and other artists in needlework at Cockade's studio. Research revealed that a practical joker had contrived to gatecrash the ceremony; he was faithfully included among the figurines, in his yellow silk robes of a Chinese Mandarin!

At each end of the showcase was a slowly rotating display surmounted by ostrich plumes, containing dioramas and transparencies of contemporary scenes by Elizabeth Corsellis and Grace Bryan-Brown. From loudspeakers issued the somewhat fortissimo strains of Handel's Halleluja Chorus – as performed at the original ceremony.

Throwing our entire energies into the production of Cockade's features at the Festival was an exhilarating experience. One cherishes memories of the men and girls concentrating on the design and production of the exhibits and the multifarious problems of transport and installation. There was, predictably, a considerable feeling of strain as the opening date drew near. For some reason the Board of Trade, in its infinite wisdom, decided to arrange the opening of its annual British Industries Fair to coincide with the opening of the Festival of Britain. In consequence, our designers had to work on, and I had to supervise construction of, no fewer than seven large exhibition stands at Earls Court, Olympia and Castle Bromwich. My sleeping was mainly confined to naps taken on night trains between Birmingham and London – while on the South Bank I frequently saw dawn break over the Thames.

There was tense drama when a heavy piece of equipment fell from the summit of the high Shot Tower and crashed through the specially moulded curved glass roof of the Centenary pavilion. The master glazier, seeing the expression of utter horror on my face, said quietly, 'Don't worry sir. For these special jobs we

Marie Hill with Queen Victoria and other model figures made for the Centenary pavilion.

always produce duplicates of the glass panels – just in case.'

On the 4 May 1951 the heavens opened and gave the Festival their blessing and baptism with a deluge of rain. The roof of the Transport and Communications pavilion proved somewhat leaky. I remember standing there with our managing director, Mr Moll, ruefully gazing down at the rain streaming on to our £1,000 model of the BBC Television Centre – delivery of its protective showcase had been delayed.

Yet these tragedies were almost forgotten when, in the height of summer, I took my eleven-year-old son on a tour of the Festival – he was clutching a silver Crown piece, newly minted on the site. Needing to rest, we sat down to watch a tennis match in progress at the Sports section. Every few minutes, however, we were deafened by 'HA – lleluja!' . . . 'HA – lleluja!' from the loudspeakers at the Centenary pavilion. The jubilant chorus most assuredly echoed my own sentiments – but with rather too much emphasis. I went in search of the sound technicians.

A minor mannerism in art history

CHARLES PLOUVIEZ

Employee in the Festival Office

ALMOST FRESH from university, I came into the Festival of Britain Office in 1950 like a small child into Santa's workshop. Santa himself, the late Cecil Cooke, Director of Exhibitions, was my boss. I sat in his anteroom with two secretaries, a mass of files and only a vague idea what my job was. From the back rooms of our converted mansion flats at Savoy Court, we could see our main enterprise, the South Bank Exhibition, taking shape; and the people who were creating it wandered in and out of my office with plans, maps, drawings, documents and (increasingly, as the opening date approached) crises. Hugh Casson had the office opposite, but Misha Black worked from his own firm in Mayfair and sent ceaseless memoranda. 'I never know where to file them,' said Casson's secretary, 'so I've opened a file marked "Mishallaneous".'

All the Festival exhibitions were supposed to be 'thematic' – to tell a story. Cecil had virtually invented the thematic exhibition while at the Ministry of Information, with his very successful 'Britain can make it' Exhibition at the Victoria and Albert Museum. But this was more ambitious: five simultaneous exhibitions, all thematic and all at least loosely coordinated in theme. The Director of Science, Ian Cox, had written the overall 'story' for the South Bank, the Science Exhibition in South Kensington and the miniaturized travelling exhibition on board HMS *Campania*. Then theme conveners developed their own sections of the story and organized exhibits, while architects, designers and caption writers realized their conceptions in the round.

All this took an enormous amount of co-ordination, and the thing that suffered worst was financial control. We were still in a period of post-war building inflation and materials shortages, and most of the pavilion architects ran over budget, which meant that the design budget was curtailed. One small pavilion used the entire display budget for the building shell, and we had to hunt around for a sponsored display to go inside which would cost the Festival nothing.

Apart from dogsbodying for Cecil Cooke, my job settled down into running the caption-writing programme, troubleshooting for exhibits stuck in the bureaucratic machine, and dealing with the public on matters relating to the exhibitions. We were still being offered incredible inventions and souvenirs from 1851, right up to opening day. One or two were accepted – a music typewriter developed by Miss Lily Pavey, and a large embroidered panel on the history of the past century made by women's organizations. The former went into the Lion and Unicorn pavilion, and I found a home for the latter on the stairs of the old Shot Tower.

The Council of Industrial Design, as it was then called, looked after exhibits from private firms – this was the embryonic form of what later developed into the Design Centre. But national museums had their own regulations and their own problems, chiefly manpower shortage. It took a lot of everybody's goodwill to get everything there 'on the day'. One exhibit that nearly wasn't there was Constable's *The Salt Box, Hampstead Heath*, on loan from the National Gallery. On 3 May – the day before the South Bank opened – we got a message that the picture could not be released from the gallery.

It was a beautiful bureaucratic deadlock. The gallery was not permitted to release any picture until being assured that full insurance cover had been provided. The FOB Office, equally rigidly, was not permitted to insure anything, all the exhibits being covered by a blanket government indemnity. Since all my directors were at celebratory functions that afternoon, I went to see the deputy keeper and formally took note of the gallery's requirements. We agreed that Sir Gerald Barry and Sir Kenneth Clark would be able to sort out the paperwork later, the urgent thing was to get the picture to the exhibition. So the keeper kindly called me a cab, and I escorted a fully uninsured Constable to the South Bank.

Laurie Lee was officially Chief Caption Writer, but he had written most of his allotted captions when I arrived, and been swept into organizing the Eccentrics' Corner of the Lion and Unicorn pavilion. His office up the corridor had become a small museum of oddities, and he was for ever showing off his latest finds. He sauntered into my office one day with a violin and mandoline made from used matchsticks, and together with Jim Holland, one of the chief designers, gave a spirited performance of a Telemann concerto.

The other caption writers were mostly freelance, and it was my job to get briefs to them and see that the captions were delivered and 'subbed' by the editor. Officially, this was Lionel Birch, but after his sudden resignation from *Picture Post*, his place was taken by Tom Hopkinson, who could go through a sheaf of captions with his stubby pencil faster than I could read. The most reliable writers were the poets – Laurie himself, Alan Ross and Douglas Newton. Some of the journalists were not so good, and as time got shorter I wrote quite a few captions myself. By that time, everybody was doing whatever came to hand.

On 4 May, King George opened

the South Bank. The exhibition was by no means complete, and in the Homes and Gardens pavilion a section devoted to interior lighting was in total darkness. Turning to Mr Attlee at his side, the King said, 'Another of your power cuts, Prime Minister?'

Five years after the Festival, Sir Hugh Casson was writing: '"Rather Festival of Britain, old man, isn't it?" you can still hear somebody rather nervously say about a building, an interior or a piece of furniture . . . and everybody knows exactly what he means.' Twenty years later still, I heard somebody say the same thing, not nervously at all, and I knew exactly what he meant. 'Festival of Britain' has become a minor mannerism in our art history, and at the moment a moderately despised one.

Yet it was in the field of architecture and design that the Festival achieved most. As an exhibition, the South Bank was a failure. The thematic treatment fought with the exhibits, and the whole was too indigestible for the visitor to absorb. And the exhibition itself as a communications technique was already on the way out, displaced by better colour printing, easier travel and – above all – TV. What the Festival did was to legitimize a complete generation of design thinking with the British public. In 1950 the only public building in London with pretensions to being in the modern international style was Peter Jones store in Sloane Square. LCC estates still had Peabody proportions and Georgian trim. After the South Bank, that all changed very rapidly. For better or worse – for better *and* worse – the Festival opened the door to the future. The same was true in furniture design. The furniture in the exhibitions may have been spindly, splay-legged and austere – cleaned-up 'Utility' – but even that was hard to find in the shops where sham-Jacobethan 'borax' still ruled. G-Plan took off where the South Bank ended.

At the time, and still today, the most significant achievement of the South Bank, however, was in what would now be called environmental control. The Design Group chaired by Hugh Casson planned and coordinated everything, from the Dome of Discovery to the litter bins, and especially the spaces and vistas in between, with a skill and imagination that subsequent planners have rarely shown. Perhaps there was something in the anarchic atmosphere of the department, or perhaps it was the unconscious realization that we were already a lost cause.

Because we were. Where 1851 had been deliberately international, 1951 was deliberately chauvinistic. It might almost be said to mark the beginning of our 'English disease' – the moment at which we stopped trying to lead the world as an industrial power, and started being the world's entertainers, coaxing tourists to laugh at our eccentricities, marvel at our traditions and wallow in our nostalgia. Labour's Festival of Britain begat, after a difficult gestation period, the Conservative Swinging Sixties.

And even the chauvinism turned sour. The Festival had been conceived by a vigorous Labour administration: when it ended it had become a mild embarrassment to a dying one. Press reaction had not been enthusiastic, and the *Daily Express* had been bitterly hostile throughout. American tourists had been far fewer than anticipated, because of the trauma of the Korean War. There was a row over the cost of the Festival Gardens project at Battersea. Receipts justified keeping the South Bank open into 1952, but political considerations didn't, and a series of forlorn auctions began to clear the way for the Shell Centre.

A broadcasting marathon

AUDREY RUSSELL
Radio commentator

It was stimulating from the start. It was the first time since the war that things were being planned, designed and created because they were decorative and imaginative rather than useful and economical. At early press conferences, held primarily to whip up interest and enthusiasm, the mass media cautiously watched the Festival grow. While the project had to run counter to the harsh economies of the time, even the most grudging of newsmen and women found it difficult not to get swept along by the explosion of ideas that emerged at these meetings on how to commemorate the Great Exhibition of 1851 and to pull ourselves up by our own bootstraps at the same time. Clearly it was to be an enterprise of complexity and sophistication, shot with a charming simplicity. During a long meeting on street decoration plans, one of the young designers on the platform suddenly said, 'I would like to have a bunch of flowers put in the hands of all female statues on the day of the opening ceremony.' The prospect of including, say, Florence Nightingale, Mrs Pankhurst and Lady Godiva in the festivities seemed irresistible, but from the sheer volume of notions flying around, I fear this idea was one that got away.

The BBC made extensive plans for full coverage. There was to be a radio and TV centre built into a converted garage somewhere at the South Bank Exhibition. It was also to serve the Pleasure Gardens at Battersea Park. Nearly all the main exhibition buildings were equipped with 'plug in' outside broadcast points for on-the-spot broadcasts, all of which were used extensively by broadcasters from overseas, as well as ourselves. The fact that the whole of Britain was involved in the celebrations made it a broadcasting marathon of arts, music festivals, pageants, gymkhanas and carnivals from Aberdeen to Brighton. The word 'Festival' must have appeared more frequently than any other in issues of the *Radio Times* that summer.

I have a jumbled recollection of one lengthy commentary outside London, at the Dickens Festival at Rochester. It was scenes from *Nicholas Nickleby*, done as a pageant in the grounds of Rochester Castle. I began the broadcast under the impression that it was to be a dramatization of *David Copperfield*. I scanned the green sward for Betsy Trotwood, Mr Micawber and David himself, but to no avail. I still hope that the early entrance of Mr Wackford Squeers saved the broadcast from utter disaster. No one wrote in to complain so I thankfully assume my mistake wasn't noticed.

I have other memories of a touching transformation in the middle of the town of Dover, where I had spent some time during the war. This was the inspired idea to turn the unsightly shell holes into pretty flower gardens until more permanent restoration could be begun. The most modest contributions to the Festival received recognition. A Rural District Council voting for some new litter bins or a bus shelter in honour of the occasion knew the gesture would be recorded in the huge official Catalogue and that a mention in a BBC Regional News Bulletin was most likely.

On 3 May, in the Home Service, Richard Dimbleby and I were the commentators at St Paul's Cathedral for the Service of Dedication and the Opening Ceremony by HM King George VI from the steps of the cathedral. He was surrounded by a few civic and church dignitaries and the rest of the Royal Family: the Queen, Princess Elizabeth, Prince Philip and Princess Margaret, and by the outstandingly tall upright figure of HM the late Queen Mary, who followed her son's speech with rapt attention. Although it was a cloudy grey day, it was a brilliant stroke that the King should perform the ceremony out of doors. One really felt that the occasion belonged to the whole of Britain and not merely to the capital. As a broadcast, it was an international event, described in more than thirty languages by visiting broadcasters from all over the world.

The South Bank was ready on time, waiting for the visitors and their reactions. My first impression was that the overall design of the terraces made me more aware of the river frontage than ever before, with water buses plying to and fro between the South Bank and the Pleasure Gardens at Battersea. Because the river was so much part of the scene, a great many outside broadcasts were done from high-speed motor launches (and they always seemed to go too fast for all the words I had to use to describe the animated scene on the bank). It is sad and perhaps curious that the great potential of the Thames revealed at that time has not been realized since to the same degree.

The Festival architecture made use of new materials, exciting shapes at strange angles that stood up without visible means of support. The exhibition emblem led the way in this. The Skylon was a sliver of a silvery splinter of light against the night sky. Looking back now, it was a prophetic glimpse of a soaring rocket at Cape Canaveral. The extensive use of glass was new to most of us at that time, giving a transparency to the buildings, creating fantastic vistas of a luminous, sparkling city by the river at night. It was much more than a temporary theatrical spectacle. The most important and only permanent structure on the site was the Royal Festival Hall, the first public building to be built in Britain after the war.

The first concert was held on the evening of 3 May in the presence of the King and Queen and other members of the Royal Family. The King unveiled a small commemorative plaque in the entrance hall. With his careful attention to formality and ceremony, he pointed out that this unveiling was *not* the official opening. 'I opened the whole Festival of Britain this morning,' he declared, 'I don't have to open anything else now, I am just attending the first concert.' It was an evening of elation and exhilaration. Few people had ever been in a British building with glass walls and split level floors. Everyone marvelled that the concert hall could be so successfully insulated from the noise, a few yards away, of the trains on Hungerford Bridge.

The programme of music was familiar, patriotically triumphant and magnificently performed, with Sir Adrian Boult and Sir Malcolm Sargent as conductors of an orchestra made up from no less than five very distinguished orchestras and combined choirs. The quality of sound was astonishing. As *The Times* put it next day, 'The words of the choirs were actually intelligible.' It was a bravura performance that included Handel's Zadok the Priest; Sir Malcolm Sargent's arrangement of Arne's Rule Britannia; Vaughan Williams' Serenade to Music; Elgar's Pomp and Circumstance no. 1; and the Hallelujah and Amens of Handel's Messiah.

Everything that evening went quite beautifully, everything, that is, except for one small hitch. On his way to the mayoral box, the Lord Mayor of London, Sir Denys Lowson, with his Lady Mayoress and all the aldermen and sheriffs, got stuck in a Festival Hall lift. It came about because everyone wanted to be in the same lift as the Lord Mayor. It took the engineers at least fifteen minutes to wind the lift down to ground level. By then the concert was under way and very few members of the audience were aware of the happening. Perhaps it was only the two commentators who spotted the strange sight of a mayoral party tiptoeing into the auditorium as unobtrusively as possible.

One of the things that made the greatest impression on me at the South Bank Exhibition was the aluminium Dome of Discovery (described in a quite un-British fashion as 'the largest Dome in the World') which was a tribute to the British genius for exploration and scientific discovery. It held many pointers to things we now take for granted. A major exhibit in the Dome was a giant conventional 74-inch telescope, made for Mount Stromlo Observatory in Australia. A large caption read: 'The explorers of outer space are the astronomers'. I remember wondering at the time if man would ever walk on the moon. We were rightly impressed and probably puzzled at a first glimpse of the new science of radio astronomy, watching the return of radar impulses from the moon, beamed from the top of the old Shot Tower and reflected on a screen in the Dome.

It is said that the fanciful, decorative and amusing Lion and Unicorn pavilion is the one thing people remember most about today. In terms of exhibition technique, it was certainly ahead of its time for it managed to express abstract ideas through carefully chosen exhibits. It was about our attitude to life, our love of free speech, our penchant towards eccentricity, and the ability of different social strata to be amused at the antics of each other. It reminded one of *Punch*, especially as it made use of writers and artists such as Stephen Potter, Laurie Lee, Heath Robinson, Pont, Edward Lear, Rowlandson and Max Beerbohm. It might be thought that only the intelligentsia would be charmed by all this, but there was an unerring touch in the choice of objects and in their juxtaposition. I can remember a 365-day clock by Thomas Tompion, an original edition of Dr Johnson's Dictionary, an edition of Shakespeare, one of the Bible, a tailor's pinking scissors, a model of the White Knight, with acknowledgments to Sir John Tenniel, and a corrected page proof of Winston Churchill's *History of the Second World War*. And there was greatness in the three masterpieces of English painting near the exit, forever to be remembered, by Gainsborough, Constable, and the contemporary painter Paul Nash.

This pavilion, more than any other, fulfilled the organizers' claim that the Festival was an 'autobiography of the British people . . . written by ourselves'. It certainly reflected what we were like at that particular time. We had then an innocent appreciativeness; we were hopeful for the future.

When the Festival closed on 30 September an auction sale of fixtures and fittings was held on the South Bank during the dismantling of the pavilions. I had my eye on one of the most imaginative features of the Lion and Unicorn pavilion: the flock of plaster doves, which were released from a wicker basket and looked as if they were flying straight through the glass. I managed to acquire two of those doves for a guinea apiece. I gave one to Richard Dimbleby as a souvenir of the many broadcasts we had shared. I also bought an elegant white wrought iron garden chair. When I received my purchases I realized how fragile were the plaster doves and how heavy the chair. There were no taxis to be seen and half way across the now deserted concourse the chair had to be left behind. The dove is still my souvenir of the Festival. I wonder what became of the chair.

Naming the Skylon

MARGARET SHEPPARD FIDLER

Poet; suggested the name 'Skylon' for the vertical feature on the South Bank

When the idea of the Festival of Britain was born, we were moved by the belief that a new and expanding life was opening around us after the years of war's agony, and that the joy of living would grow in our hearts again – that we could create new ways of life for all, better than the old, and that our efforts for peace would be even more glorious than our grim determination to fight to the death for freedom. A new era was beginning: we were all seeking happiness and self-expression, new opportunities to create new and exciting things – to enjoy leisure, beauty and freedom, in a society of friends who had striven together and who would now like to relax together, and then work together towards a new tomorrow.

When Mr Gerald Barry, Director of the Festival of Britain, spoke on the radio about his hopes and ambitions for the Festival, he mentioned the proposed 'Vertical Feature' – vivid, bright and shining, hanging miraculously in mid-air on the South Bank of the Thames – a symbol of hope, triumph and gaiety, piercing the sky. My husband was then the chief architect of one of our New Towns, Crawley, and we felt deeply involved in the making of the new Britain symbolized by the 'Vertical Feature'. With our son, home for the day from his prep school, my husband and I were sitting by the fire, listening to Gerald Barry's broadcast and his suggestion that a better name might be found for the 'Vertical Feature'.

As a poet, I love words, so I rallied my family to try to think up a good name for this inspired and inspiring design. We toyed with words like Skyhook and Pylon and, of course, visualized it in the London sky. Suddenly it seemed that 'Skylon' would be a good name for this beautiful and exciting adornment of the London sky, shining by day, and at night piercing the darkness with no visible means of support. We were, of course, very thrilled when this name was chosen.

My first visit to the Festival site, on the South Bank of the Thames, was on a very cold bright morning in March 1951. The BBC invited me to be present when the erection of the Skylon was almost complete. Wynford Vaughan-Thomas was to be hauled to the top of the mast in a builder's skip, so that he could broadcast a radio message to Britain and the world. I was asked to give him a few words of 'send off' and to explain how I came to suggest the name Skylon. This broadcast was relayed to other countries and I was thrilled when I learned that, by chance, my sister in New York had heard my voice on the air.

Margaret Sheppard Fidler after broadcasting with Wynford Vaughan-Thomas (right) who ascended the Skylon for a broadcast on the BBC Home Service on 30 March 1951.

Later, we visited the exhibition very often, by day and in the evening, when it glistened with light in the darkness, for it was truly a living symbol of rejuvenation. Everyone felt the stirring of new hope, because all the buildings were touched with the magic of inspiration, all the exhibits were alive with novelty and ingenuity. They were full of life and colour and really suggested the rebirth of all our hopes. They were light-hearted too, and that is why even the most staid citizens began to dance in the open air by the Thames, in the very heart of our London that had suffered and survived so much. The names of the pavilions were magic – after Dunkirk and the Blitz – the Dome of Discovery and the Lion and the Unicorn! Pubs, cafés, restaurants, with the Thames shimmering in sunlight or shining in the lights of London which had for so long been dark and secret, wounded and bleeding.

One of my quietly happy memories is of an evening on the South Bank when I was watching a glassblower making a series of beautiful glass swans. Starting with the molten glass, he built up the graceful shapes – the wings, the tails, the necks, the bills – a whole family of swans which seemed to float on his demonstrating-table in the darkening evening light. Then, giving a slight bow to his admiring audience, to my surprise, he placed a cigarette between his lips, twisted a spill of paper and looked round in vain for a light. Then, to our amazement, he touched his latest swan with the tip of the paper spill. The spill burst into flames and, to our enthusiastic applause, he nonchalantly lit his cigarette with great style. Somehow, he epitomized the whole spirit of the Festival: effort carried out with seeming ease, Phoenix proudly flaming from the ashes of war!

Design after the war

DIANA ARMFIELD

Textile designer

MANY OF US whose training had been interrupted by the war had a second chance when it was over. This second opportunity of a training in art, and the pleasure of meeting other mature students, brought a most invigorating atmosphere to the schools. Few wasted their time. Groups of close friends were made, who stimulated each other to work and study with tremendous seriousness, and these contacts were kept later in professional life.

We emerged, trained, many with quite exceptional talent, to find that the textile and wallpaper manufacturers were simply not ready for us. Some firms did have buyers, but they were drawn from the pre-war generation who had been in the habit of getting their collections from abroad, and were looking forward to the day when they could renew the pleasant twice-yearly trips. In any case, they explained, their firms had been unable to use the designs bought before the war, and they protested that it would be a waste to buy new ones before these had been gone through.

There appeared to be a total lack of design policy in some firms and even a slight mistrust of the English art-school product, who, admittedly, had not been trained to present work in the highly professional and therefore reassuring way that the French designers had done. (It used to be rumoured that French designers visiting English firms spent their evenings ironing their designs!) Things looked grey for a while, but on all sides there were people determined that the designers should find a respected place in our economy.

The new generation of designers persevered; some went into the firms' own studios, some worked on their own, some in groups. My own experience was to form a partnership with a fellow student. We became Armfield-Passano, designing, hand-printing and selling printed fabrics for furnishing and dress. We found our markets by holding exhibitions of our work in small West End galleries. Obtaining cloth to print on entailed a certain amount of jiggery-pokery as this was still the era of clothing coupons. To sustain our business it was necessary to make contact with valuable people in the textile trade who found it possible to get supplies of material in ways we didn't ask about. There was one occasion when the source temporarily dried up and we were obliged to buy best quality architects' tracing linen, dissolving away the dressing to reveal the basic fine material – an expensive way out, but necessary.

Looking back, the whole venture seems improvised, as a great deal that was enterprising was at that time. We used linoleum from battleships for block printing, which was carried out on the floor of the studio, the pressure being applied with the feet. For screen printing we had a long table made out of oak planks; we made our own screens and mixed our dyes in buckets and baths on the gas stove. Orders came from such diverse customers as the Finnish Legation, the organizers of the exhibition '40,000 years of Modern Art', the better London and provincial stores, and countless private customers. These last were supposed to provide clothing coupons for the material they bought, but were rarely in a position to do so. Fortunately the authorities – a department of the Board of Trade – never bothered us unduly about this, as long as we handed over a number of coupons each month as a gesture. There was a great deal more latitude in all such matters than can be imagined today in the age of Value Added Tax. Nylon was introduced at about this time. It was rather harsh and springy, and we had to make many experiments in order to get the dyes to 'take' properly on this new material, which a corset firm wanted printed with our designs.

The Society of Industrial Artists became very active in setting standards of work and professional conduct. The Council of Industrial Design worked to further our interests, and a few firms launched promotional schemes, one of the first being John Lines, who bought wallpaper designs and encouraged the young designers with publicity.

The training in the design departments of the art schools – much of which, in fact, pre-dated what later became known as Basic Design in Fine Art departments, some twenty years later – brought about a type of small textured pattern for printed cloth and wallpaper. Alongside this emerged the influence of mobile sculpture; carefully balanced 'mobile' motifs appeared in designs everywhere. The third trend was based on personal study of natural forms; some of the results were beautifully drawn, a fact noticed by the new generation of textile firms' buyers, who were a pleasure to take a portfolio to. These new men had an attitude not far removed from the designers themselves; they were often, in fact, people who might have liked to be artists themselves and had often had some art training. They, in their turn, were replaced some years later by men with a keener eye for fashion and business, but that was after 1951.

Into this tentative new climate came the Festival of Britain, gathering up everything of interest that was going on, stimulating and giving standards of professionalism. In its turn it crystallized some of the emerging trends. Certainly the textured and the mobile-inspired design became very much part of the Festival ambience, and, compared with many of today's fashions, lasted a long time. The Festival also marked the beginning of the current emphasis on the young; instead of being directed at the established and the middle-aged, fashion from then on set its sights on youth.

Porridge wallpaper was served notice

JOHN WRIGHT
Artist designer

CITRUS YELLOW! That is my first thought when someone mentions the 1951 Festival of Britain. This colour seemed to dominate from the moment one crossed the Bailey Bridge, which was the main approach from Charing Cross. The seats of the Ernest Race chairs, the coloured balls projecting at all angles, sections of wall, a ceiling, it was citrus sunshine all the way.

The two years prior to 1951 were, I realize now, halcyon days for the young designer just starting his career. The Design Council, then known as the Council of Industrial Design, had their offices in Petty France with balconies giving an excellent view of Buckingham Palace. By careful planning of one's visits it was a splendid place from which to watch state processions, or, alternatively, to dash round to the Westminster Catering College for lamb chops with braised chestnuts at 3s 6d. The Council of Industrial Design, during this period, was a hive of activity: 'go and see this designer or that architect', 'could you design abstract shapes for a suggested fantasy garden at Battersea?' How we worked, colliding on stairs with portfolios packed with new ideas, what excitement and how many opportunities! One now realizes with hindsight that a Festival such as that of 1951 is an oasis in one's career.

During the months preceding the Festival many letters appeared in the press, both national and provincial. I well remember a battle of words in our local paper between myself and a lady councillor; 'a sheer extravagance, a waste of public money', she declared. To a great many people however those acres on the South Bank became a vision of hope for the future: a rekindling of energy sapped by five years of war. The Meccano-like constructions which gradually took shape, this futuristic city of colour and light set amid the drab aftermath of war, became the 'site to watch', whether across the Thames or leaning out of a carriage window crossing Hungerford Bridge.

Once again life had come to this great river. For a fare of 3d passengers were conveyed by water bus to and from the Festival site, by night, passing under bridges garlanded with coloured lights to 'all the fun of the fair' at Battersea Pleasure Gardens. Visitors to the Festival could dine in the Regatta or Thames-side Restaurant. From there one admired the vast sweep of the North Bank against whose inky blackness the famous buildings of London, from St Paul's to the Houses of Parliament, took on a magical quality with the many coloured floodlights, a spectacle which became an attraction for thousands of people.

The Festival showed many aspects of industry and demonstrated new technology gained during the war. Unlike the exhibits on display in the 1851 exhibition, which portrayed the achievements of Empire and the Industrial Revolution, 1951 had a lightness and gaiety combined with a spirit of adventure which captured the country's imagination. Many of the decorative features soon became multiplied in the mushrooming coffee bars. Those coloured projecting balls on white wire were transformed into coat-hangers and lighting fitments. How we tripped over those insecure coffee tables shaped like a boomerang or toppled a pin-legged chair! Like the Festival, they were transitory.

The permanent influence upon design of 1951 was, I feel, slight. It fathered much that was bad in the mass market. Well thought-out ideas by now leading designers were exploited by many manufacturers and soon distortions of Festival impedimenta appeared everywhere. The impact of colour however remains and no longer is it considered avant-garde to have a coloured ceiling or a coloured wall. The legacy of the Festival of Britain has been to make people's homes more enjoyable by the use of colour, shape and light. The days of varnish, brown paint and porridge wallpaper were served notice in 1951. We were no longer afraid to start with white and then use any colour or combination from the rainbow. It was great fun and continues to be so.

An advertisement on wheels

DAVID J. WEBB
(assisted by Robert Wilkin)
Former London Transport employee; member of the European Bus Tour, 1950, to promote the Festival

IN JULY 1972 a group of enthusiasts, many of them London Transport employees, bought for preservation a 1950 London RT 1702 type bus. Just an ordinary old London bus you may think, but in fact it is a bus with a very interesting history. In 1950 London Transport and the Festival of Britain organizers selected four of their latest buses to publicize the forthcoming Festival by a tour of Europe through Norway, Sweden, Denmark, Germany, Holland, Belgium, Luxembourg and France, covering 4,000 miles in three months. RT 1702 was one of these vehicles, and it is the only one remaining today.

The vehicles had the words 'Festival of Britain 1951' as their destination, and over the entrance hung a Union Jack. In the space along the sides of two of the buses, between the upper and lower decks, there was an announcement in seven languages. The English version read: 'The Festival of Britain 1951. – A nationwide demonstration, by means of exhibitions, arts festivals and other events in all parts of the United Kingdom, of Britain's continuing contributions to civilisation and of her faith in her future place in the world'. Three of the vehicles had been turned into exhibition galleries with models and illustrations of the Festival. An information centre had been laid out in one of the lower decks, complete with counter, Venetian blinds, specially built furniture and thick fitted carpet, together with a record player and records of national anthems including God Save the King. The fourth bus was used for carrying spares and staff. A crew of eight London Transport staff were selected for the historic venture, the party leader being Mr Frank Forsdick.

On the 28 July 1950 buses and crew were lined up on Horse Guards Parade for the sending-off ceremony; along with them were seven of the busmen's wives to wish them goodbye. The buses were shipped from Hull and London. The first stop on the trip was Oslo in Norway where a great reception awaited them, as it did everywhere else on the tour. The trip was not all easy going, however, as the buses in some parts caused serious traffic hazards. In Oslo the overhead cables which powered the trams had to have their power switched off and the wires lifted to enable the convoy to get through. Tram services were delayed for a considerable time. Between Stockholm and Gothenburg on the west coast of Sweden traffic coming in the opposite direction had to be stopped for a distance of thirty miles.

Wherever the eight busmen stopped they were praised very highly. Letters had been sent to the Festival's Paris office and to British legations and embassies. In addition they spread fame for British busmen's manners and sense of humour. One Festival official said, 'Although they don't speak a word of any foreign language they have helped handle the crowds visiting the displays – just like a London bus conductor helps old ladies on and off.'

British tastes must surely be unique. 'The food isn't up to English standards,' said Frank Forsdick. 'We have been to many banquets and had strange dishes, but give us a bit of old English roast beef or a plate of fish and chips.' 'Wine! Give us beer,' grumbled another. His plea was answered, for when they arrived in Paris casks were waiting for them.

The vehicles finally arrived back in Britain on 30 October 1950, and the tour can only be described as a fantastic success. In three months the bus exhibition was open for 485 hours and visited by 122,000 visitors. The figures are indeed impressive: Sweden 10,000 visitors, Denmark 4,500, Germany 3,750, Holland 10,500, Belgium 17,000, Luxembourg 4,000 and France 62,750. Telegrams of congratulation were sent by London Transport, Park Royal (who made the bus bodies), AEC (engines and transmission), from the Festival organizers and many well-wishers. The buses were put on display for the next year, giving even more publicity for the Festival. After it closed the buses were converted back to their original status and looked the same as any other London bus except for two outstanding features.

Interior of European publicity bus, 1950 *(see p. 16).*

On the rear of the buses remained the original GB plates, and on the interior of both decks hung a plaque which informed passengers that they were on a bus which had travelled 4,000 miles publicizing the Festival of Britain. RT 1702 still carries both GB plate and plaques.

The years passed and the vehicles served the public admirably, but eventually, one by one, they were retired and disposed of. In 1972 it was RT 1702's turn to be withdrawn from service. Employees at Catford garage, where the bus spent most of her working life, had grown to admire the old bus. A group of them decided to buy the vehicle, fully restore and keep her for preservation. Many people heard of the venture and wished to involve themselves, so the RT 1702 Preservation Society was formed. Now members, who amount to twenty, spend much of their free time restoring and servicing RT 1702. The bus can be seen at various rallies up and down the country and has had the honour of winning a few trophies. Mentions have also been given in the local and national press.

An active part

MARGARET KNOWLES
Researcher

I GOT TO WORK for the Festival secretariat by way of a remark from a friend when I said that I would like my next job to be on exhibition work. 'What about this new Festival of Britain,' she said. I soon pined for a more active part than that at a desk in the secretariat, then run by Leonard Crainford. He was later to take on the planning of the Festival Gardens in Battersea Park, following the Regency designs of the former Rotunda adjoining the Royal Hospital – across the river – in my opinion the most tawdry of the three units: the exhibition on the South Bank; the *Campania* travelling exhibition on a converted aircraft carrier; and the Festival Gardens and Amusement Park in Battersea.

We worked from Lennox Gardens where we compiled an information library of materials, fire protection, decoration, etc. for reference by architects and designers. Then I worked as a 'non industrial and scientific research worker' or, more simply, for exhibits on free loan from individuals and museums. Industrial exhibits were dealt with by the Council of Industrial Design, and information of suppliers and their goods became the embryo of a card index used thereafter. Research included many items from the 1851 exhibition, requested by the designers, such as wrought iron railings – which we traced to the boundary of a garden at Frant. We would prepare history sheets for each item including the name of the loaner, description of the object and where it would be placed, value (for insurance – sometimes difficult to assess) and to where and when objects had to be returned. Their free loan was acknowledged in the Catalogue where they could be traced.

I was responsible, in this connection, for the Sea and Ships pavilion and silverware exhibits on the South Bank, and for the travelling exhibition on the *Campania*. The main exhibit in the Sea and Ships pavilion was a model of the *Thermopoli*, the tea clipper sister of the *Cutty Sark*, complete with the original anchor and other equipment, information for which had been difficult to find in the papers charred in the recent fires of the Blitz. Many models of ships were loaned by the Science and National Maritime Museums. My most interesting source was the Look Out, a museum of merchant seamen's trophies in converted cottages on the waterfront at Gravesend, collected, as a hobby, by a Captain Silver and his wife, charming people who were very generous with their loans.

On arrival at the Look Out, flags were hoisted on a masthead over the door, signalling 'Welcome – Come aboard'. Every room was called by the name of part of a ship, and the ship's bell rang at the appointed times. The char went by the name of 'stewardess' and when the flags on the outside and inside of the loo door were decoded, they read: 'I have sprung a leak. Leak repaired.' One long room contained the greatest collection of figureheads in the world, from the beautiful all-white Lady of the Rose and General Gordon to a luscious rosy 'Barmaid'. I felt it an occasion to walk the passage between the two rows of figureheads facing towards me. Some are now housed in the *Cutty Sark* at Greenwich.

Embarrassing moments come to mind, such as an appointment with the Head of the Crown Jewellers whom I had asked for the loan of a sceptre, requested by my designer for display in one of his sections. Seated at a very large desk, equipped with magnificent silver appointments, he froze me with his remark, 'If you proceed with your request I shall have no other resort but to report it to the Lord Chamberlain.' I did *not* proceed. Another vivid recollection is of ascending an ice-clad ladder on to the stripped deck of the aircraft carrier *Campania* moored at Liverpool, and afterwards travelling through a snowstorm through Wales to Holyhead, where there was sunshine and a disused beam engine in a dock to be measured and photographed and used as a pivot in the exhibition. The industrial research worker had been unable to trace one, and had handed the buck to me. What *was* a beam engine? I found one on view in the Science Museum. Luckily I was able to negotiate the beam engine found at Holyhead with the captain of the marine section of the railway company, over a cup of tea in his office at St Pancras Station.

Exhibits found and negotiated, the muddy site on the South Bank became my work area for the next few months. Buildings were fast going up. It was wet and cold at first, but eventually a sort of office was found for us underneath the arches of the railway bridge; next door were the security police and at the other side, in the open arch, Topolski day by day worked on a mural. It was exciting seeing the 'revolutionary' Dome and other pavilions go up. Sculptures and fountains of strange shapes appeared overnight, for this was to be an exhibition of new ideas. Instead of concrete, stone slabs were used extensively for greater foot comfort; but distances were great. I remember one morning trying to count the hundreds of model doves hanging from the ceiling of the Lion and Unicorn pavilion (before payment to the supplier) and remarking to Laurie Lee, who did so many of the captions for the exhibition, 'I shall *never* count these correctly.'

Eventually the Festival Hall and all the pavilions, each telling its separate story, were completed and equipped, the site cleared of rubbish, and the new staff to work on the exhibition site moved in. We who had worked on the preparation 'broke up' on the opening day, and to my knowledge there has never been a reunion since.

A supervisor's duties

K. MOLLIE MONCKTON

Personnel supervisor, South Bank

I WAS A personnel supervisor, in charge, together with one other of the same grade, of two hundred women working on the site for the South Bank Exhibition in all kinds of capacity – *and* of some four hundred keys, amongst other things! My duties began three weeks prior to the opening and I remained there for a month after the closure of the exhibition to assist with the clearing up – which was vast.

It was an unforgettable experience. I had forfeited the chance of becoming established in the Civil Service, in which I had worked for eight and a half years, in order that I might be able to say that I had played a part in this exhibition, the like of which would not, I knew, be seen in my own lifetime again. It took two years of relentless badgering to get them to accept me. My qualifications at the time did not match those for which they were looking. Eventually, after joining the staff in one capacity, three weeks later I was promoted to supervisor in another!

Beautiful doves hung from the high roof of one of the largest pavilions (which one escapes me). At the entrance to this one was a verse by Laurie Lee carved in stone. Inside were many interesting exhibits, quite a number on loan from the present Queen Mother. When the exhibition closed, these doves were sold. I bought two, one for a friend, and could barely stagger under their combined weight. They were extremely heavy and very well made.

In the Agriculture pavilion, I was personally responsible for getting on display two fine Shire horses from London's Dust Cart Corporation. My late husband photographed one of them *en route* from his stable in Waterloo to the show box in the pavilion. The horse was a perfect showman – no need for his keeper to lead him, he followed like a dog. Tail and mane were fully decked out, plaited with tiny pieces of straw and ribbon. He loved being on show and played up to the audience.

Many interesting people visited the

site during the six months the exhibition was open. From the verandah of the building in which we worked we became quite adept at estimating the number of visitors and could usually get to within a few hundred of the correct figure. Every evening the Royal Marines came to close the exhibition at 10 p.m., immaculate in their lovely uniforms. The last evening of all was so touching; I think there were few dry eyes by the end of the bugle's last note.

Festival spearhead

EILEEN BAILLIE

Member of staff, information desk, Ocean Terminal, Southampton

Festival of Britain information desk, Ocean Terminal, Southampton.

NOTHING COULD have been more appropriate than to place information desks relating to the Festival of Britain in the two waiting halls for passengers disembarking at the grand new Ocean Terminal at Southampton. The decade of the fifties was a golden one for shipping. The first Jumbo Jet – ultimate destroyer of the *Queens* – was not to fly the Atlantic until 1957; in Festival Year it was considered uncomfortable, risky and slightly eccentric to make the crossing by air. Yet people yearned to travel. Fettered for too long by the war, or borne compulsorily in uniform to unknown destinations, they were now free to go where they liked – and for pleasure they went by sea.

They streamed across the Atlantic in the great *Queens*, now magnificent in their Cunard livery after the grey of wartime; they came by shiploads from South Africa and South America and up from the Antipodes in splendid new liners just off the slipways, or in their old favourites restored to former luxury; and most of them landed at Southampton. Gerald Barry, when he asked the Women's Voluntary Service to staff his information desks, was right to tell us that we would be the spearhead of Festival propaganda in Britain itself.

We were busy enough in 1951, overstretched, in fact, with the demands of the Korean War: troopships twice a week or more to embark or disembark their Service families; the NAAFI Club – where we ran a different sort of information desk – crammed with soldiers waiting to sail for that distant port, supposed to be so secret, whose name was on everybody's lips – Pusan. However, the WVS are not in the habit of saying 'No' when their help has been requested; and we said 'Yes' to Gerald Barry.

The Festival opened officially in the spring; and at 8 a.m. on a fine April morning our carefully chosen teams came on duty for the first time at the Ocean Terminal. Wearing our very best uniforms, we stood behind the newly erected, gleaming desks and faced our first customers: passengers from the *Queen Mary*, just in from New York.

She was a full ship, which meant that it would be an hour or more before the baggage was ashore and sorted in the Customs Hall. Meanwhile, we hoped to attract the passengers' attention – but to our growing dismay, they took practically no notice of us. They flocked round the snack bar, the bookstall, the travel agencies, the exchange offices, the telephone booths; lounged on the tastefully coloured leather banquettes, listened to the soft piped music, looked at everything – but us. It might have been the unfamiliarity of our uniforms, for we were successively asked if we were policewomen, a first aid unit or – once only – hot gospellers.

For the next six months the valiant WVS missed neither an arrival nor a departure. As our experience grew, we realized sadly how little many of our visitors would see of Britain. The rich, with car and chauffeur waiting for them, we sought to entice from the usual tourist treadmill – London, Windsor, Stratford-on-Avon, Edinburgh – into the lesser-known byways and beauty spots. Sometimes we succeeded; and weeks later, on a sailing-day, grateful Americans and Australians would thank us with genuine warmth.

For me, the unflagging thrill was always the arrival alongside the terminal. Choice pilots, either Cunard or P & O, always seemed to bring these giant beauties in at speed. Through the glazed frontage of the Terminal one saw them sweep past, apparently about to steam on up Southampton's High Street. Miraculously, they would be stopped and berthed at exactly the right moment. Another load of passengers would shortly stream down the gangways into the waiting hall; and the WVS, automatically straightening their green-clad backs and settling their berets at a better angle, would brace themselves for action.

The Temple of Mystery, Battersea

FRANK TAYLOR ('Roy Ricardi')

Magician; performer at the Festival Pleasure Gardens, Battersea Park

THE TEMPLE OF MYSTERY, run by the late Amir Bux, an Indian magician, was situated directly beneath the well-known Big Dipper and did not open until 25 June 1951. Bette, a first-class acrobatic dancer and one of Frank Kirby's Flying Ballet aces, was my partner in a magical act; we joined Amir Bux in time for the opening of the Temple of Mystery. The company consisted of speciality acts only – dancing girls, magicians, jugglers, balancers, acrobats and the like. The pace was killing, with up to eighteen performances a day. Ten artistes came and went in two weeks and by Saturday 7 July we were left with five performers only, two dancers, Amir Bux, Bette and myself. But the show went on. Performers continued to come and go, but seldom lasted for more than two weeks.

Despite the arduous nature of fairground work, there is a fascination about it which makes one carry on, and here at the Pleasure Gardens the hypnotic influence was even greater. From the very moment I arrived, I was thrilled with its vastness. The funfair alone extended over 6 acres and included such famous rides as the Big Dipper, the Emett railway and Peter Pan Railway, the Rotor, Sky Wheels, Moon Rocket, Waltzer, Mont Blanc, Dodgems and many more, besides over a hundred smaller sideshows and the Boating Lake. This was all very exciting by day; when lit up at night it was absolutely fantastic.

The front 'flash' at the Temple of Mystery will be remembered by many visitors to the Festival. It consisted of quite an attractive stage from which the inside show was publicized. My partner Bette was a natural 'flash' well used to the business and capable of using a microphone to advantage. The various dancers not immediately engaged inside the theatre were expected to be on the outside stage as display, whilst Bette or Amir 'spieled' and entertained to 'coax' the people inside. Bette would perform a few acrobatic tricks or a conjuring trick, Amir Bux spieling in broken English and displaying his snake basket – and very occasionally a snake. However, more often than not his snake basket was empty, and I used to wonder what would happen should one of the crowd challenge him to show the snake. One night this did happen. A fairly large crowd were listening and watching Amir with his 'empty' snake basket, when a voice yelled out, 'Come on, let's see the snake then.' Amir Bux was quite unruffled and replied with no hesitation, 'Sorry, RSPCA tell me no show snake after seven o'clock.'

I entertained under my stage name of Roy Ricardi. I was called Mister Roy by Amir Bux, and was frequently honoured by being invited to sit on the floor in Indian fashion and share a meal with him. He was quite a good cook and on one occasion presented quite a banquet of exotic Indian dishes, cooked by himself in honour of Bette's birthday.

My act was a very shortened version of my stage repertoire and was mostly sleight-of-hand, so after each performance I had to quickly re-set everything for the next. The main items consisted of the Cut and Restored Rope, which was purely sleight-of-hand, originated by the well-known Eddie Victor; a sleight-of-hand version of Sympathetic Silks, where six, thirty-six inch square silks of different colours magically tie and untie themselves; and a fascinating version of Diminishing Cards, where a full pack of cards gets smaller and smaller until it finally disappears. I ended each performance with the Oriental Wrist Chopper, in which the audience see the guillotine blade slice a potato cleanly in half. The potato is then replaced by the wrist of the victim, the magician's assistant. As the blade comes down quickly the victim lets out a scream, and the audience gasp as the blade is seen to cut right through the wrist. The wrist is then shown to be quite undamaged. The effect was created by Jack Hughes – and yes, there was an element of danger in the performance.

Amir Bux also presented magic, again mostly sleight-of-hand, his *pièce de resistance* being the Miser's Dream. I can still seem to hear his broken English as he told the audience, 'You watch. Keep your eyes. I take nobody's money but mine own.' Then reaching into the air coin after coin appeared at his finger tips. He would then walk down into the auditorium, taking coins from behind the ears of the bewildered audience. Returning to the stage, he would invite a boy or girl to join him and ask them to cough into the tin, when a shower of coins would be heard to fall. Finally he would make as though to throw the contents of the tin into the audience – only proving the tin to be completely empty – the Miser's Dream. Yes, this was Amir's big act and I would like to pay him tribute as being the finest exponent of this act that I have ever been privileged to watch.

Notwithstanding the brilliance and glamour of the Festival Gardens, bad luck seemed to dog the Festival. It yielded no financial profit, and it cost the tax-payer over eight million pounds. During its run came the fall of the Labour Government and the start of the Korean War. The Festival Gardens itself had the setback of an unusually wet summer. A number of accidents took place, the most tragic catastrophe occurring on the Emett Railway. The Emett miniature railway would appear to have been the safest of rides and was usually packed with children and a fair sprinkling of adults. The engines, carriages and Far Tottering Station were all built on lines devised by *Punch* cartoonist Roland Emett. I recall the names of two of the three engines being *Neptune* and *Mother Goose*.

The tragedy which took place on Wednesday 11 July had nothing to do with the railway's design, but with human error, when two of the engines were accidentally driven on to the same track and came into a head-on collision. Fire broke out, a number of children were injured and one woman died in the wreckage. First aid, ambulances and fire engines was quickly on the scene, the fire hoses lying directly in front of the entrance to the Temple of Mystery. Performances came to a halt and a gloom settled over all of us, in fact over the whole of the Festival Gardens as the tragedy became known.

We had little opportunity of seeing the many attractions of the Festival as we were busy performing each day, except during occasional breaks and towards the back end of the season when the crowds began to fall off. One most interesting side-show presented a unique stunt. A girl in the minimum of attire, just panties and bra, was sealed in a block of ice. The ice was hollowed out sufficiently to take the girl horizontally. A nurse, or at any rate a female dressed as one, was always at hand and kept a close watch on the girl, giving the order when to release her. I cannot recall the length of time the girl would remain in her casket of ice, but I know the time was recorded and an attempt was being made to beat a previous record. Professional secrets are closely guarded, and even if I knew whether this was a fake or not, I would not reveal it. But I do not know.

A week in the life of a cow

V. L. FORD

Farmer, whose cow was chosen for show in the South Bank Exhibition

THIS IS THE STORY of Carswell Orange Blossom, one of the Jersey cows who achieved distinction by being selected for exhibition at the 1951 Festival of Britain.

She came from a very old family in a very old herd, started originally in 1912 by my parents, with the purchase of two Jersey cows, to provide rich milk and cream for the household. My parents had recently acquired the lovely old house of Carswell Manor, in Berkshire, a house whose antecedents were said to go back to the Domesday Book, and where Alwold, Chamberlain of William the Conqueror, is reputed to have lived. Subsequently more Jersey cows were bought, and the Carswell herd was founded, domiciled at Carswell Home Farm.

The herd consisted mainly of two families of cows and their descendants. The first name of one family, after the herd prefix of 'Carswell', was always 'Pax' – the first Pax was born on Armistice Day 1918 – and that of the other family 'Orange'. Carswell Orange Blossom's ancestress was a lady called Elm Orange, who was born in the Island of Jersey in 1917, and joined the Carswell herd in 1920.

The herd had rather a sad history. The original owner and founder was killed on active service in France in 1917, and his son, who inherited it, became a bomber pilot in World War 2, was posted missing on a raid over Germany and never heard of again. The herd then passed to the last owner's sister – writer of the present article – and her husband. It was transferred to Great Bramsket Farm in Hampshire, where Carswell Orange Blossom was born in March 1943, a lively, healthy young creature with a rapacious appetite.

Her life during her early years was peaceful and uneventful – save for the flying bomb which passed over the farm one day, but fortunately came down in a field some miles away. Then her owners, who had become very interested in the forthcoming Festival of Britain, decided to offer a choice of their two best cows for exhibition there. A panel of judges, one of whom was the president of the Jersey Cattle Society, came to the farm to inspect the two animals, and their choice fell upon Carswell Orange Blossom.

When the day came for her departure to the South Bank – she had never been off the farm before – she was loaded on to the cattle transporter sent to fetch her without raising any objection to the procedure, and off she went on her great adventure. She spent a week at the Festival, during which time she was very well looked after, and was taken for a walk every day. During her stay, she was visited on more than one occasion by her owners, but she gave no indication of pleasure at the sight of them.

After the Festival, it was decided that she might do well in the showring, which proved to be the case. She attended many shows, including the Royal Show at Windsor and the Dairy Show in London, and won a number of cups and other prizes. But she was not only distinguished by good looks. She gave over 100,000 pounds of milk during her lifetime, and produced a number of children of both sexes, though none of them of the calibre that she was herself.

Eventually the day came when the years caught up with her, and she ceased to bear children or even to give any more milk. However, she and her aged half-sister, Carswell Thrift, lived on peacefully together at the farm, where they both ended their lives on the same day in February 1959.

I will conclude by recalling the very enjoyable memories I have of that 1951 Festival, the most outstanding exhibition of that nature I have ever been to – chiefly because the sight of so much that was new and unusual, bright and beautiful, after all the shabbiness and shortages of the war years and afterwards, was, in addition to being extremely interesting, such a tremendous uplift to morale.

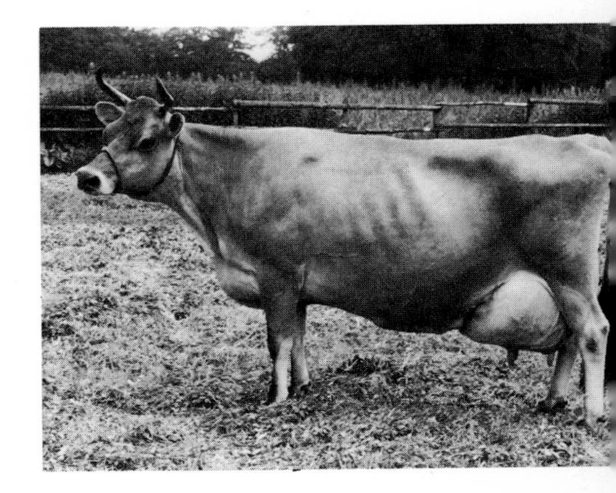

Carswell Orange Blossom, a Jersey cow.

Visitors and Abstainers

Seaside section, South Bank: visitors enjoy the river scene.

South Bank

This poem, written by George MacBeth as a schoolboy, won third prize in the North-East Regional Festival of Britain Competition.

I pass through pavilions, the slightly bored visitor,
Nibble an ice at a kiosk, obtain my souvenir.
Where do we go to next? We consult the guide:
'Homes and Gardens' it seems. The emphatic Theme,
Officiously omnipresent, exploits our apathy.
Gaping like sheep we shamble admiringly round,
Dutifully paying our little coins of praise:
'So well proportioned, down to the smallest detail' –
'Quite a treat' – 'O marvellous, really, my dear!'
I hear faintly. The vaguely phallic statue
Surreptitiously scratches itself. I smile,
In the lovely hair of the Nereid spotting lice:
The rather depressed look of the dome: its diffidence:
The finicky skylon confessing its failure on legs:
The Festival Hall on its very best behaviour.
I yawn, moving inside. Each hired exhibit
Self-consciously poses for me, an embarrassed nude.
I slide out. Evading the vigilant Theme
I turn to the main fairway and make for home
While the crass fountains spell Mock in the air.

G. M. MacBeth

A monument to the future

BRIAN ALDISS

1951 IS NOW AN ancient enigma which we decode with difficulty.

If today's generation could walk round the South Bank of 1951 today, as we can walk round Stonehenge, they would find themselves asking – as we do of Stonehenge – 'What was it a monument *to*?'

Unlike Stonehenge (presumably), and unlike its illustrious predecessor, the Great Exhibition of 1851, the South Bank Exhibition was a memorial to the future. The Skylon and the Dome of Discovery, architecturally non-functional, were structural expressions of a hope that the British would break through their psychosis of war and austerity into freer air. But what was 1951 a monument to?

We were hardly out of uniform in 1951. Indeed, we had started re-arming; army lorries still trundled through Britain's grey villages as in the forties. There was a war in the Far East which could at any time involve us all. Many of us were not long demobbed, and the talk of the time was still about the war, its heroisms, its shortages, its excitements. I turned up at the South Bank in my old demob mac; with its football buttons, belt, shoulder straps, it looked much like a uniform.

What I was after was a glimpse of the future. All the bright and flimsy architecture was great – anything different was great – but what I most wanted to see was Grey Walter's electronic tortoises. So, first, to the Science Museum where they were housed. The electronic tortoises were animals begot between a new science, cybernetics, and a new technical development, automation (both labels coined during the forties). These chelonian hybrids were clumsy creatures of metal, not at all prepossessing to look at, but they did something that no mechanical had done hitherto: they pottered about their cage and, when they were feeling hungry, returned to their power source and replenished their batteries of their own accord. Not only did they have feedback; inbuilt infra-red cells ensured that they did not bump into each other during their wanderings. Suppose these creatures to be the first lumbering amphibians of the Devonian period, then the Apollo space rockets of the seventies are the ferocious allosaurs of the Jurassic; evolution among the servo-mechanisms has been amazingly rapid, and one of the hallmarks of the past quarter-century.

Although I understood how the metal tortoises worked, I wanted to see them for myself – to feast my eyes on them, in that expressive phrase. So I did. Squat, unlovely, but full of significance, they sat in their unlit tank, unmoving, gathering dust. A notice on the exhibit said 'Out of order'. More than I knew, it was the shape of things to come. The hibernation was not of technology but of British industry.

Under the Bovril advert in Piccadilly Circus there was at that time a dramatic sign which read 'Export or Die'. Some years after it was gone, an American friend, who presumably felt nostalgic for it, asked me, 'What happened to it?' 'We died,' I said. Despite the bravado of the Festival, Britain never quite recovered from the war, for reasons compounded of all manner of factors, psychological, socio-political, technological and geographical. But in 1951 we were convinced we were convalescent; the Festival was our first walk out of hospital alone, getting a breath of fresh air.

The South Bank Exhibition was laid out as an educational spread. There was a correct way to go round the exhibits, a specific way which would make everything clear. Lord Reith no doubt approved. Deviate from page order of this mighty scrapbook and, warned the catalogue, 'some of the chapters will appear mystifying and inconsequent.' My first wife and I were in London for a few hours only, had scrounged a day off work to come up, and were unable to take the proper route. As a nation, we were still used to discipline, but the long queues made recommended procedure impossible. Besides, being mystified was pleasurable.

The chaps who took the 'Elevator to Outer Space' with us were mystified. They were mystified by the splendid working model of the solar system, which showed the planets with their full company of satellites. 'Coo, don't they come close,' one man said and, after a moment, 'That's us in the middle, the big one with the others going round it.' Copernicus had lived and died in vain. His friend contradicted him. 'No, it's not, because where's the moon, eh?' (authentic 1951 dialogue, transcribed in my diary at the time).

In the Transport pavilion were cars with glass bodies, revealing their Morris Motors intestines, as well as a Cyclemaster. I was pleased to see that. I had just acquired a Cyclemaster, 'the magic wheel that wings your heel'. It fitted into the rear wheel of your bicycle and sped you along at fifteen miles an hour, making your turn-ups oily. Everyone thought everything was wonderful. The front of the Science Pavilion had stepped off a science fiction magazine cover. I bought a postcard of it. I still have it, together with some cuttings from the *Daily Telegraph* of the time, the headlines of which appealed to me. 'Pig Shoots Butcher', and, my favourite, 'In Laughing Fit I Killed Her'. And there's a story about an Irish lodger who hid under his landlady's floorboards for three weeks because he couldn't pay the rent.

The science was well presented. It reinforced my feelings that technology, and the western way of thought shaping and shaped by it, was an integral part of life, not just one of its departments. Evidently the message did not get across on an effective scale; people still think of science as something apart – like religion, perhaps. It is a pity that the exhibition could not have been permanent; the South Bank was more stimulating than the windy expanses of concrete which replaced it. The Land of Britain was a particularly striking exhibit, with a display designed by James Holland. It showed the history of the earth in brief, dramatic form. Although it could offer nothing as overpowering as the typhoon you walked through in the Mitsubishi Tower at Expo 70 – unforgettable, that – I came away with one piece of knowledge which illustrates graphically the brevity of man's history. Following full-size models of Stone Age men doing their stuff with flints and antlers, was a Bronze Age group: fine-looking people, ornamented and bronzed (what else?). A notice told you that this was only two hundred and fifty generations ago.

It is a very brief period. Humanity does not evolve as rapidly as electronic tortoises.

We had taken sandwiches to the exhibition to save expense. We ate them on a bench in light drizzle. It was only the weather that took our pleasures sadly – we enjoyed the tipping fountains, spilling gallons of water at random intervals. We took photographs with my father's Ensign camera, all of which turned out badly. Many Americans were there, photographing continually. In those days, you could tell Americans because they were healthier and wore at least two cameras to punctuate their broad stomachs.

Later in the afternoon, we took a water bus to the Battersea Pleasure Gardens, passing the fairly new power station on which I lavished what was then my best prose:

> No human hand had touched this devil-dedicated palace. Up and up it rose, unadorned, windowless and soulless, complete in its own surly strength, with four great chimneys capping it, chimneys like pillars supporting – nothing. Before it, dwarfed by it, yet dwarfing us, stood six cranes like skeleton vultures from an interstellar age, silent, black, unmoving.

At the gardens, we watched a punch-and-judy show. And we admired the Piper and Lancaster kiosks, and the Emett railway to Oyster Creek and Far Tottering.

Then it was time to hurry for Paddington and the train home.

The fifties are remembered as a time of greyness, when the austerities of war were imposed on us without its mitigating drama. We had rationing, with 2d a week lopped off the meat ration in 1951, clothes and sweet coupons, petrol restrictions, endless shortages. Another war raged in Korea, and many of us on 'Z' Reserve who had served in World War 2 were expecting to be called up again to fight the Communists in that miserable peninsula hanging from the frozen belly of Manchuria. As the Festival opened, the British Government sent a cruiser to cow Abadan; the Shah laughed and nationalized the oil industry. We were conscious of rapid changes but the threat of the H-bomb shrank our imaginations.

The cities of England in 1951, not least its capital, were dominated by gloomy nineteenth-century buildings and bomb sites. Today we may be fond of Victorian architecture because it no longer appears to menace us with its funereal-and-marzipan pomposity; we have diluted it with beautiful structures like the Vickers Building and Centre Point. I'm sure a trip in a time-machine to 1951 would re-awaken a hatred for the overdressed pretentions of Victoriana. To it, and the rat-infested ruins created by the war, the clarity of the South Bank in '51 came like a bite of lemon at half-time.

Our response to the past is necessarily personal, for in a sense we recreate it in our own image, or recall only our own spoor through its jungles. Yet that decade, 1945–55, would surely get the vote for one of the dreariest decades in recent history.

I'm convinced that when we look at the ugly photographs of 1951 we see not only the war that threatened, the war that was over and the war before that, but also the long war which had been England's peace, and which raised the meanest houses for those who did the most essential work. We now have to decipher 1951 like Linear B, with its cryptic references to the once-living: George VI, Baden-Powell, Stalin, Tommy Handley, Aneurin Bevan, Trygve Lie, Gillie Potter, Klaus Fuchs, Farouk, George Orwell, Betty Grable, Smuts, my father. How should we call it back?

Best to cross ourselves, think of the phallic Skylon, and pass on.

We saw the future

JOHN MACKAY

I STAGED A PROLOGUE to our visit to the South Bank Exhibition by first taking my wife to Aldgate Tube Station.

In the closing phases of World War 2 I had been moved from the north of Scotland to Rainham in Essex and on short leave took the Tube to London. Having heard of the devastation in the East End, I chose Aldgate for a stopping place and clearly remember coming up to street level, looking across the road at an apparently whole office building to wonder what all the fuss had been about – until I crossed the road and looked west . . . there, no building stood between me and St Paul's Cathedral. And its great dome seemed a long way off across that desert of broken masonry.

The scene in 1951 looked exactly the same. On that visit to Aldgate we saw the past. The late evening of that same day, we stood on the Embankment, on the north side of the Thames and, looking across the river at the myriad lights on the South Bank mirrored in the water – there we saw the future.

Next day, we went to the exhibition. Twenty-five years on, memories persist in a mixture of unimportant detail and enduring impression. Did we really walk through the floodlit foliage high on the trees in Battersea Park? And sail back on the dark river to Westminster? Did we actually see John Slater telling a story on the still novel medium of television – his face repeated over and over again on a collection of expensive sets on one of the stands?

More enduring, that feeling akin to awe on approaching the Dome of Discovery, and of walking into an empty Festival Hall, those strange balconies, the *newness* of everything, typical of that whole strange complex on the South Bank. There was, too, some sense of pride in knowing that Scottish artists and architects had contributed – and with that, a further-back personal memory of myself in the 1930s as an evening student at the Edinburgh College of Art, having a young man pointed out to me as a lad of promise: 'That's Basil Spence', I was told.

There was the grace of a past world too. Was it in Westminster Hall that the story of Parliament's history was mounted? All I can remember was how splendid, how unique the manner in which all was unfolded and (to use an outdated phrase), in this Heart of Empire, how appropriate the background music of Walton's *Crown Imperial*.

In that same vein, the exhibition in the *Punch* offices off the Strand: the courteous way we were personally taken up and shown the table where the next week's cartoon was traditionally discussed – the carved initials of famous contributors on that table and the display of original drawings of long admired masters of the pen and ink – admired for their draughtsmanship as well as their humour.

The sound of Walton's *Crown Imperial* still marching across the memory and that visit to *Punch* – that was the *good* past. The South Bank was the future; and that is the abiding impression of that brief visit to London, of how the exhibition would influence the arts and industry in the years to come. That hope for a new and better Britain, at least the promise of it was there, then.

Sailing to the 'Fostivol'

ANGUS McGILL

I SHOULDN'T have been hard up in 1951. I was a reporter on the local paper and earning £7 19s 6d a week, an enormous sum, and I was living at home. I didn't drink much or smoke at all and I didn't know any wild wild women so where did all the money go? My mother said it just burned a hole in my pocket but, as I tried to explain, everything was very expensive in 1951.

For instance my new drape jacket had cost me £5 17s 6d and my new suede shoes that I hadn't dared wear yet for fear of being whistled at cost £3 10s. It was prices like these that had left me with next to nothing to spend on my holiday, my great holiday, long planned, much discussed and now only a few days away, the holiday that was to take me to the Festival of Britain.

We knew all about the Festival of Britain in South Shields. The *Gazette* was full of it, and on the BBC Home Service Mr Stuart Hibbert seemed to talk of little else. The Skylon, the Shot Tower, the fantastic Dome of Discovery, the astonishing Festival Hall, they were famous all over the world, and in only a few more days I'd be seeing them for myself.

But money! What was I to do for money? I had £11 in the Trustee Savings Bank, far more than usual, but the fare to London was £3 13s 8d, third class return, and bed and breakfast at the Strand Palace Hotel, where I intended to stay, was a whopping 17s 6d a night. Would £11 last me a week? 'It just burns a hole in your pocket,' said my mother.

Then I had two tremendous breaks and every problem disappeared.

First came my friend Frank's announcement that he was coming too. He was also a reporter on the paper but he came from London and his parents lived in Hampstead and they said we could stay with them. Free. Fantastic.

Then I was sent to interview an old sea captain, the master of a collier, on the verge of retirement after sixty years at sea. He was a small, square man with a red face and thin white hair, and he had spent his entire career in one sea lane, the one connecting the Tyne with the Thames. Every week for sixty years he had sailed from South Shields to London with a cargo of coal and back again with a cargo of ballast and now his next trip was to be his last.

As he talked I had a wonderful idea.

'Do you,' I said casually, 'ever take passengers?'

'Sometimes . . .' he said.

'Do you think it might be *possible* . . .?'

And yes, he did think so. If the owners agreed. I rang them up the minute I'd handed in my story. Yes, they said, why not? No charge but tip the steward ten bob for his extra work. Have a nice time. Why not visit the Festival of Britain while I was about it?

So it was that the following Monday night Frank and I boarded the old boat at Tyne Dock, me with my new drape jacket and my new suede shoes carefully packed in my demob suitcase, also new.

The captain seemed surprised to see us.

'What do you want then?' he said.

I said we were the reporters from the *Gazette*. Didn't he remember? We were his passengers, I said.

'Passengers?' he said. '*Passengers?*'

A small fat man appeared at his side. He seemed in a very bad temper.

'What's this then?' he said.

'They say they're passengers, Alf,' said the captain.

'Oh *no*!' said Alf. 'They haven't sent us bloody passengers! That's the limit, that is, that's the bloody limit, that's all, that's what that is.'

'Well you'd better look after them,' said the captain, wandering off.

'Oh yes,' said Alf. 'It's *me* that has to look after them, oh yes!'

I said I was awfully sorry but I had rung up the owners and . . .

'*Oh* yarss,' said Alf. 'Ay'm offlay sorray. Well won'tcher kayndlay step this bleedin way.'

We followed him to a small cabin and lay on our bunks for the next hour, sure that the dreadful Alf would be back at any minute to chuck us off.

Then we heard the engine throbbing and felt the boat moving off. We raced to the deck. We were moving splendidly downstream towards the gap between the piers and there was the Town Hall clock and there was the groyne and hello lighthouse and then with a lurch and a shudder the North Sea grabbed us and shook us. Now they couldn't put us ashore. We were truly on our way to the Festival of Britain.

We soon exhausted the possibilities of the deck. The ship seemed mostly black tarpaulin and the coast a low black line of nothing in particular. Sunderland, I supposed. So we went back and lay on our bunks again until Alf poked his head in and said he hadn't got all day so *come on* won't you.

We followed him to the saloon. An elderly man and a boy were eating bacon and baked beans. They didn't even look up.

'This is the engineer so watch it,' said Alf mysteriously and produced bacon and baked beans for us too. And thick white bread and butter and hot sweet tea. It was delicious.

We ate in silence. Finally I ventured a remark.

'We are going,' I said, 'to the Festival of Britain.'

Alf gave a whoop of delight. 'The Fostivol of Broton! We'ah gooing to the Fostivol of Broton!'

I didn't speak again until I got back to the cabin. 'Do I really speak like that?' I said, fuming.

'Yarss,' said Frank.

Next morning we awoke to a curious silence. The engines had stopped. So had everything else. We pulled on some clothes and went on deck – you never saw such fog! It swirled around us just as it did in movies about Jack the Ripper.

Alf materialized with mugs of tea.

'Look,' I said, 'how long is this going to last? I mean we've only got a week's holiday.'

Alf raised his eyebrows and drew down his lips in a parody of Edith Evans as Lady Bracknell.

'The Fostivol,' he said, 'will wait.'

This was, as it happens, some comfort. We sat there on that bit of sea all day and all night and all next day and all the day after that. We may have moved forward a bit but if it was more than six inches I'd be surprised. The engineer and the boy never uttered. The master was nowhere to be seen and Alf got more and more sarcastic.

'Oh here-ah we come,' he would say as we arrived in the saloon for supper. 'On ah way to the Fostivol of Broton.'

Frank and I lay on our bunks and lay on our bunks. We ran out of things to read. We ran out of things to say. The trip had assumed a dreamlike quality. We would spend the rest of our lives in that fog patch on the North Sea.

'Why didn't we go by train,' said Frank. 'If only we'd gone by train. If we'd gone by train we'd have been at the Festival two days ago.'

'The Fostivol,' I said, without conviction, 'will wait.'

On the fourth day we woke up to feel the boat surging magnificently forward and there, out of a porthole, was a warehouse sliding past. Then a crane. Then a mud flat. Could we believe our eyes? We were actually going up the Thames. We'd arrived!

We raced to the deck and alleluya, there, directly ahead, was Tower Bridge. We sailed under it and under another bridge and another and then it was Waterloo Bridge and, my God, there they were, the Shot Tower, the Skylon, the fantastic Dome of Discovery, the amazing Festival Hall.

It had taken us just four days to get there. It was four *hours* by train. But the money we'd saved!

Alf appeared. He actually smiled at us.

'There we are then,' he said, nodding to the Festival Hall. 'I thought I'd go this afternoon. Why don't you come?'

We paled. What a shame, I said, I had to see an aunt and Frank said he didn't think that he'd bother with the festival after all.

'Oh dear-ah,' said Alf, himself again. 'Ay won't both-ah with the Fostivol!'

We were there that afternoon of course. But we didn't see much. We spent all our time thinking we'd spotted Alf and hiding round corners.

We saw a lot the second time though and we really enjoyed ourselves the third time. Alf, as we well knew, was half-way back to South Shields by then.

A Festival visitor malgré lui

GEORGE CLARKE

WE CAUGHT THE TRAIN (8.40 a.m., I think) from Preston to Euston on Thursday, 17 May 1951. Joe Dale and I had been friends from early school days and now here we were travelling to Aldershot to report to our King who desperately wanted us to join his Medical Corps. Our principal qualifications for this were that we were eighteen and had been certified fighting fit by a host of doctors who had examined us in what used to be the local skating rink.

On the same day, there were hundreds of us converging on London, and the majority of us carried the common badge of the National Serviceman – a brown paper, Co-Op carrier bag. It was pointless taking a case because we were not to be allowed to wear civilian clothes for six months and, to ensure this, the clothes in which we travelled would be sent home by the Army as soon as the King had given us our first suit of denim overalls to be worn over his gift of a green vest, green knickers and barbed wire socks.

In preparation, we had all had a special haircut (in the hope that it would save the Army the trouble) and so it was fairly easy for us to identify kindred spirits as they straggled along the platform at Euston. Only one or two of us had ever travelled on the Underground before and so, using our travel warrants as tickets, we shepherded the now swelling party into the labyrinth of tunnels. Not all of us were reporting to the RAMC depot – our conversations had revealed that some were going into the Lancers, some into the Guards, some into the REs and some into the Royal Artillery. We sat facing one another in the Underground like parachutists waiting to drop through the hole in the floor of the fuselage. The potential Guardsmen left the train along the route and we, Aldershot and Woolwich bound, alighted at Waterloo.

The tension was building up and the carrier bags were looking much the worse for the nervous clutching they had suffered on the journey. It was something of a relief when a very smart officer in a grey uniform faced, as I recall, with red piping, approached us and asked where we had come from. 'Lancashire, sir.' 'Good,' he replied, 'follow me.' He turned about and our 'party', now numbering twenty to twenty-five, fell in and tried to look soldierly as we followed him up a rather grand, decorated stairway at the top of which stood another officer, similarly dressed. This wasn't too bad; nobody had shouted at us yet; no mention had been made of our inadequate haircuts and the fellow at the top of the stairs was actually smiling.

In a fairly friendly voice he called out 'Have your tickets ready now!' Tickets? We exchanged baffled glances and then Joe quickly set the correct example by brandishing his travel warrant. We all followed suit and arrived at the top of the stairs where our 'officer' turned round with his back to a turnstile. Spreading his arms, he instructed us to lead on through the turnstile. Well, this was novel – joining the King's army resembled going to the Saturday football match.

The first man to join stepped up and offered his travel warrant – 'What's this?' said our 'officer' in a less friendly tone; 'aren't you Lancashire chaps on a bulk ticket?' Plainly, something was wrong and it took a few questions and some heated answers to clarify the situation. Our 'officer' was an attendant at the Festival of Britain: he had met the wrong Lancashire party and taken us to the special entrance into the Festival site which led from Waterloo Station.

Of course, I visited the Festival again – later in the year, September or October, when I had been transferred to the Army X-Ray School at Woolwich; but, as a 24s a week soldier, I was somewhat limited in my ability to enjoy the side-show and entertainment aspects of that wonderful display of British public relations capability. Certainly, that autumn, it became a place where the many soldiers based in and around London could always rely on finding some feminine company.

Grotesque to say the least

BERESFORD EGAN

THE FESTIVAL OF BRITAIN 1951 suggested to my pictorial mind a female skeleton arrayed in a Josephine coat of Commonwealth colours, banging a tambourine with Salvation Army zeal, and hiding her grinning skull behind the toothpaste smiling mask of a dumb blonde. Grotesque, to say the least of it; tawdry in its conception; macabre in its timing.

There is no shadow of a doubt that we were not yet at peace with the world. Husbands, fathers, brothers, sons and lovers were still being slaughtered in Korea – which struck me as a somewhat discordant note in the tin-pan symphony of jubilation. What, indeed, was there to be jubilant about? The fact that bomb sites were abandoned to the weeds, while the Dome of Discovery and the Skylon were being erected on the South Bank? Anyway, for all actively concerned, it must have been enormous fun squandering public money on ineffectual frivolity when there were so many more important things requiring immediate attention.

But what of us ordinary citizens in this extraordinary era? It would be misleading to picture the entire population hopping and skipping, popping balloons, brandishing bunting, shouting 'Rule Britannia!' and strewing the landscape with paper streamers. Not everybody crossed the bridges of Hungerford and Waterloo, Chelsea, Albert and Battersea to gawp and gambol on the bedizened South Bank. To many of us, in view of the circumstances, the Festival of Britain 1951 was an altogether un*fun*ny af*fair*.

An incident in the Grotto

GWENDOLINE WILLIS

FOR MANY YEARS after 1951, Chinese lanterns along the Battersea waterfront symbolized the colour, warmth and gaiety to be found in the Festival Gardens and Funfair, constructed in

Battersea Park for the Festival of Britain. At night, the lanterns glowed romantically and the sound of music drifted across the water to Chelsea.

It was fun to cross Chelsea Bridge and enter the enchanted world of the gardens, hung with fairy lights. Romantic, too, to ascend the Tree Walk and wander – some 20 ft above ground – among the branches of the tall trees that bordered the main drive through the gardens. Glow-worms lit the way and there were fairy folk at the turnings. The return to earth was made with some reluctance.

Further along was the Mississippi Steamboat, moored on the riverside promenade. Paddles churning, hooter sounding, it realistically evoked the American Deep South; so much so, that I often wished it were even more real and could steam up and down the Thames.

Striped-canvas booths in the main drive sold souvenirs of all kinds as well as candyfloss, toffee apples, rock, sizzling hamburgers and coffee. You could even have your fortune told.

The funfair itself was a mad whirl of merry-go-rounds of all kinds and the traditional side-shows of a fair. A favourite of mine was the Water Splash, where half-a-dozen cars ascended a steep ramp, circled on the level at the top, and then descended a slope at ever-increasing speed to splash down in a large pool of water! The spray they sent up was exhilarating.

Also in the funfair was the Crazy House, leaning drunkenly to one side in a rather endearing manner. Within, all was hilarity as people encountered incongruities and absurdities – such as cobweb curtains – not usually met with in a house.

In the afternoons, the Guinness Clock in the gardens was a mecca for nursemaids and their charges. Just before the hour, at which all the characters on the clock's face came out and performed, they would gather round. The show took some while, and then it was time to go home for tea.

The Children's Zoo was also very popular. Here, a charming chimp once offered me some of the cake it was eating from its dainty paw. I did not accept, as she (I am sure it was a she!) was in an enclosure, and it might have been dangerous to do so, but it was a very sweet gesture.

Pony rides along a sanded path in the Festival Gardens, among the always beautifully tended flower-beds, were another attraction to the young. Ecstatically clinging to the most adorable ponies, they were led up and down by dedicated young women in jodhpurs – sometimes by young men.

In this part of the gardens was the mystic-sounding Grotto of the Four Elements (Earth, Air, Fire and Water). An amusing incident occurred when I visited it. It was a quiet afternoon and I noticed only one other person as I descended into the Grotto through mist, past a waterfall and gigantic vegetation, seeing the flames from a distant volcano and hearing its rumblings. Having got to the bottom, I thought I would return to the top and, as there was hardly anyone about, see it all again from a different angle. Accordingly, I rose up through the vapour and greenery – to the consternation of a party entering at the top who must have thought they were seeing the Grotto's nymph! However, I gave them a very substantial smile on reaching the top, and they seemed relieved to find I was human!

Encouragement for artists

G. S. WHITTET

DATES DON'T ALWAYS produce much in the way of print-outs from the memory computers of our minds. 1951 by itself signifies little. 'The Festival' on the other hand conjures up instant 'frames' from that great visual epic. Once in the forties the South Bank had been lit up by a great bonfire display (friendly this one) to celebrate the victories of Europe and Asia. In 1950 it was still a mess of seedy slums, bomb sites of rubbish made tolerable only by the magenta blooms of the ubiquitous bay horse meadow sweet. The good new days had not yet arrived, but a feeling in the atmosphere signalled they were on their way. It took a journalist to set the optimism alight, disproving the accusation levelled at our profession so often: 'They know everything and understand nothing.' I did not meet Sir Gerald Barry then but some years later we were both members of a press party flown from Gatwick to Manchester, guests of Granada and Lord Bernstein, and Barry's personality was such that I wondered how he had inspired such a brilliant event. But there it was, growing every day. I was then managing editor of *The Studio*, and if I were lunching in a Strand pub near my office I often looked across the river and saw the new exciting horizon taking shape beside the old Shot Tower. It was a good sensation.

Prior to the opening I frequented the Festival Press Office and two vivid recollections stay with me. One was a jolly interlude when the small room rang to the twanging guitar and rubicund voice of Laurie Lee singing what seems at this distance to have been a rumty tumty Gloucestershire calypso. Maybe *Cider with Rosie* would have made a good musical. It struck a note of the spirit of gaiety that pervaded everything. Believe it or not, I don't think there was a bloody-minded strike of any dimension. I can't even remember a Tory MP bleating about the waste of public money even though the meat ration was only 1s 2d, equal to about six new pence. How in the name of little apples did we live and, relatively, so well? Beer was flowing, of course, and I quaffed a Festival Ale or two. Another impression that lingers is of a press conference when a question was asked about the Festival and the spokesman called upon to answer did so with such brisk, assured and fluent delivery, in a fluting tintinnabulation of tones suggesting Rhondda via Oxbridge, that I made a mental note that he would go far. In the sound-wave propagation of the spoken word – now seen to be spoken so beautifully – he has soared. The voice and the persuasive manner were those of Huw Wheldon.

My field being contemporary art, the Festival made a day and more. Then as now I wrote a monthly critical commentary on London art exhibitions. All the South Bank pavilions had their murals, some more than one. Those that made their mark in print I find were James Boswell's fishes in a section of the sea, Victor Pasmore being decorative and interesting in his spiral whorl motives for a riverside restaurant, Josef Herman setting his seal on coal miners that made his name and fame for the record.

Portrait Group *by Rodrigo Moynihan, ARA.*

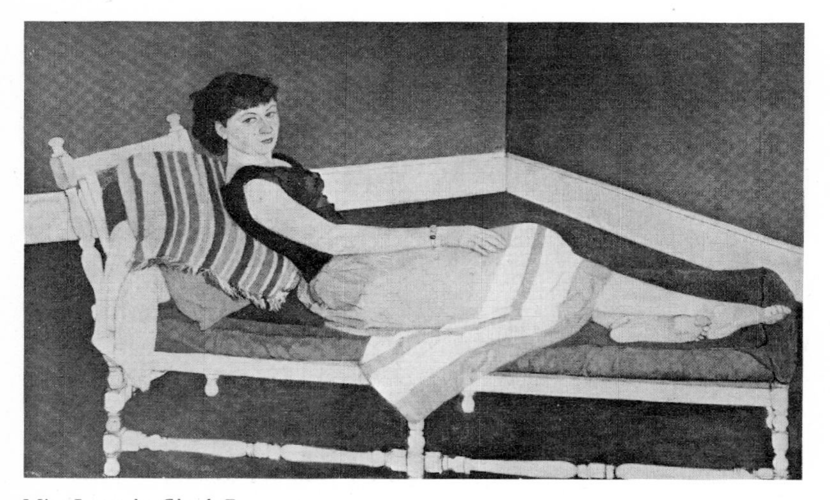

Miss Lynn *by Claude Rogers.*

Naturally the figurative artists came off best in the public arena. For the only occasion in my experience painting and sculpture became even the tiniest bit proletarian in the sense that people read contemporary work without the help of pseudo-philosophical interpretations by superfluous critics.

The painter having the biggest ball was Feliks Topolski, peripatetic Polish émigré long resident here. He covered the wall of a Hungerford Bridge railway arch with a pageant of Empire peopled by peacock characters from his notebook repertoire of thousands. His smiling gaze picked up the highlights and painted them in the myriad delights of a new Bayeux tapestry in effect.

Not all art was on the South Bank, of course. The West End dealers put on special exhibitions. The Arts Council came up with a worthwhile idea – not as at present by issuing handouts of thousands of pounds to provide sabbaticals from wearying pedagogical duties for deserving but unsuccessful artists – by offering to buy five of the large paintings submitted by fifty-six invited artists. The judging was by a Dutch museum director, a *Times* critic and an Australian collector. Across the intervening quarter of a century the choice looks not half bad – though which half is debatable. Lucien Freud's *Interior near Paddington* is well known and for many people represents Freud. It is reality not only observed but a Creation of man – with a lower-case m. I don't think the artist would be ashamed of it today though personally I prefer his recent portrait of Lady Beaumont, one breast exposed. Bill Gear's *Autumn Landscape* actually caused some ructions, hard to imagine today, because the loosely abstract treatment was something more than the title implied. But '£500 for that!' was the Puritan protest. Claude Rogers' *Miss Lynn* was a safer bet, the model reclining on a day bed, her feet and arms bare. She looked familiar. Everybody knows a Miss Lynn. How painters change is evident when one looks again at two unrewarded entries. One is Rodrigo Moynihan's *Portrait Group* of members of the senior common room of the Royal College of Art with Carel Weight gazing thoughtfully at seated Johnny Minton (he seems marked for the tragedy to come) and Ruskin Spear, his sanguine eye taking it all in. And the other is Patrick Heron's *Christmas Eve*, something he would probably prefer forgotten. One can only describe it as a badly scrambled Braque.

Sculpture was more diverse. In Battersea Park the London County Council, as it then was, held its second open-air exhibition with quite a lot of panache. Henry Moore was having a large retrospective at the Tate and the Arts Council had commissioned twelve sculptors for special works. Best on the South Bank was Moore's *Reclining Figure* in bronze, pared to its minimal skeletal torso, its curving rhythms alive with sensual movement and vital erotic presence. But the dominant sculpture of the Festival was the 300-foot high Skylon, flying a metal pennant to the future and implying a sailor's farewell to the past.

Of all the skills and talents in the making of the Festival of Britain, especially the South Bank Exhibition, the most effective were the designers'. Design for display had been almost ignored pre-war but in 1946 the 'Britain can make it' Exhibition held aptly enough at the Victoria and Albert Museum struck a welcome note of novelty in putting ideas and objects in compact and stimulating sets. Key designer for 'Britain can make it' was James Gardner – he deserved and received his OBE. His ideas and chiefly his attitude brought the public into view of the histories and fantasies of industries and localities. Writing about Gardner in 1948 I called him 'the Compleat Designer' saying: 'As the 1951 exhibition looms ahead Britain

Three cartoons by Belsky in the Daily Herald.

has need of many Gardners.' In the result he had several superb followers.

An outstanding exhibition was the ICA anthology 'Ten decades – a review of British taste 1851–1951'. Each of the 250 works displayed had a catalogue entry quoting contemporary critics' remarks. One of mine appeared in relation to the triptych *Resurrection: Waking up* by Stanley Spencer about which I had written: 'The exhibition included several more paintings on the theme of the Resurrection with their puzzling insistence on the ugliness of the persons depicted.' Getting to know Spencer and his work better I realized there was no insistence. His models were the people of Cookham as Pieter Bruegel the Elder's were those of a Flemish village and neither were concerned to flatter them.

It was a fun time too. Two years previously Ronald Searle introduced me to Franta Belsky and his wife Margaret – or Cooee as she was called by her friends. He was starting on his successful career as a sculptor, in fact he worked on the Dome of Discovery on the South Bank, and she was beginning to make a name as a brilliant comic draughtsman. Having just got the job of front-page cartoonist on the *Daily Herald* she was worried if she could think up enough ideas for pocket-sized cartoons on events of the day. She asked me to help and there began a routine that ran for years. At 4.15 p.m. I would buy the afternoon editions of the evening papers, retire to the lavatory, skim through them for joke ideas and ring them through to Cooee. Inevitably the Festival featured in many of them and browsing through a dog-eared cuttings album I can still raise a smile from the following.

Two swallows fluttering around the tip of the Skylon with wisps of straw in their beaks: 'We might build our nests here, dear, so the children can get a good bird's eye view of the exhibition.'

Female battle-axe at the turnstile to gateman: 'I'm sure I'm the millionth visitor to the Festival – I demand a recount.'

Two bee farmers beside a 'Honey for sale' sign: 'Yes, I'm thinking of expanding. I'll probably make an offer for the Dome when the Festival closes.'

Looking back to those hard times, the Festival was like a shot in the arm. We need another today.

No artistic enjoyment

W. Y. CARMAN

My recollections of the 1951 Festival of Britain are mixed, for my hopes were not matched by the actual event. As a struggling (at the time) working man, who hoped to see recovery after the war, I had looked forward to the Festival as an inspiration, an event perhaps on the lines of the 1851 Great Exhibition of which I had read exciting accounts of the vast collection of inventions and artistic products. It is true that certain 'gimmicks' like the Skylon and the ingenious tumbling fountain remain in my mind, but I enjoyed more the exploration of the old Shot Tower. The complex display structures gave me no artistic enjoyment, although the half-lifesize figures of the Story of Britain were very good. I can recollect much more of the features of the British Empire Exhibition of 1924 and 1925 at Wembley, but no more of 1951.

Those are my thoughts. Perhaps if I had been younger and gone to Battersea Park, it would have been better, but as an ex-soldier I did not find enthusiasm or inspiration in the other parts of the South Bank.

Almost surreal confusion

MARGARET BEAN

The slatternly waitress with a dirty dishcloth over her arm took our order, and an enormous helping was dumped on our plates. An order for wine caused consternation. 'Wine!' she said in horror and went away to confer with a higher authority, returning with the news that nothing was available except British sherry or (I think) someone's Invalid Port. She was disappointed when we turned them down. Afterwards she wrote out the bill and stuck the pencil behind her ear, and we paid at the desk.

The furnishings and tableware for this meal embodied a novel system of decorative pattern, derived from the diagrams made when scientists map the arrangement of the atoms in crystals studied by X-ray methods. The occasion was luncheon at the Regatta Restaurant on the first day of the 1951 South Bank Exhibition. The odd contrast between the building, designed by a distinguished modern architect, and the elegant fittings, and the catering, let out to a north-country firm with old fashioned ideas, is one of my clearest memories.

The architecture was the thing; that is what remains in my mind about the 1951 exhibition after twenty-five years. Britain's modern architects and designers, starved during the war years, here had a chance really to let themselves go, and whereas the pavilions were elegant, striking and original, the actual contents of the exhibition left a general impression of almost surreal confusion. Looking at the official guide again today I wonder whether, if I could now revisit the exhibition, the complicated maze-like pattern, flitting dreamlike over every possible aspect of the country and the people, would make more sense. I do not think so.

It was all so huge, so full of information, photographs, diagrams, machinery, history, agriculture, science, art, and yet there were strange gaps, displays which looked as if they were an afterthought. The Dome of Discovery I recall as being particularly muddling. The enormous theme was 'the intensive exploration and development of the present time', and there were such a lot of exhibits and descriptions, the mind boggled and the feet gave out.

I remember too, going eagerly to the section on sport. Miserable little cases labelled 'Tennis' or 'Cricket' contained some tastefully arranged groups of rackets or bats and balls, and not much else. Some were empty too, but of course it was the first day, and no exhibition is ever really ready on time. Still, the feeling was that those responsible for the display really hated any kind of sport except darts and shove ha'penny.

Later on I revisited the exhibition, and some of the cases were still empty. I specially remember an exhibit of different kinds of bread in the Dome of Discovery, for which real bread had been used; but no one had remembered to replace the loaves so they were quite green with mould.

Living on the North Bank, directly opposite the exhibition site, I had watched with sorrow the disappearance of the romantic and much painted view, beautiful but useless. The Shot Tower remained alone on a temporary reprieve, and not long after the 1951 celebrations ended it was demolished to make way for the new permanent developments which became the present grey waste of concrete, and joined the rest of the old South Bank in limbo. Only the Lion surmounting the old Lion Brewery survives, rescued by special command of King George VI, and today it is to be found mounted on the south end of Westminster Bridge.

Regatta Restaurant veg cook

FRANK NORMAN

When I came home from the Army in 1951 it was no surprise to find that things had changed little around Soho during the two years I'd been away. Iron Foot Jack was still smoking hand tailored cigarettes made from dog-ends gleaned from the gutter; No Nose Charlie was still selling newspapers on the corner of Soho Square; the streets were still infested with bad-faced Messina tarts and the priest of St Anne's was still vowing to defeat the wages of sin.

Of no fixed abode, a work shy layabout, with precious few coins between me and the gutter I faced the future with lethargic apathy. I was twenty-one years of age and finding it no easier to wrest food and drink from an unwilling world than I had in my teens, but the Welfare State was still in its infancy and it was not yet illegal to be destitute. Soho, in those days, was an enclave of indolence in a city still licking its war wounds. Poverty was acute and how any of us survived is still a mystery to me.

The Festival of Britain was greeted with little enthusiasm by the denizens of Soho, but the 'clip joints' did all right out of the influx of tourists. The street walkers, framed in the stone shadows of darkened office buildings, were prepared to unzip for two quid and dispense cold-blooded 'knee tremblers' to passing men.

A few weeks after the commencement of the festivities on the South Bank, an improbable creature bounced along Charlotte Street trundling a motorized tea trolley on the side of which, in a bold half moon of red letters, was printed 'Festival of Britain' and beneath it the name of a world-famous caterer.

'Hello, Wozzo,' I said as he hurried by. 'Where yuh goin' with that thing?'

'Bin floggin' tea and cakes to tourists,' he replied, without slackening his pace. 'Got to get this fing out of sight before they tumble it's gone missin'.'

Wozzo was a ragged layabout who had been around the 'manor' since before the war and was in no way the kind of bloke that you would expect to see decked out in a snow-white coat and forage cap to match. I fell in with him and taxed him further.

'How did yuh come by a motorized tea trolley?' I inquired mildly.

'Nicked it.'

'How?'

'Well, yuh see, the fing is they've got this Festival of Britain labour exchange down Denmark Street wot's bin set up so's the South Bank kayfs don't run out of dish washers and cooks,' he said. 'So bein' as 'ow I didn't 'ave anyfing particlar lined up just now, I reckoned I might as well offer 'em me services on a strickly casual basis. So I chatted 'em up and they give me this job shootin' around the festivities wiv this tea trolley. I dun it for a week then it come to me, all of a sudden, that it was a mug's game floggin' me guts out for some millionaire when I'd be a lot better orf workin' for me self. So when the geezer on the tradesman's entrance weren't lookin' I ducked out the gate wiv me tea trolley. And now all I gotta do is a paint job on it and convert it into a roast chestnut barrer and I'll be larfin'.'

There could be no denying Wozzo's ingenuity, but it occurred to me that if the law took an interest in the tea trolley before he'd done the conversion job I'd get arrested as an accomplice, so I abandoned him at the corner of Tottenham Court Road and scurried back to Dean Street.

Inspired by Wozzo's success I myself joined the queue at the Denmark Street employment agency the following morning. In the fullness of time a man in a suit took down my particulars and asked me what sort of job I was after.

'I want to work on the Festival site,' I said.

'Yes sir,' he said. 'We have all sorts of jobs. What training do you have?'

'Depends.'

'On what?'

'What you're prepared to offer,' I grinned at him across the counter. He glanced at a card index.

'There's a vacancy for a veg and omelette cook at the Regatta Restaurant.'

'Oh yes, I've been one of them,' I cried.

'You sure?'

'Sure I'm sure,' I lied. 'Done two years spud bashing in the Army.'

He gave me a dubious look, shrugged and wrote me out a card.

As luck would have it I showed up at the Regatta Restaurant at the peak of the lunch hour rush. The kitchen was a hive of insane activity – an army of sweating chefs slaved furiously over a battery of hot stoves to keep up with the orders that poured in from the packed restaurant above. 'Two rump steaks and chips, one rare! *Morue Aux Tomates* and chips! *Coquilles St Jacques Au Vin Blanc* and chips! Two spaghetti and chips!' cried the harassed waiters as, weighed down with clattering plates, they propelled each other through the swing doors marked 'IN' and 'OUT'.

The whole place was such a turmoil of writhing bodies that it was twenty minutes before I could get anyone to hold still long enough to ask the whereabouts of Monsieur de whatever-his-name was, *le maître chef des cuisines de* Regatta Restaurant. But I tracked him down eventually, in a secluded corner, concocting some delicate sauce and doing his nut.

'I've come about the veg cook job,' I said and waved the employment agency card under his nose.

He gave it a cursory glance.

'Can you start first thing in the morning?' he asked. 'Seven o'clock sharp?'

I gaped at him in astonishment – I had expected to be quizzed closely about my previous employment or at least asked to show my diploma. I'd thought up a really fine story and was disappointed at being deprived of the pleasure of telling it. I later learned that the restaurants on the South Bank were so short staffed they were prepared to take on anyone with reasonably clean hands.

'Anything else?' he said, when he saw that I was still rooted to the spot.

'What's the money?'

'Ten pounds a week and your meals,' he replied and hurried away to deal with an argument that had flared up between two waiters and a chef about who had ordered what.

It was not without the greatest difficulty that I was eventually able to persuade Gregorius Kalacholis, the proprietor of a Soho greasy spoon, to lend me a chef's hat and coat. But he relented in the end and the next morning, with no more knowledge about cooking than it took to boil water, I stood at the long kitchen range flanked by experts.

As I learned a few years earlier, when I'd applied for a job in a packing factory as a perforator of talcum-powder tin caps, a rudimentary competence in semi-skilled work was more a matter of panache than expertise. A man who could boil water could easily disguise the fact that he hadn't a clue how to boil cabbage and potatoes. I coasted through the morning without mishap, chucking buckets of spuds into my steaming copper and stylishly stirring the greens with a massive wooden spoon. Then suddenly came the lunch hour rush and life began to get sticky.

It wasn't so much my lack of experience in omelette making that threatened to give me away, but the alarming rate at which they were ordered. It seemed as though the entire clientele of the restaurant had taken it into their heads to eat an omelette of some kind. I was soon swamped and if it hadn't been for the generosity of my neighbours, who swiftly came to my rescue, it is likely that my career in the exotic world of *cordon bleu* fry-ups would have been short lived.

The following day my luck continued to blossom. I was taken under the wing of a jolly little fellow with a thick Transylvanian accent, who boasted that he had made omelettes for the crowned heads of Europe, and in no time at all I was as dexterous with the frying-pan as a gambler with dice. Indeed, it was two whole months before I got sick of the job and two further weeks before I could bring myself to ask for my cards.

Slight though my contribution to the Festival of Britain may have been, it was a rewarding experience, and the two stone that I put on kept me warm throughout another hard winter of laying about.

Not one word of praise

SHELAGH SPARKS

I KEPT A DIARY in those days and, on pages stuffed with superlatives, bad shorthand and worse French, a visit to the Festival of Britain did not merit one word of praise. A dozen of us went by train to London, armed with spending money which the company chairman had thoughtfully provided for the occasion. We were rude about that and we were rude about the Festival all the way home. 'Bread and circuses', my colleagues said and, 'it's all about beating the Socialist drum for a new Britain.' Others remembered 'the smelly huskies', or 'just the smell', or the crowds queuing obediently as they had done in the war.

'Lunch in Lyons', I read on, trying to conjure up the events of the day, 'then to Festival. I got "lost" and went round dome and country exhibition etc., saw King Haakon of Norway (went to see Emett railway), Festival Hall and illuminations. Went to Funfair by launch, saw centrifugal force arrangement, went back by launch, went to Buckingham Palace. Back to terrible restaurant. In by midnight.'

When I cudgel my brains I can recall the Skylon, the Dome of Discovery – but nothing of its contents – and a Henry Moore sculpture sitting on a piazza. No one could forget the clinical aspect of it all, the masses of concrete and the litter. Still, it was a day out, a rare visit to London, and it was a bit of ersatz fun, an attempt to slough off the gloom which beset everybody who was not young and silly.

My twenty-year-old contemporaries looked on the Festival as a big con to take parental minds off austerity but, really, neither they nor I cared. It was small beer in a social whirl with the Bachelors' Ball, yacht club regattas and agricultural shows earning the top marks and fulsome descriptions. Looking back, I wonder how any of us found time to work. We did, anyway, getting £3 to £4 for a sixty-hour week; a rise of 16s 6d brought out all the superlatives again. Such largesse was far more exciting than the Festival – as far as we were concerned there was only one and that was located on the South Bank – up in Town as we self-consciously called London.

Part of our energies throughout 1951 were employed in avoiding provincial sops to the Festival spirit, for athletics meetings, country dancing and musical competitions were all got up in its name. I saw *Hamlet* at the Arts Cinema in Cambridge, as part of the Festival programme, and there seemed to be more dancing than usual in the market squares of the little towns in East Anglia.

What really brought out the purple passages was the run-up to the general election in October. Even mayors mattered in those days and we were always in a state of ferment over the local political scene let alone the national. Talking cost nothing and money was always tight, although we did manage, modestly, to take advantage of the sweet ration which increased that year. With that, tripe and onions every Tuesday night in the digs, and a diet of tea and buns in run-down cafés, it is no wonder we all suffered from puppy fat, even if we did walk everywhere or use public transport. Girls with boy-friends who had cars were considered one-up on the rest.

If we had been less self-centred we would have realized what a philistine lot we were. Middle-aged pursuits, and that included the Festival, were none of our business. People, preferably young and preferably single, did. My diary confirms this but I wish it would reveal exactly who were Harry Flintoff, Chitty Moss and Polish Fred.

Alarmingly like a private club

BARBARA DORF

MY WARTIME YEARS as a youngster were spent in a north-west London suburb. We were 'kept going' by the propaganda that, 'after the war', there would be some sort of magic time when all would be lovely. The 1951 Festival, then, was to herald the new era. It was summer time, but the day I went it was very cold and the wide cement spaces made the Festival exceptionally draughty. Apart from the pavilions there was nowhere one could comfortably shelter or sit down. And heaven help the poor tourists, nowhere to get any sort of refreshment except tea and stale swiss roll.

And the more one looked, the more one asked oneself: the Festival of Britain? *Britain?* Whole vital areas of Britain were apparently ignored – the Midlands, the North – unless one counted some pleasing if prissy Wedgwood china as representing Midlands industry. And there was a fair amount of artwork, like mosaics and appliqué, the charm of which lay in its *lack* of professionalism and its Hampstead amateurishness. One assumed that this artwork was commissioned from friends of the organizers.

Very much of the Festival was alarmingly like a private club. Particularly odd was the pavilion of British humour. Who, in heaven's name, was supposed to laugh at jokes that in 1951 were still based on class? In no way did this attract foreign tourists and I remember shabby British tourists wandering about, bewildered. Then there was the pavilion that contained the 'best' in British design. There were mock-ups of rooms. This was not quite the era of spiky legs and sludge green but fast coming on that way. It was deeply disconcerting that, supposing one *had* wanted the stuff, it was quite unavailable to us in the shops. No one looking at it really liked it much, there was in those days still a genuine preference for Angela Thirkell chintz.

One could not but agree with those who complained of lack of proper facilities. The atmosphere at the Festival wasn't dissimilar to that at the 1946 'Britain can make it' Exhibition. We queued in incredible discomfort to see the show, only to wonder why it was done. The same question hung over Festival of Britain 1951. What in all conscience were we trying to prove? Who were 'we'? Festival of Britain 1951 certainly *tried.* But it wasn't really much of a festival – it wasn't much fun. Souvenirs were rubbishy or arty and very expensive. One was very aware, even as a teenager, of the sort of mumblings that were a background to it all. 'They' were getting something 'out of it' for themselves. Perks and handouts were for 'them'. Considering the amateurishness of many of the art exhibits there might well have been some truth in it. One also heard mumblings regarding the Festival of Britain estate that 'they' were going to put their friends into the flats. What, most people wondered, were we celebrating? There was still rationing. Were the Government seriously suggesting this was to show we were a major power, when their administration was making it perfectly certain we could never be again?

The Festival was appallingly awkward to get to; an uncomfortable journey and discomfort once you got there. But if you came back by night you saw, from Charing Cross Bridge, London floodlit. Dear old London, grand, dignified, bomb-scarred, rubbish floating, spoiling the Thames. People were wandering home, blandly indifferent. The things that mattered about Britain you could not exhibit or celebrate.

A wonderful day for £5

SYLVIA I. JENKINSON

I HAD TAKEN the keenest interest in the Festival. It was so stimulating to read about it during the years of preparation. After the long war years and the drabness of everything it was something that caught our imagination and gave us hope. It did something for us all at that time. We were young and had been starved of colour and spectacle for so long it was just what we needed. I saved the special magazines and the national press reports of the official opening by King George VI and I looked forward impatiently to when my husband and I with our eight-year-old son could go and see for ourselves all we had read about. At last the day arrived and we set off at 6.45 a.m. by car from the small Lincolnshire town where we lived for the nearest main line station for London.

When we arrived home from London, I wrote some notes about our visit to the Festival.

'Left home at 6.45 a.m.

Left Peterborough 8.10 a.m. train to King's Cross. (Fares £2. 12. 6.)

Bus from King's Cross to Whitehall Place from whence we walked to the exhibition over the Sapper Bridge. Admission 10/– each: 5/– for Philip (25/–).

Stood underneath the Skylon!

We found the Transport pavilion and the Power and Production most interesting. Among other things we saw being made were:

1. Ice wafer biscuits by Peak Freans
2. Paper making
3. Printing

4. Silversmith
5. Glassblowing
6. Painting on Royal Doulton ware
7. Shoes being made (Dolcis)
8. Axminster carpets
9. Metal strips being made into rings
10. Paton & Baldwin wool
11. Weaving loom
12. Sweetwrapping machine (Pascall)
    Cricket bats (Slazengers), Festival Rock.

We saw an old car (Lanchester 1902 model) in the Transport pavilion – also some smashing new models! Jet gas turbine engines used in aeroplanes.

We saw the Robot (Post Office) Underground Railway. We went by boat from Nelson Pier to the Pleasure Gardens at Battersea Park. It was very pretty and gay – we liked it very much. We had a ride on the Emett railway and H. & P. went on the children's Peter Pan Railway.

Arrived home at 9.25 p.m. and the day cost us £5.'

I can remember my first sight of the fountains and the excitement of *seeing* the Dome of Discovery and actually *standing* underneath the Skylon! I took a photograph of my husband and son standing on the steps of the Dome of Discovery, and my husband took a snap of my son and I near the Skylon and then another of the Skylon.

We walked round recognizing all the pavilions we had read about. I can remember the locomotives in the Transport pavilion: there was one called 'City of Durban', I think. I also recall the displays of aircraft engines – I believe there was one of a 'Merlin'.

It was all so absorbing but we left at 3 p.m. to go by boat from Nelson Pier to see the Pleasure Gardens at Battersea Park. I remember it was drizzling as we left the South Bank, but that didn't dampen our spirits! I can remember the Tree Walk and the flowers and the happy holiday atmosphere. The Guinness Festival Clock was great fun and we stood with the crowds waiting for the time when the figures would appear. We saw the Festival Clock again in 1955 when we were holidaying at Clacton.

I bought a horse brass as a souvenir which shows a helmeted head and has the lettering 'Festival of Britain' round the top and the year at the bottom. Also a picture postcard of *Neptune*, one of the engines of the Far Tottering and Oyster Creek Railway.

I remember the Festival very well indeed and I have enjoyed recalling these memories of a truly wonderful day when we were all together. My husband died last year from cancer and my son is in the Arabian Gulf. He is a civil engineer. Perhaps the Transport pavilion or the Power and Production pavilion had something to do with his choice of career!

Bright and bragging and English

ROY FULLER

My memory is bad and I keep no journal, so what follows must be taken with a pinch of salt. In 1951 I was still under forty and hadn't yet published a novel for adults: I was a 'minority' writer, as I had always been. One of the (to me) surprising features of the Festival was the opportunities (and financial rewards) given to a few of my friends, about my own age, who I had hitherto regarded as firmly in the minority category. Keith Vaughan was commissioned to paint a mural for one of the South Bank pavilions; Laurie Lee's fantastic cast of mind was translated into curious actualities in the Lion and the Unicorn feature there. This kind of patronage, financially welcome but rather superficial and pointless, perhaps set the pattern for a good deal of future public-money-spending on the arts, just as the whole South Bank concept, self-consciously bright and bragging and English, led to the flourishing of a certain kind of theatre – and of Carnaby Street.

There was also a Festival of Britain poetry competition, run by the Arts Council, for long poems and sequences of short poems. Prizes totalled £1,100. There were 2,093 entries, one of which was my sequence 'Ten Memorial Poems'. The judges were distinguished: Sir Kenneth Clark (as he then was), Sir Maurice Bowra, Lord David Cecil, John Hayward, George Rylands and Basil Willey. They chose a mixed bag of winners (Gerald Bromhead Walker, Clive Sansom, J. P. Fletcher, Jack R. Clemo, Robert Conquest, J. C. Grant, Theodore Nicholl and L. A. Redford) whose entries were published together as a Penguin – again, a remarkable act of would-be popularization, for those were days long before such series as the Penguin Modern Poets. This was not, however, a volume that made the whiskers rise up; though looking at it today I wonder somewhat why it roused in me so much wrathful scorn.

I visited the South Bank Exhibition one day with my wife and son but with no anticipatory relish. Nevertheless, the spouting water and fluttering flags made a cheerful impression. Possibly deeper optimistic feelings were induced, though I'm sure only momentarily. One was struck by such things as 'artistic' litter-baskets, but behind the colour and novelty little of fresh and permanent significance could be discerned.

You came away feeling you could dance just like Kelly

ARNOLD WESKER

What do I remember? What everyone remembers: brave colours, exhilarating shapes, thrilling designs – the communication of courage. No, not that quite, rather the revelation that one had the spark of something within oneself. You know, like seeing a good film-musical, you came away feeling you could dance just like Kelly and, for a few moments, along the road, with one's friends, you actually did step more lightly and leap a little.

Most vividly, though, I remember going into the decorating shop on the corner of Urswick Road E.8., Atlas I think they were named, and asking why didn't they have the new wallpaper designs? Wouldn't sell down here, they told me. I was furious. There was always that kind of insult around.

But I did buy a stunning three-piece suite for my mother, and some rugs, on HP. The rugs came from Heal's. Now *that* was courage – to go from Hackney to Heal's. On a 653 trolley bus.

I'm sorry I didn't hoard anything from those days. But the three-piece suite is still around and I think the rug is in our country cottage. Oh yes, and I bought curtains to match. She thought I was mad, my mother.

No clothes . . . no fashion

HARDY AMIES

I HAD OPENED my own dress business in '46 and had made several visits to America. I thought of Britain as a centre of design inspiration. I was immensely proud of the Festival. It was the first time I had ever seen an exhibition that had been designed as a unit. As a schoolboy I had visited the Wembley exhibition, which was hideous. My most vivid recollection of that was Pears Soap Hall of Beauty with famous beauties sitting in glass cages.

And yet, impressed and moved as I was by the decor of the Festival of Britain, I was less interested in the contents. *There were no clothes: there was no fashion.* There was nothing in it which presaged 'swinging London' or the renown of a Mary Quant. 'Swinging London' in the 1960s demonstrated an attitude to dress which *was* uniquely British and which had a world-wide influence. Yet the advertisements in the Festival of Britain 1951 catalogue are fascinating. Manufacturers of mens' slacks today have a renewed interest in pleats on the front of mens' trousers; but they fear that designers will be accused of going back to the fifties too soon.

I remember a generously proportioned American millionairess who ordered a crinoline in silver lace from us in 1951. When I enquired of a French fitter how the fitting had progressed, she replied, 'Monsieur, it vas zie Dome of Discovery.'

Plant pots and 3-D

M. JUNE MAGGS

I SPENT SEVERAL Saturdays on day trips to the Festival. I had started work in December 1950 at the Royal Aircraft Establishment, Farnborough, and day return rail fares were cheap. I can't recall *how* cheap, but my hostel board for the week had only just risen from 25s to 30s, and I think my pay was about £20 per month after stoppages.

The things I always remember about the Festival grounds are the truncated cone concrete plant containers, which seem to have been dotted about the grounds freely, and to which I have always referred as the 'Festival of Britain' pots, when they subsequently appeared all over new towns and shopping precincts.

I also remember seeing 3-D films in what later became the National Film Theatre, wearing those red and green lens specs which are so awkward when you already wear glasses. There was also closed circuit TV showing people entering the foyer to customers already seated, waiting for the next performance.

On one of the terraces near the river, a sculpture cum fountain had metallic scoops which filled with water and tipped into a series of similar scoops. It was the clanking, pouring noise, rather than the visual impact, which I remember. Most of the exhibits had a Rowland Emettish, 'Schweppshire' comic element about them – the British laughing at themselves. I remember eating a meal in a restaurant, which a few years later became a departure lounge for BEA.

I didn't go on any rides in the funfair, and though I remember weary feet from trailing round the exhibition halls, none of the serious exhibits remain clear to me. I am somewhat surprised at this, because at the time I was very interested in the technical future. Perhaps I saw too many of them *not* developing. I worked on Guided Weapon tests at Farnborough until 1957. Perhaps I am one of the reasons we are *not* in the Space Race?

Rubber table mat souvenir: some design remained uninfluenced by Festival example.

Souvenirs were snapped up for use

D. E. WARREN

THE CLIMATE OF OPINION at the time of the Festival was rather hostile, as most people thought better use could have been made of the money – to help clear up bomb damage, for example. The then Labour Government was acting on its usual premise, that 'it's a poor heart that never rejoices', and went ahead with the opportunity to build the Festival Hall and the rest of the complex on the South Bank.

The Festival turned out to be a pleasant and justifiable diversion; besides keeping a lot of people in employment, it also used surplus war 'scrap' in the making of such things as souvenirs. The country was heartily tired of wartime utility goods – white crockery and plain textiles, among other things; a lot of Khaki dye was used for a long time afterwards. I still have a cushion cover of this basic colour brightened with rather scant embroidery. Metal containers were almost non-existent. Large biscuit tins were returned by stores to the manufacturers for re-use: as a ward Sister I had great difficulty in hanging on to large tins for ward use. Luxury commodities like tins of biscuits, tea and sweets were slow to enter the shops, and so such things displayed at the South Bank Exhibition were snapped up very quickly. Wages were incredibly low and there wasn't a lot of money to spend, but I think there was a good attendance by our near foreign neighbours and the Americans.

My own purchases were a small tea caddy and scoop. The scoop, in white metal, is in excellent condition, the handle decorated with the Festival sign in red, blue and white enamel and of excellent workmanship. The tea caddy, 'a long time want', is I'm afraid too battered about the lid to exhibit. The black lacquer-type paint has been partly washed off, but the Festival insignia is intact. The lower part has a festoon of pink roses – the whole probably made from aircraft aluminium scrap.

The Skylon on the South Bank site was most attractive at night. Its very simplicity was 'new'. The Science Museum in Exhibition Road was in charge of the engineering section. The accompanying 'muzak' in the photographic section was the waltz from *Swan Lake*.

Battersea Park Festival Gardens remained with us longer. The Emett construction got very dilapidated by weathering as did the Guinness Clock, a great source of delight. There was also a splendid iron stork which surmounted the pavilion of the Children's Zoo. This was made by the Chelsea blacksmith Ivan Margery who then had his old forge at the Kings Road end of Dovehouse Street. He was at one time a Chelsea Borough Councillor and died a few years ago. He had to leave the old forge when the new Fire Station was built. Mr Margery made all the armatures for the Chelsea sculptors and his iron stork was quite a lovely work of art.

The Coronation festivities eclipsed the Festival of Britain with its greater variety of souvenirs. As I have explained, there was such a need of things that the Festival supplied (scarves, fancy tea cloths, pots and crockery, glassware, book matches, etc.) that they have probably worn out with use; the more durable things, however, like pen-knives, metal dishes and ashtrays, trays, tea and jam spoons and brooches, may well still be around in abundance.

On not visiting the Festival of Britain

EDWARD LUCIE-SMITH

WHY DIDN'T I GO to the South Bank, and sample all the marvels Festival publicity promised us? Looking back, at a distance of a quarter of a century, I find it hard work to disentangle the real reasons. Some of them were entirely to do with my own emotional development, but some others, I suspect, were shared by a great many other people who failed to go.

Better to begin with the personal reasons. I was eighteen, and at eighteen one is suspicious of all forms of innovation. Though the Festival made play with the idea of 'tradition', I was right in thinking that it was in essence innovative. Where I was wrong was in not respecting innovation for its own sake. In addition to this, I felt, at some deep level, that I might be presented with more excitement, more ideas, than I could comfortably absorb. I had arrived in Britain as recently as 1946, coming from the very different environment of the West Indies, and I was still in the process of coming to terms with the country where I now lived.

And yet, and yet – there were perfectly genuine reasons for resisting the Festival. I remember about it, or about all the propaganda for it, an air of enforced jollity. It approached one, through the media, with the fixed grin of a scoutmaster: determined that one should enjoy oneself, equally determined that one should learn something in doing so. I had been the most disastrous boyscout anyone ever remembered, and all my reef-knots were grannies. And, on the whole, I preferred then, as I do now, to take my education straight, preferably between the covers of a book. I find it a more efficient way of learning things.

In addition, the Festival had a slightly hypocritical side – the hypocrisy of a second-class power still masquerading as a first-class one. I couldn't have formulated this as precisely then as I do now, but I am sure the objection lay at the roots of my contempt for the Festival's traditionalist pretensions. They were too obviously fancy dress, and rather scanty costume at that – so diaphanous you could still see the bruises.

Yet I mustn't give the impression that I made a deliberate decision not to attend, any more than most of the other absentees. I looked at the site from across the river, Skylon piercing the air, and kept resolving to make my way there. I even went to the funfair at Battersea Park, as a way of getting up my courage for the real thing, and attended the old-fashioned music hall, which I enjoyed whole-heartedly. But still I didn't go.

Of course, when the opportunity had been irretrievably missed, I kept quiet about my delinquency, and have continued to keep quiet about it until this moment. I did, however, indulge in one act of vicarious penance. My mother was furnishing her house, and I persuaded her to buy, and place in the drawing room, a small settee designed by Ernest Race. Few pieces of furniture can have exemplified the Festival Style more neatly or more uncomfortably. Perched high on splayed aluminium legs, it had a thin, hard seat cushion placed on springs so tense they tried to throw you overboard every time you sat on it. 'Sports-car handling', commented one guest tersely, after losing an unequal struggle with it. It resembled a sports car, too, in that the space it offered was so exiguous that two people could not occupy it both simultaneously and decently unless they were either married, or engaged to be married, to one another.

The fate of this sofa still seems symbolic of what happened to the Festival idea. Its weakness proved to be its most traditional element – a covering in pure wool. Undeterred by its up-to-the-minute appearance, a family of moths attacked it, and, with a sigh of relief, my mother threw it out. If it has survived, an artefact so characteristic of its period is surely well on the way to becoming a valuable antique.

9 The Style: 'Flimsy . . . Effeminate'?

REYNER BANHAM

'THE INFLUENCE of the 1951 Festival of Britain on contemporary architecture', wrote Osbert Lancaster in *Here of All Places* (his cartoon history of architecture) 'was out of all proportion to its actual success. On the credit side, colour returned to façades for the first time since the daring experiments of Mr Halsey Ricardo in the early years of the century, the Teutonic preponderousness which had weighed down so many examples of the modern movement was modified or banished and much ingenuity was shown in the employment of such materials as chicken wire and asbestos sheeting for purposes for which they had never been intended.'

That was published only eight years after the Festival and was already a work of pious mythography, rather than a witness of truth. The fact that the same passage could be quoted as an example of the author's perceptiveness and accuracy in 1975 (in newspaper reviews of the paperback edition) shows that there is no myth so persistent as a British Establishment myth. The word 'establishment' is used here warily, but it is difficult to find a better collective noun for all those salaried spokespersons of the Council of Industrial Design, the editorial 'We' of the *Architectural Review*, and other former officers and gentlemen whose common triumph 'the Festival Style' undoubtedly was – and who later and almost unwittingly became the guardians of the myth.

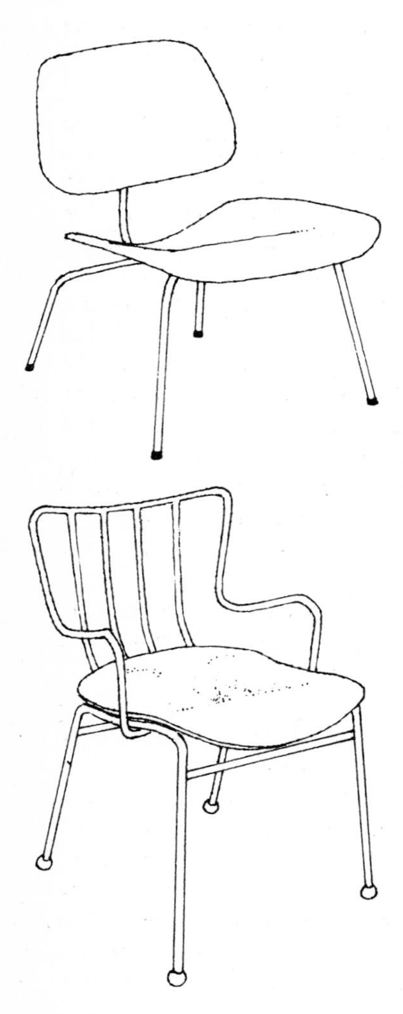

Chairs by, top, *Charles Eames and*, above, *Ernest Race. The Race 'Antelope' chair was designed for the Festival.*

Reduced to its two basic propositions, and baldly put, the myth proposes that: the Festival of Britain created a style that was new and valuably English; and that this style was influential, especially on popular taste. The first proposition is so easily falsifiable, and was known to be so even in 1950 before the Festival existed, that one must now wonder about the second, but both have been so tenaciously held that their value as 'official legends' is almost as interesting historically as the romantic fallacies they enshrined. The meaning of the Festival myth is a topic which cannot be avoided in this discussion, but it is more appropriate to begin by examining its *content*.

To begin with the first point: the Englishry was real, if not new, but was not in the style (in the restricted sense of 'an idiom of design') and the style itself was not all that new. Whatever was English about the Festival was in the content, the iconography which the idiom of design was meant to carry. This disparity between style and content can be seen in Festival objects as diverse as the Emett train at Battersea or the Race 'Antelope' chair on the South Bank site. The chair, for example, conforms to the spindly, splay-legged 'insect-look' silhouette most authoritatively propounded by the American Charles Eames in his famous DCM-1. As a prototype this steel and plywood chair was known in England through the pages of the California magazine *Arts and Architecture* (the most ruthlessly pinned-up and cribbed-out-of magazine of the hour) and well known enough throughout the rest of the world for imitations to have appeared in Roberto Aloi's *Sedie, Divani, Poltrone* at the beginning of 1950. The most obviously 'Italian' of these imitations is Paolo Chessa's with its wild exaggerations of the forms of the original. What is unmistakably 'English' about the Race derivative is that, within this wiry style, it makes visual reference to a traditional type of English chair; it is like a drawing of an armchair done in steel rod, but still in the Eames style.

The case of the Emett train is, obviously, more complex. What now seems so striking about it is that while it, like the Race chair, makes visual reference to beloved English topics – in this case George Stephenson, dead seagulls, Heath Robinson and faked-up period detailing – it does so within a general idiom of skinny and tapering space-enclosing frameworks and curved roofs that is far closer than any of us could see at the time to the 'international' style of the more serious structures on the South Bank.

Top, *drawing by Gordon Cullen for the* Architectural Review*: the people are looking up at the Skylon.* Above, *hanging platform canopy at Milan Fair, 1948.*

In spite of the observable internationalism of these structures, some foreign writers were keen to emphasize their Englishness, and their originality. Not all, however; some were quick to point out borrowings from Scandinavia, others from Italy. The Italians themselves seem to have been in two minds; Manfredo Nicoletti made a careful comparison of the Transportation pavilion and the gabled silhouette of the half-timbered structure of Choplloyd's house in Chester. This, however, may have been put into his head by deliberate (if unofficial) British pre-Festival propaganda, some of which was so chauvinistic and uninformed that it finally provoked at least one strong, polite but withering riposte.

This came from the authoritative but short-lived Roman magazine *Spazio* in August 1950. Under the helpful title *Soccorso agli Inglesi* it offered to come to the aid of the British who (according to an article by Trevor Stanley in *Tempo do Milano*) were having difficulty in describing the proposed South Bank architecture because it was so original that there were no words for it yet. Patiently, *Spazio* pointed out that the Italian language already had *tensistruttura* for structures in tension, and no fewer than three words – *puntone*, *fuso* and *falcone* – for what the *Architectural Review* had been forced inelegantly to call a 'raking strut'. The reason why the Italians were so well provided with such words was that they had been using such structures (or proposing to) for some fifteen or sixteen years, and knew that they had borrowed them in the first instance from Le Corbusier.

Even discounting the jingoist rhetoric that begins the last paragraph of *Spazio*'s comment – *Italiano dunque il principio estetico della struttura in tensione . . . e italiani gli elementi formali della modernissima costruzione* – this rebuke was effective; the visual evidence was to hand. Renzo Zavanella's tension-hung pavilion roof at the Milan trade fair, its suspension cables fluttering with pennants, and carried from the apices of lattice-framed 'raking struts', had been illustrated in the *Architectural Review* itself as early as March 1949, a full year before the first of Gordon Cullen's perspectives of remarkably similar proposed South Bank buildings appeared in the same magazine (*the* magazine as far as the Festival was concerned). *Spazio* simply reproduced four of the Cullen perspectives, and needed to do no more for its Italian readership, because the whole aesthetic of exhibition architecture was visibly the same as Zavanella's.

Festival veterans themselves tend to look baffled when presented with this seemingly irrefutable evidence of blatant plagiarism. Some see the matter as a pure verbal quibble ('What else can you call a tension

Roof supports of the Dome of Discovery.

structure in Italian?'); others, without claiming ignorance of Zavanella's work (difficult that; it was in all the magazines), tend to imply that the dates are too close for effective cribbing, given the very short time in which the South Bank buildings had to be designed. With hindsight one might suspect that simply because time was so short, a readily available design idiom would indeed be *Soccorso agli Inglesi* in their hour of need, but hindsight also suggests that this might indeed be a striking coincidence, or something, at least, whose origins lie further back.

The clue may lie in *Spazio*'s reference to Le Corbusier, who had indeed used raking, openwork *puntone* for the *tensistruttura* (to wit, tent) for his *Pavillon des Temps Nouveaux* at the Paris Expo of 1936. Anything done by Le Corbusier was guaranteed 'seminal', and would almost automatically become part of the official programme of the modern movement, especially after it had been officially codified by that movement's official codifiers who included Sigfried Giedion, the secretary of les Congrès Internationaux d'Architecture Moderne (CIAM).

In 1943 Giedion (together with the Spanish architect J. L. Sert and the painter Fernand Leger) indited *Nine Points on Monumentality*, a matter which might seem to have only negative relevance to the Festival, whose lack of monumentality was proclaimed on every hand. Yet nearly all the nine points seem to have at least oblique bearing on the layout of the South Bank site, and the ninth, which gets down to material specifics, comes so close to what was actually built that the effect is uncanny:

> Modern materials and new techniques are at hand: light metal structures; curved laminated wooden arches; panels of different colours, textures, sizes; light elements like ceilings which can be suspended from big trusses covering practically unlimited areas.
>
> Mobile elements can constantly vary the aspect of the buildings. These mobile elements, changing positions and casting different shadows when acted upon by wind or machinery, can be the source of new architectural effects. . . .
>
> Elements of nature, such as trees, plants and water, would complete this picture. We could group all these elements in architectural ensembles; the stones which have always been used, the new materials which belong to our time, and colour in all its intensity which has long been forgotten. . . .

To say that this was just the conventional wisdom of the modern movement (and it was, just about, by 1950) is not to put down the wit and wisdom of Sigfried Giedion, so much as to destroy any real claims for originality in the architecture of the Festival of Britain. Those words are too good a fit for what actually happened; however little their actual phraseology may have been known in Britain, they look remarkably like the intellectual programme out of which the actual Festival structures could have been conjured.

Whence the legend of the great originality of the Festival Style, then? Patriotism? Ignorance? Selective amnesia? It is instructive, now, to look again at what Osbert Lancaster said in 1959. The concordance between Giedion's prescriptions for a new monumentality and Lancaster's observations of the Festival Style is so close that one can only boggle at Lancaster's insistence that he had heard a 'roar of disapproval from the ancestral voices of the modern movement prophesying woe from the splendid isolation of New Canaan'. Nothing could have been further from the truth; but then one observes that the illustration which faces Lancaster's views on the Festival shows a block of flats, brilliantly observed and highly typical of the fifties, in which not one single detail is notably traceable to the Festival (even though they are captioned 'Festival Flats'), while the overall effect is unmistakably derived from the work of Berthold Lubetkin, who did nothing at all on the Festival of Britain.

It is indeed a mythical Festival that Lancaster celebrates, an alleged liberation from an ancestral modern movement tyranny that had been lifted a decade earlier without him noticing. The 'ancestral voices of the modern movement' (none of whom were based in New Canaan Conn. at the time) were all in England in Festival year, for the CIAM congress which took place in Hoddesdon that summer, and none, that I recall, prophesied woe. Most of those to whom I spoke personally (including Giedion), while hardly raving with enthusiasm, reckoned that they had been diverted by Battersea, found Lansbury worthy, and approved of the South Bank, if only because of its obvious relevance to the main topic of discussion at Hoddesdon: the Core of the City. What, for some English pundits, had been an overwhelming demonstration of the superiority of the English Picturesque tradition over all other planning dogmas, was for these 'ancestral voices' simply an English version of their own corporate vision of the future city, perhaps even a welcome return of the British to the true path of modern urbanism – at least to judge from some rather enigmatic remarks of Ernesto Rogers comparing the layout of the South Bank with Le Corbusier's plan for St Dié of 1946.

The lack of any raving enthusiasm on the part of the guardian spirits of modern architecture may well have been due to a sense that there was nothing very new about what could be seen at the Festival – though the British deserved a bit of a pat on the back for having finally caught up. The catching-up seems, with hindsight, to be real. In spite of the semi-official line that the Festival was by British Originality out of Stockholm 1930, the exhibition it most visibly resembled was the Triennale di Milano of the same year. It could even, in some details, be construed as being a little behind, say, 'Rotterdam Ahoy', mostly designed by J. B. Bakema, of the previous year (in spite of the fact that many of the Festival team had been over to see it, which accounts for the importance of Philips of Eindhoven in the lighting of the South Bank) and even, in its conception of display techniques, a bit behind the exhibition 'Growth and Form' at the London Institute of Contemporary Arts in Festival summer itself.

The officer-and-gentleman establishment had, in historical fact, just caught up with a particular stylistic package that was about exhausted. At least one of them, indeed, saw the Festival Style as early as August 1951 as a style at the end of its tether:

It is easy to see that this style of the fifties will be thought flimsy and effeminate by the next generation, but we should lose no sleep on that account. It reflects a public mood just as the New Look did, and we have reason to be certain that in its way, and of its kind, it had real quality. One's only fear is that it

Detail, Sea and Ships pavilion.

has reached a degree of refinement from which there is no advance except by a complete change of direction that nobody wants. It is to be hoped the leaders will not think it necessary to right-wheel or left-wheel until the whole column is out into the straight.

The military language and assumptions of leadership sound like the New Establishment, but who among that gentlemanly body dared pull the flush on the Festival while it was still open to the public? The author of these remarkably perceptive views was Lionel Brett, least involved of his connection, in a general review of 'Detail on the South Bank'. He was right, too – even about his own generation, as one can see by looking at what Casson, Misha Black *et al* did within a year of the Festival in their interiors for the new Time-Life building in Bond Street, all dark, heavy and plushly upholstered.

For the next generation, both its spokesmen like Joseph Rykwert, and its practitioners like James Stirling or the Smithsons, the Festival Style was anathema. Suspicious of the *Architectural Review* and all its works, they looked for leadership to Le Corbusier and his newly revealed *beton brut*, or to Mies van der Rohe and his eternal steel stanchions. By the time Brett's words had appeared in print, the Smithsons, for instance, had already designed their Miesian school at Hunstanton and their Coventry Cathedral project. The latter was compared by David Sylvester to the Dome of Discovery, chiefly in terms of a supposed lack of axiality in their internal planning, but it was never so 'Festival' as the design which actually took first prize in the Coventry Cathedral competition, by Sir Basil Spence. Planned in a manner remarkably like his Sea and Ships pavilion on the South Bank, and detailed in an expensive 'butch' version of the manner that Lionel Brett had suspected of effeminacy, it carried the Festival Style deep into the surprised sixties, but this was less an example of long-term influence than a fossilized survival. Influence-wise, the Festival died a-borning.

There is no reason why it should have done otherwise, if indeed it was only a passing mode like, as Lionel Brett had suggested, the New Look. Yet the alleged influence of the Festival was a major issue for some years, and an essential part of the official myth. In 1961, for instance, the Council of Industrial Design staged a ten-page retrospective on the Festival Style in *Design* magazine enquiring, among other things, 'Has this style made an important contribution to subsequent developments in Design?' They got some dusty answers from their four symposiasts – Sir Gerald Barry, Misha Black, John Murray, Richard Hamilton – which was hardly unexpected, since most design manifestations of the twentieth century are at their nadir of public esteem ten years later. Nevertheless, the CoID had so much capital tied up in the reputation of the Festival and their own version of the *Führerprinzip* attitude to leadership in public taste, that they had to do something to retrieve a position that was being seriously eroded.

It was in the public and private discourse of Paul Reilly, the director of the CoID, that the status of the Festival as a 'turning point in public taste' was most frequently cited, coupled with genteel appeals to the solidarity of men of good will – 'After all, we're all on the same side, really, aren't we?' In fact, the idea of established leadership in taste was under heavy attack from both Right and Left at the time; John Berger, for instance, maintained that the function of the newly opened

Design Centre was to impose middle-class standards of taste on the people. In time confidence in this leadership was undermined culturally by the Pop Art movement, and in more material terms by the demonstration in some consumer publications that odd items approved and listed in the Design Index were ill made or less functional than they looked.

Whatever occasional failings the Design Index might exhibit, it remained one of the Council's most valuable properties and its most important heritage from the Festival; the reputation of the index was bound up with that of the Festival. The CoID was thus an organization to which the myth of Festival influence was crucially important. In the upshot, the Council could have drawn little comfort from the views expressed by their symposium. At one extreme, John Murray, who clearly clove closest to the traditional CoID view of design leadership by pace-setting manufacturers, denied that there was any such thing as a Festival Style, merely good design; at the other extreme, Richard Hamilton was able to show influence only in objects that all four would clearly agree in finding excruciatingly ill designed.

Even Gerald Barry, in spite of his fundamental involvement in the Festival, had to admit that 'South Bank quickly deteriorated into a cliché for every coffee bar or renovated pub. . . . The trouble is that it seems to have got stuck – design has not gone forward from where the South Bank (deliberately an experimental style, remember, evolved for an exhibition) left off.' Misha Black declined even to accept that the style was experimental, and seems to have been prepared to agree with Lionel Brett that it was a style on its later (if not last) legs: 'The Festival spotlit and gently pushed forward an already existing style – it did not create one.' Hamilton rubbed the message in even harder: 'The most successful objects in the Festival, stylistically, were the buildings – but here the style was borrowed, not indigenous. . . . The Festival was an elegantly prepared platform from which to jump into a newly designed future – unfortunately the leap found us just where we were.'

Richard Hamilton was, of course, a representative voice of that 'next generation' whose hostility to the Festival and its style had been foreseen by Brett. More importantly he was a survivor of a round of later exhibitions which had begun to reveal a change of attitude that was more than a change of fashion. Shows like Richard Buckle's 'Diaghileff' of 1954, 'This is Tomorrow' of 1956 (in which Hamilton had himself been involved, as he had also in 'Growth and Form') were all, in Mario Amaya's phrase, 'environmental shows', in which the distinction between exhibit, display technique and surrounding space had been largely dissolved in a manner that would probably have been inconceivable as well as organizationally difficult on the South Bank (though something like it had been tried out in parts of the Science show at South Kensington).

Worse, what survived of any 'living tradition' from the South Bank had been badly tarnished by the British Pavilion at the Brussels Expo of 1958. Whatever the alleged popular success of the contents of the British Pavilion, the building itself, designed by Howard V. Lobb, who had been Controller of Construction on the South Bank in 1951, caused most British architects and critics considerable embarrassment (and acrimony, leading even to threatened libel actions). Yet according to Gerald Barry, the pavilion 'was directly descended both in style and

The Moat Garden, landscape architect Peter Shepheard, Lion and Unicorn Café.

standard from the South Bank', and that was fundamentally what was wrong with it in the eyes of most observers.

So, if the Festival Style had bottomed out in 1961, where does it stand now and why is it worth staging a major commemorative exhibition of it in 1976 – a project in which I heartily concur and for which, in expansive moments, I might claim some responsibility. Partly, there is now a kind of mixture of sentimentality and astonishment about the whole enterprise. The idea of leadership in public taste with an almost formally constituted establishment is now almost as incredible as it is, to some minds, attractive – especially in the picture it presents of an apparently orderly structure of social castes who 'knew their place' in a way that teenagers, trade-unionists and trend-setters, among everybody else, no longer do. The mythology of the Festival's originality and influence now begins to exhibit the same kind of period charm as the designs themselves. It is not only profitable nostalgia-mongers and snappers-up of trivia, 'more tattersey than Battersea', whom the Festival fascinates.

Indeed, a ground-swell of interest in the Festival as a national phenomenon in social, organizational and cultural terms precedes any revival of interest in the style *as such* by several years – the tat-collectors are Johnnies-come-lately in Festival scholarship. It was, in some sense, the 'Children of 1944', raised in the Welfare State and educated under the Butler Act, who turned to the Festival in search of the origins of their world and found in it the origins also of the umbrella stands, light-fittings and wallpapers of the homes in which they had grown up.

For, if the Festival was not a 'turning point in taste' itself, it was part of the raw material that fed the influence that did help to modernize public taste: the media. Television – above all, commercial television, instituted in 1955 – and increasingly sophisticated popular illustrated magazines are ever voracious for new modes and new visual material. The Festival Style was to hand, along with Scandinavian modern, *lo Stile Espresso*, space technology and other funds of imagery to feed the Media Revolution, so called. At the beginning of commercial television, the Festival was the most handy of all such image-funds in Britain, was heavily pillaged and acquired enough exposure to gain some penetration into the public mind, especially when something that looked like it could be bought from your neighbourhood 'G-plan' outlet. Indeed, in this sense, the Festival may have had some real if marginal influence on public appreciation of 'good design' since, as Leslie Julius of Hille Furniture could be heard to say at times in the middle fifties, 'Anything that sells more G-plan enlarges the market for modern design generally.'

More importantly, however, the first few 'annual cohorts' of the Children of '44 actually *saw* the Festival: not as architects or even as architecture students, but as impressionable but beady-eyed schoolchildren and teenagers. Some may only have seen the local manifestations in Belfast or Glasgow, but a remarkably large proportion of them made the pilgrimage to London with their parents or in school parties and saw the South Bank – and were changed!

Unprepared and unprejudiced, not subject to the satirical remarks of junior architecture-school staff who were already teaching their charges to despise the Festival and its 'mouldy picturesque', nor singed by the crusading fire that would lead others to de-Festivalize the Festival

Hall and try to return it to a true Corbusian purity it was never intended to have, they were almost ideal viewers of that festive scene. For them it was not instruction in the appreciation of good design nor a new awareness of our great national inheritance of dotty humour and professional eccentricity. It was a turn-on, man! It is striking how many of that generation have told me in recent months that it was the Festival that turned them on to modern architecture, or made them want to be architects for the first time. It was a preview of the human environment as a zone of enjoyment and its design as an occupation of pleasure.

They did not imitate the Festival Style; but when the British became self-confident enough again to rejoice without having to be ordered to by Herbert Morrison, sophisticated enough to enjoy themselves without needing instruction from kindly ex-officers and gentlemen, and affluent enough to do it without threatening national bankruptcy, then there was a generation at hand – from Archigram to the Beatles to almost anyone else you like to name in the late Swinging Sixties – to whom the Festival had shown the way if not the style. The Festival was probably one of the most essential foundations for that half-decade or so up to 1970 when British architecture and design had its greatest ever influence and prestige since the beginning of the twentieth century. It may even, in a negative way, have laid the foundations of the fame of the pre-Archigram generation, that of James Stirling, by giving them something solid enough to react against, and with enough character to tell them which way to react. In a frivolous but enjoyable time, the Fathers of the Festival could have taken pride in this unexpected achievement – but most of them were too busy trying to face down 'the Challenge of Pop' or to explain away James Stirling's architecture as 'too showy to be truly English'.

There remains one other matter which ought to feature largely in any assessment of the importance and influence of the Festival and yet hardly ever does. It was neither effeminate nor flimsy; in fact it is solidly with us still, for the most persistent of all the objects that appeared at the Festival has never gone out of use since and is now so common that it is difficult to imagine the British scene without it: the Festival flower-pot, that broad stable concrete cone designed by Maria Shepherd that is now almost as familiar a denizen of the urban scene as the red pillar-box or the Belisha beacon.

Whether or not one regards the extirpation of 'Cotswold detailing' as being as essential to the mental health of the nation as did some pundits of the fifties, the fact remains that municipal gardening has not been the same since the Festival. This is hardly surprising; the philosophy of treating all exterior spaces on the South Bank as being of almost equal importance (and complication!) with the enclosed buildings between them, and the mustering of a roster of design talents that reads like a *Who's Who* of landscaping, would have guaranteed something special, but the performance demanded of that landscaping left no room for messing about.

Physically it had to stand up to almost as much wear and tear as the steps and footways it framed (the rest of the landscaping team would certainly agree with Peter Youngman that the hard-standing is in fact as much part of the design as the greenery). Visually it had to equal, and occasionally stand in for, everything from wallpaper to free-standing sculpture, from snob-screens to fountains. At the time it did not get the attention it deserved because it was, inevitably, embroiled in the contentious subject of 'Floorscape' which was effectively dividing the generations, and thus coming under any anathemas against the Picturesque which were then current. Curiously though, even outside parochial British polemics, the landscaping was little noted at the time, and few foreign observers felt required to comment on it.

Yet, if one tries to recall the experience of the South Bank as an inhabited environment, if one looks at the backgrounds to the family snaps and the surviving footages of film, the landscaping is omnipresent in a way that it was not at any other great expo. You saw it (often obstructing the view), smelt it, walked on it and (with varying degrees of legality) sat on it. Of all that was designed and done, it was one of the great triumphs of imaginative professional skill at the Festival. It was probably more truly English and more genuinely innovating than much else that was more loudly praised at the time and more thoroughly forgotten since; almost alone of all that was in the Festival it has had, in concrete and growing reality, the kind of long-term influence that the rest has had only in gentlemanly mythology.

Direction signpost, designer Robin Day, lettering designed by Milner Gray.

Acknowledgments

PHOTOCREDITS · The majority of the photographs appearing in this book are official photographs taken for the Festival of Britain Office. However, grateful acknowledgment is made to the following individual photographers:
Aerofilms Ltd, Brian Aldiss, *The Ambassador*, the *Architectural Review*, the Associated Press, Barratt's Photo Press Ltd, the British Transport Docks Board, Camera Press Ltd, Campbell's Press Studios Ltd, Alfred Cracknell, the *Daily Herald*, the *Daily Mail*, the *Evening Standard*, Faber & Faber Ltd, V. L. Ford, Fox Photos Ltd, Future Books, Halifax Photos Ltd, Margaret Harker, Angelo Hornak, Hulton Press Ltd, Edgar Hyman, Peter H. Jones, Keystone Press Agency Ltd, the Labour Party Library, J. F. Lawrence, G. Macdomnic, John Maltby, Manor Studio, Millar & Harris, Patons & Baldwins, John Physick, Planet News Ltd, *Punch*, Peter Ray of Paul Popper Ltd, S & B Miniature Railways Ltd, W. F. Sedgwick Ltd, the 600 Group of Companies, Henk Snoek, John Still, Studio St Ives Ltd, J. Underwood, Colin Westwood, John Winter, Zanton.
To those photographers whom we have been unable to trace, we offer apologies in the hope that they will not be displeased to see their photographs reproduced in this volume.
Acknowledgment is also made to J. M. Dent & Sons Ltd, and the Trustees for the Copyrights of the late Dylan Thomas, for permission to reproduce the extract from *Quite Early One Morning* by Dylan Thomas; to the Southampton City Art Gallery for permission to reproduce *Miss Lynn* by Claude Rogers; to the Tate Gallery for permission to reproduce *Portrait Group* by Rodrigo Moynihan; and to the Walker Art Gallery, Liverpool, for permission to reproduce *Interior Near Paddington* by Lucien Freud.

Index

Page numbers in italics refer to illustrations; roman numerals denote colour plates.

ABERCROMBIE, Sir Patrick 138, 142
Adams, G. A. 51
Agricultural pavilion 79, 80, 106–7, 172
Aldiss, Brian 176–8
Amies, Hardy 188
Angrave, Bruce 128–9
Architecture Council 110
Armfield, Diana 169
Arts Council 36–7, 49, 62, 70, 110, 131, 182
Arup, Ove 71
Attlee, Clement 35, 36, 166

BACKHOUSE, George 161–3
Bailey Bridge *25*, 78, 79, 80, 83, 111, 170
Baillie, Eileen 173–4
Barlow, Sir Alan 152
Barlow, Harry 125–6, 127
Barry, Sir Gerald 12, 13, 14–16, *16*, *19*, *20*, *22*, 20–3, 26–7, 52, 76, 88, 89–90, 96, 118, 120, 194–5
Battersea Festival Gardens 29, 53–4, 118–22, 124–9, 130, 150, 166, 171, 173–4, 177, 180–1, 187, 189
Bawden, Edward 98, 101
Bean, Margaret 183–4
Beaverbrook, Lord 13
Beddington, Jack 118
Bell-Scott, Donald 163
Bell-Scott, Harold 164
Belsky, Margaret 183
Benoy, J. M. 61
Bevan, Aneurin 32, 33
Bevin, Ernest 27
Birch, Lionel 84, 165
Black, Sir Misha 11–12, 51, 58, 61, 70, 77, 78, 80, 82–3, *82*, *83*, 110, 150, 166, 194
Borthwick, Alastair 152
Boswell, James 181
Braven, Arthur C. 152
'Britain can make it' Exhibition 58–9, 182
Bronowski, J. 144–6
Bryan-Brown, Grace 163, 164
Building Research pavilion 112, 143
Butler, Reg 83
Bux, Amir 174

CADBURY BROWN, H. T. 84
Campania 13, 40, 65, 68, 70, *72*, 150–1, *151*, 162, 165, 171
Campbell, George 76, 120
Carman, W. Y. 10, 183
Casson, Sir Hugh 11, 12, 15, 30, 58, 71, 76–81, *77*, *82*, 91, 96, 110, 118, 120, 123, 150, *160*, 163
Casson, Lady Margaret 163, 164
Centenary pavilion *12*, *116*, 164, *164*
Central Office of Information 62–3, 150, 161
Chadwick, Hulme 152
Chadwick, Lynn 83
Charoux, Siegfried 50, 83–4, *109*
Churchill, Sir Winston 13–14, 29, 162
Clark, H. F. 84, 110
Clarke, George 180
'Cockade' 163–6
Coia, Jack 152
Cooke, Cecil 76, 120, 150, 165
Corsellis, Elizabeth 163, 164
Costain 91, 92, 93
Council of Industrial Design (CoID) 36–7, 51, 58–61, 62, 65, 88, 110, 165, 169, 172, 190, 194–5
Country pavilion 106, *106*, *107*, *113*, *115*
Coventry Cathedral 54–5, *55*, 194
Cox, Ian 34, *62*, 62–9, 76, 165
Crainford, Leonard 120, 171
Cripps, Sir Stafford 26–7
Crystal Palace model 12, 118, 164
Cuneo, Terence 51
Cunliffe, Mitzi 83

DESIGN GROUP 76–81, 83, 85, 110, 112, 166
Design Research Unit 102
Design Review 59, 60
Detling 40, 55
Dickens, Ronald 146, 150
Dickinson, Frederick 163
Dobson, Frank 80, 83
Dome of Discovery 49, 51, 52, 64–5, 69, *69*, 71, 78, 79, 84, 85, *86*, *87*, 91–3, *91*, 110, *113*, 163, *163*, 167, 176–7, 184, *192*
Dorf, Barbara 186
Drew, Jane 70, 71, 92, 103–4, *104*

ECCLES, David 38
Edgington, Benjamin 121
Edgington, John 121
Egan, Beresford 180
Elleano, Charles 81, 90
Emett, Rowland 53, 71, 121, 125–7, *125*, *127*, 174, 191; X
Epstein, Jacob 50, 54, *56*, 80, 83–4; VI
European Bus Tour, 1950 16, *16*, 170–1, *171*
Exhibition of British Popular and Traditional Arts, Whitechapel *129*, 130, 131–2, *131*
Exhibition of Industrial Power, Kelvin Hall, Glasgow 68, 70, 152–4, *152*, *153*, *154*, 162

FAR TOTTERING and Oyster Creek Railway *see* Emett, Rowland
Farm and Factory Exhibition, Belfast 70, 155–8, *155*, 157
Festival Pattern Group 51, 60
'51 Bar *105*, 110, *112*
Figgins, Thorne and Austin 114

Fisher, Archbishop 26, 35
Ford, V. L. 175
Forshaw, J. H. 142
Frayn, Michael 28–9
Freeman, Sir Ralph 79, 91–3
Freeman, Fox & Partners 79, 91–3
Freud, Lucien 49, *50*, 182
Fry, Maxwell 70, 71, 92, *104*
Fuller, Roy 187

GAITSKELL, Hugh 32
Games, Abram 40, 55
Gardner, James 11, 12, 58, 77, *77*, 80, 84, 118–22, 123, 124, 125, 128, 150, 164, 182
Gear, Bill 182
Gibberd, Sir Frederick 72, 104, 138–41
Godfrey-Gilbert, Jack 10, 82, *160*, 160–1
Gooday, Leslie 78, 81
Goodden, Robert 84, 96–9
Gray, Milner 150
Guinness Clock *132*, 181, 187
Gutmann, Robert 164
Guyatt, Richard 96, 163, 164

HAMILTON, Richard 195
Handisyde, Cecil 140
Harrison, Dex 124
Harrison and Seel 126
Hart, Barry 97
Hartland Thomas, Mark 51, 59, 60–1
Harvey, J. D. M. 51
Hasler, Charles 114
Hendrick, T. W. 163–5
Henrion, F. H. K. 52, 70, 106–7, 118
Hepworth, Barbara 50, *56*, 80, 83, 103, *113*
Herman, Josef 49, 182
Heron, Patrick 182
Hippisley Coxe, Antony D. 88–90
Holland, James 11, 77, *77*, 80, 150–1, 165, 177
Holland & Hannen and Cubitts (HHC) 91, 92, 93
Homes and Gardens pavilion *50*, 72, 84, 88, 110, *111*, 166; IV, VI
Hopkin, Roger 163–4
Hopkinson, Tom 165
Hulme Beaman, S. G. 49
Huws, Richard 50, 52, *70*, 84–5

IRONSIDE, Christopher 98, 163, 164
Ironside, Robin 98, 164
Ismay, Lord 13–14, *14*, 29, 76

JAMES, R. T. & Partners 79, 92

Jenkinson, Sylvia I. 186–7
Jennings, Humphrey 49
Johnston, Thomas 152
Jones, Barbara 10, 129–32
Judge, Peter 129

KATZ, Bronek 84
Kirk & Kirk 92
Knowles, Margaret 171–2
Kroll, Natasha 99

LANCASTER, Karen 123–4
Lancaster, Osbert 54, 121, 123–4, *123*, 190, 192–3
Land Traveller Exhibition 70, 129, 148, *148*, *149*, 162
Lansbury *see* Live Architecture Exhibition, Lansbury
Laski, Marghanita 11
Lee, Laurie 84, *98*, 165, 172, 181, 187
Levin, Richard 129, 148, 150
Ling, Arthur 140
Lion and Unicorn pavilion 52, 65, 81, 54, 96–9, *97*, *99*, *100*, *101*, 111, 129, *163*, 164, *164*, 165, 167
Live Architecture Exhibition, Lansbury 72, 111, 138–43, *139*, *140*, *143*, 160–1
Lobb, Howard 76, 80, *82*, 93, 195
London County Council (LCC) 49–50, 70, 91, 111, 122, 140
Long, George 90
Lonsdale, Kathleen 60
Lucie-Smith, Edward 189
Lynch-Robinson, H. 156

'M'-SERVICE 60
MacBeth, George 176
McGill, Angus 178–9
Mackay, John 178
McLean, Ruari 17
Maggs, M. June 188
Majo, Willy de 155, 156–8
Manasseh, Leonard 110
Margery, Ivan 189
Marini, Marino 50
Medley, Robert 49
Megaw, Helen 60
Minerals of the Island pavilion 49, 51
Minton, John 49, 83
Mizen, Fred 97
Monckton, K. Mollie 172–3
Moore, Henry 50, *56*, 80, 83, *113*, *115*, 182
Morrison, Herbert 13, *27*, 27–38, 59, 77, 80, 120, 162
Moynihan, Rodrigo 182, *182*

NASH, Paul 99

'Newtonian House' 67, 68–9, 150
Nicholson, Ben 49, 83, 103–4, *103*
Nicholson, Max 37, 76
Noble, Wycliffe 78
Norman, Frank 184–5
Nugent, Sir Roland 155

PAGE, Russell 120–1
Paolozzi, Eduardo 50, 103
Pasmore, Victor 49, 51, 54, 83, 102, *102*, 181
Peake, Brian 146
Philips, Hubert 97
Pick, Beverly 118, 150
Picton Jones, Miss 131
Piper, John 11, 49, *50*, 54, 55, 80, 83, 121, 123–5, *123*, 127
Plouviez, Charles 10, 165–6
Port of London Authority 77, 103
Potter, Gillie 126
Powell and Moya 71, *72*, 78, 93, 110
Power and Production pavilion 111, 186
Presentation Panel 88, 110

RACE, Ernest 170, 190, 191
Ramsden Committee 27, 34
Ratcliff, John 11, 80, *82*, 93, 110–12, 160
Ray, Peter 150
Regatta Restaurant 51, 61, 83, 102, 183, 184
Reilly, Paul 58–61, 194
Riverside Restaurant 103, *104*, 160
Roberts, Gilbert 93
Rogers, Claude 182, *182*
Rowntree, Kenneth 80, 98
Royal Festival Hall 30, 70, *115*, 167
Russell, Audrey 166–8
Russell, Sir Gordon 59, 88, 118
Russell, R. D. 84, 96–9

SACHS, Leonard 121
Samuely, Felix 71, 93
Scarfe, Laurence 83
Science Council 65–8, 110, 152
Science Exhibition, South Kensington 65, *66*, 67–8, 144–6, *145*, *146*, *147*, 165
Science pavilion 177
Sea and Ships pavilion *39*, 53, 83, *108*, *109*, 111, *113*, 172, 194
Seaside pavilion 88–9, *89*, *94*, 110, 129, 130, *176*
Sendall, Bernard 76, 88, 91, 150
Shephard, Maria 84, 110, *117*, 197
Shepheard, Peter 84, 110
Sheppard, Guy 121

Sheppard Fidler, Margaret 168–9, *168*
Shot Tower *18*, 20–1, 53, 69, 77, 80, 85, *116*, 150, 164, 165, 183
Skylon *24*, 51, 52, 71, *73*, 78, 84, 93, 110, *113*, *117*, 167, 168–9, 176, 178, 183
Smith, Albert 152
Society for Education in the Arts 131
Sparks, Shelagh 185–6
Spence, Sir Basil 54, 83, 91, 152, 194
Spencer, Stanley 183
Stephen, Douglas C. 152
Strong, Roy 6–9, 10
Sutherland, Graham 49, 55, *55*, *57*, 80, 83

TALLENTS, Sir Stephen 163
Taylor, Basil 51
Taylor, Frank, 'Roy Ricardi' 174–5
Telecinema *24*, 72, 96, *112*
Television pavilion *24*, 72, 129, 130
Thomas, Dylan 16–17
Thomas, Margery E. 40
Thorleys 132
Topolski, Feliks *56*, 80, 83, 172, 182
Town Planning pavilion 112, 143
Transport pavilion *91*, 93, 110, 111, 163, 177, 186–7, 191; II
Triggs, Jack 90
Trowell, Buckinghamshire 70
Tubbs, Ralph 10, 11, 15, 71, 77, 78, *79*, 80, 84, 91, 110, 150
Tunnard, John 51, 83
Typography Panel 114

VAUGHAN, Keith 49, 83, 187
Vaughan, Reginald 84
Vaughan-Thomas, Wynford 81, 168, *168*

WALTER MECHANICAL TORTOISES 146, 176–7
Warren, D. E. 188–9
Webb, David J. 170–1
Wells Coates 72, 96, 130
Wesker, Arnold 187–8
Wetmore, Robert 163, 164
Wheldon, Huw 76, 81, 181
Whiter, John 92
Whittet, G. S. 181–3
Willis, Gwendoline 180–1
Willis, M. 131
Wright, John 170
Wright, Paul 76

YORKE, F. R. S. 140
Youngman, Peter 84, 110, 197